A Year of Remembrances

December 2013 —
To Sal & Frank
    Treasured friends from
days in Truckee &
Treasured friends now.
        Love —
Diane Young McCormack

A Year of Remembrances

A Love Story

By

Diane Young McCormack

ISBN 0-930083-47-4

Jack Bacon & Company
516 South Virginia Street
Reno, NV 89501
www.jackbacon.com

First Edition

To Don

I dedicate this book to my husband, Don.

> An incredible human being.

> An observer of human nature.

> A leader in town politics.

> A teacher to some.

> A mentor to many.

> A friend to all.

> Especially, an incredible husband.

> The legacy he left is eternal.

"What would "my life" have been without you, Don?
You were my husband for thirty-one years and ten months—to the
very day. Ours was more than a marriage—it was a love affair.
And, you were my life."

Table of Contents

PART TWO

PART THREE

Prologue

"You are a great storyteller," my friends would say to me over the past years. "You remember so much that has happened to you. I'm simply amazed at how you can recall the events with such vivid detail."

Shortly after the town of Truckee, California, held the memorial reception for my late husband, Don McCormack, I received a journal from a friend along with her note. The note simply said, "Write down your thoughts. They will help you later on as you reread them."

I had already started writing down my thoughts and memories right after Don's death on the many legal pads I had placed in every room throughout our home. As I put some of these notes into form and read them to certain friends, they said, "You really need to share your memories with others— the highs and lows that you are going through—so that, if or when, this ever happens to any of them, they may find some help, some solace."

This book is written in three parts. The first part takes place between February 10, 1975, when I received that first phone call from Don through August 23, 1975, on our wedding day. The second part of the book starts the day Don died on June 23, 2007, through the town of Truckee memorial on Sunday, July 22. The third part starts the following day as I started my progress to continue my life without Don. It is in this part that I recall my remembrances of Don and of our life together.

A thirty-two year marriage is a long story. At times, the tediousness of attempting to tell the story of Don and our marriage almost made me abandon this book. But I was a woman who had been fully loved and, therefore, the loss of my husband was felt even more. How many marriages had lasted as long as ours and how many marriages had lasted as long without either of the spouses having an affair, or even the slightest interest in another person?

At one point during the writing of this book, I asked one of my dearest friends, "How does one heal a heart that has been broken?" And then I would think, well, actually two hearts were broken, his first and now mine. And, she answered, "Perhaps by writing this story you are ending one narrative but beginning another. You are writing about the one thing that mattered the most in your life up to now—Don."

Many remembrances have been left out on purpose. Some of these would be just too personal and intimate for me to share with anyone. All the reader has to know is that for thirty-one years and ten months ours was not just a marriage—it was a love affair.

If those of you who are reading my book have that "special someone" in your life, appreciate him or her. We never really know when the chimes will stop.

Part One

Chapter 1

The Ring

It fell from the upper shelf of my linen closet. I had placed it there many years ago after my Aunt Irene had given it to me. The ring was a solid band of gold, one-quarter inch in width with engraving on the inside—*A N—2-11-12*.

"A N" was Alice Nagy, my maternal grandmother, and the ring originally was worn by my grandfather, Alexander John Tobias. It was a massive ring, probably a size 10, because my Hungarian grandfather was a huge strapping man with an expansive hand. The ring was still attached to a simple brown cotton shoe lace, knotted about 3 inches down, the way it was when my aunt had given it to me.

I had been staying with Aunt Irene and her husband in Hollywood, California, after graduation from college while I was looking for a job in fashion design. She and I had been looking through her jewelry box one day when I saw the ring and asked her about it. Without the slightest hesitation, she reached for my hand and placed it in my palm, folding my fingers up over it, saying, "Here, you should have this. Your sister is married, and you may just find the love of your life one day, and so this should be yours."

So, some thirteen years later, the ring fell on the floor. I picked it up and pondered for a moment the significance of why on this particular morning did the ring just fall from its lofty place—where it had been tucked away and almost forgotten, to land at my feet.

Was it an omen? Was it trying to tell me something? Yes, I considered myself to be "spiritual," and the falling of the ring from almost nowhere did cause my heart to skip a beat.

Chapter 2

Blind Date

It was April of 1975, and I had just returned from a trip to Houston, Texas, where I had flown to meet this Don McCormack, the man I had been talking to, writing to, almost daily and nightly…since he first telephoned me as a blind date on February 10 of that year.

He had gotten my name from a mutual friend, whose husband worked at Shell Oil Company with Don while he was going through his divorce. She and I had met in 1965 when The Wool Bureau, my employer, sent me as their representative to a Home Economics Conference in San Francisco.

I was manning The Wool Bureau booth and she was working at a booth for a San Francisco book dealer. We had lunch several times during the conference, exchanged addresses and later became close friends.

She had taken on the role as a sort of "mother hen" to Don, consoling him in his loneliness and inviting him to their house for dinner on occasion. One evening, she hinted to him she had a girlfriend who lived in New York City. Don immediately asked her for my name and phone number, but she hesitated and said to him, "When your divorce is finalized, I'll give you her name." His divorce was finalized on January 28, and on Monday, February 10, he called me.

I remember the phone call as if it were yesterday. I was gathering my papers to attend some showings with fashion designers on Seventh Avenue. But, before I was out the door my phone rang, and my secretary came into my office to say there was a Don McCormack on the phone—calling from Houston, Texas. We must have talked for an hour, and I remember when I hung up I was somewhat intrigued with this man. The phone call was totally unexpected as my friend had never mentioned Don McCormack to me. I was now late for my appointments and decided to walk the five or so blocks from Lexington Avenue and 40th Street, where The Wool Bureau had its New York office, to Seventh Avenue.

I must have been daydreaming on this beautiful, sunny and crisp winter day because before I realized it, I was almost on Tenth Avenue, nearly three blocks beyond Seventh Avenue.

Chapter 3

First Letters

Five days later, on Friday, February 14, Valentine's Day, I walked back to my high-rise apartment at Seven Park Avenue and found two pieces of mail waiting for me. The first was a Valentine's Day card from a former boyfriend in California. I had not heard from this man, an architect who lived and worked in Berkeley, in at least two years and was somewhat surprised to be receiving this card out of the blue. He had not changed; the handwritten message on the Valentine's Day card was all about him, what he was doing, where he was going—him, him, him.

I opened the other piece of mail, a simple 4" x 6" envelope containing a handwritten letter. It was on "D. C. McCormack" plain ecru stationery. His old address and zip code where he had lived with his first family had been lined through and his new address inked in its place.

~~~

Wednesday
Dear Diane—
Last night I tried to sit down and write you a letter, but I didn't like the result. When one person is trying to make contact with another to explore a relationship, the written

*word offers too many possibilities for misinterpretation.
Still, I'll try again and risk a first letter because the
thought and effort says more than a phone call. Other
letters will come easier.*

*I find myself most enthusiastic at the prospects of meet-
ing you. J___ makes you sound like a fine and dear person—
I think the word "exciting" covers a lot—and I put a lot
of faith in her opinion. I hope that we are able to arrange a
schedule that allows us to test the water before too long.
Let's make an early trip to Houston work out.*

*This weekend promises to be a nice one. I've been con-
cerned that my baby (Mary Beth, age 16) has been unglued
just a bit by the divorce and everything leading up to it, and
I'm pleased to see how eagerly she accepted my invitation
to go to Austin this weekend to visit No. 2 son (Dan) a soph.
at U of T. We'll go up on Saturday and stay overnight.*

*I have not had much opportunity to do things with
M.B., and telephone conversations just don't seem to do
much. This should be fun and good all around. She's a very
dear girl and needs some papa-love.*

*We haven't had a chance to talk about feelings (i.e.,
how I feel about me, life, dogs, anything) and maybe we
won't for a while (at least not in a letter.) Among my "likes"
are tennis (a B player), skiing, any outdoor activity (camping, packing, canoeing, but I haven't done all that much),
good food, sports cars (but I don't own one) and nice music—
popular or otherwise. My ex wife and I did not attend many
cultural things together, but I've decided that this was basi-
cally because I got so little enjoyment from doing things
with her due to a bad bad bad, unloving relationship*

*We've had a miserable winter here by northern stan-
dards—lots of grey and rain. However, I think we've turned
the corner and are coming into one of the best times of the
year. I only mention this now (it's not exactly interesting "get
to know me" talk) to say that I know the NY weather well,
and I appreciate how you feel towards the end of February.
Winter ought to be over, but you've got two months to go.
Moral and message: come south for a few days. Try it—
you'll like it.*

I'll talk to you soon.
Yours truly,
Don

~~~

For a couple of days, I pondered if and what I would write back. Thoughts crisscrossed through my mind—"Oh no, Diane, not another long-distance romance. What are you trying to tell yourself? You don't want to settle down, do you? From Spain to California and now 'he' lives in Houston, Texas."

So, I decided to cut to the chase and find out right away, before I put too much energy and time into a new relationship, long distance at that, just what this Don McCormack was all about. Ten days after receiving his first letter, I sent this letter to him.

~~~

Monday, Feb. 24, 10:00 PM
Dear Don—
I finally have some peaceful moments to myself—so now I can concentrate on writing to you.
Sorry it has taken this long to get a handwriting analysis out of me—but my life, in terms of work, has never been so hectic. Tonight was the first evening I left before 7:30—and only because I had my furniture refinishing class to go to at 5:45.
So now I'm home sitting here sipping tea with honey & lemon—and the city seems to have quieted down. I can hear the rain falling on my terrace and an occasional truck rolling down Lexington Ave. Gypsy—my faithful longhaired dachs- hund—is sleeping in my closet on my pile of dirty clothes. Such taste she has! I've had her since she was 6 wks. old and she's now going on 7, so she is a real friend to me. Yesterday I almost killed her. I was in a hurry leaving the house. She "tinkled" before getting into the car and her feet were wet because it was raining, so I made her get in the back of the

*car. I always keep her leash on her. I started off with a jolt
& heard her scream/squeal. At first I thought she had gotten
back outside and was under my wheel. I thought I was going
to die. I opened the door and she came tumbling out. Her
leash was stuck outside the door and when I started off, the
wheel ran up over it and yanked her to the door. She would
have choked if I hadn't opened the door in a hurry. Her leash
snapped in two that instant. Horrors!*

*It does seem a little strange to be writing to you when
we've never met—only the sound of your voice I know and it's
a mechanical voice. I mean, I always think I sound like a
little girl over the phone or on tape. Letter writing—I think—
can also be distorted at times. It's so easy to misinterpret
when one isn't there to say, "What do you mean by that"—or
just to pick up on thought waves by watching the person's
expressions. But, as you say, for now it's our only way of
communication—so I'll make the effort, too.*

*About me—(well, a little about me)—I consider myself
a warm person. I do get too intense over things—which is a
weakness in many cases. But I'm working on this. Work still
hasn't caused me to drink! I've come to believe more & more
in fate or faith—whatever. Things—good things—have been
happening to me, and I do feel certain contentness to life
(even thought hectic at work.)*

*I am a serious person at times—a deep thinker I guess
you would call it. I love quiet moments to taste the sensitivity to life—I guess this is why I love the "house." It is so close
to nature. I love looking out my back window and seeing
nothing but woods—or watching the frogs in the creek—or
long walks in the woods with old faithful. But, on the other
hand, I do not consider myself a "loner." Hardly! I would
never want to go on a vacation alone like a few of my friends
do. I would want to share certain things. And I love to return
to the city for its pulse or vitality—even though, sometimes
I really hate to come back—there's still an excitement here.
I love good times, good friends, good laughs—I am the original tease at times. I get that from my father and his father.
That's why I loved your "poppa line"—because I am very*

close to my father. He's a great guy. My folks have been
happily married for 40 years.

Let's see, what do I hate? I hate fast, reckless driving.
I hate cigars (are you still with me,) I don't wear furs or
believe in hunting or trapping any wild animals. I burned
my old fur jacket 5 years ago. I stop for strays and try to
rescue them, and when I can't I get very emotional about it.
I guess I am a defender of the helpless.

I love creating things—I love to cook but it's even more
fun sharing the kitchen—like making a fantastic Chinese meal
and sitting down knowing it's a creation is a "neat" thing.

I sew. I used to make a lot of my things—now it's find-
ing the time. It's been fun fixing up my grandfather's house.
This furniture refinishing course seems fun, also. I took 2 years
of weaving, 2 years of Interior Design, have a BS in Textiles.
I love flowers—even grow vegetables on my terrace in the
summer. I played the glockenspiel in the Maryland Marching
Band—had a "crush" on the base drummer until I bashed
the corner of my glockenspiel into the drum head. Alas!

And I'm sure J___ has told you about my "exciting" job
interviewing people about T.P—do you crumble or do you fold!

Well, Don, my finger is sore, it's 12 PM, and I'm ready
to turn into a pumpkin—or something. Come East, I think
it'll be fun meeting you. You write a beautiful and sensitive
letter; therefore, you must have a beautiful & sensitive
"alma" as the Spanish say.

Take care—
Diane

~~~

Years later, we would laugh about my questions to him,
indirect but with true intent, pertaining to hunting, smoking
and dogs. In fact, we even shared this story with our dear
friends the night of the last dinner…when we were sitting out
on our front deck…the night of June 22.

Chapter 4

His Immediate Answer

The mail service between New York City and Houston was certainly speedier back in 1975 than it was in 2007 between Truckee, California, and anywhere in the United States. Just a few days later, Don sat down to answer my first letter to him. He wrote it on Friday, February 28.

~~~

Friday
Dear Diane –
Such a beautiful letter deserves an immediate answer. I can't remember getting such a warm feeling from a letter before. I reread it today (I received it yesterday) before answering it. It expresses so much about you, both in style and content, that I feel I know you more from the letter than our phone conversations.

I guess what impressed me the most was the way I could sense the sounds of NY from your brief references, the anguish you felt for the near-miss with your dog and your expression of likes and dislikes. I guess it is easy to imagine that we have a lot in common, but I suspect we do. I am definitely people oriented from the standpoint of being with them, but I am also very much an active do-er as well as one who enjoys lonely moments. One of my favorite times has always been (at least here in Houston) early Sunday morning (say 8 o'clock) sitting in the sun by the pool with coffee and the Sunday paper. Nobody else was ever up at that time, and I often felt imposed upon when they were.

I also very much share the "do what you like," and not what you should. My divorce is an example, I guess, of going against the current.

Two other thoughts came back to me—teasing and folding vs. crumpling. I am a tease so be on your toes. As far as my TP habits, I do not fit the mold. Most of my characteristics are those of a folder, but I'm a crumpler. Maybe that's the best anyway—not in any mold. I have had more fun with that—it is amazing how well you can predict from observing and knowing people.

I'll chance another "feeling" I have, but I can't be sure how it will come out. I do not have self confidence when it comes to any attraction I might have to women. This is not to say that I'm bashful—quite the contrary, in mixed groups I am very comfortable with women. But I was not a particularly exciting college man, was married for eons to the same woman, and just never had the feedback that says you are attractive in that sense. If I appear to be forward in this regard, it 'ain't' so. You don't know how hard it was for me to call you, but only the first time. Once the ice is broken I feel very comfortable. (I just reread this and I don't particularly like it, but you get it anyway.)

I'm very much looking forward to early April. It seems ages away.

Enjoy,
Don

~~~

If our relationship were starting up today, would we be sending emails or text messages to each other? It's hard to imagine. February to April of 1975, the ten weeks when we had not yet met each other face-to-face, Don and I wrote to each other weekly, and many nights he would go to his office in downtown Houston and call me on the WATS line—long before the days of cell phones.

In retrospect, I am so fortunate to have our letters. It gives me something to hold onto—his words to me and my words back to him. And, of course, I can now share them in these pages because these letters were the beginning of our life together. They are part of the remembrances.

Chapter 5

Details of Our Past Lives

During these nightly phone calls, we would fill each other in with every detail one of us might have mentioned in our letters.

I was amazed when Don told me that he had been at Shell Oil Company his entire professional life. He graduated from the University of Missouri at Rolla in August of 1951 with a degree in Chemical Engineering. The Wood River Refinery in Illinois was a short distance northeast of St. Louis, on the east side of the Mississippi River, and many graduates with a background in Chemical Engineering went to work for Shell Oil, including Don. It was while he was at Wood River that he married and had his first child.

In the early 1960's, Don was transferred to The Hague, Netherlands, where he worked at Royal Dutch Shell. He was recognized as a "rising star" at Shell and this was part of a newly developed executive exchange program. He was in his early 30's and he told me it was a fantastic career move for him. The family traveled to The Hague with him, but instead of flying they decided to cross the Atlantic on an ocean liner cruise. They were on the SS Rotterdam and it took seven days

to cross. While in The Hague, his two sons, Bruce and Dan, attended the American school. Bruce was in the fourth grade and
Dan was in the second grade. His daughter, Mary Beth, was
only four and attended the Dutch Nursery School. I remember
Don telling me how she was quick to pick up the native language. He was employed at Royal Dutch Shell in The Hague
for a year during which time his family traveled extensively
around Europe on both business and pleasure trips. When they
left Europe, they departed from Italy on the SS Leonardo da
Vinci. That crossing took ten days. Don told me he was sea sick
on both crossings of the Atlantic. No wonder he never wanted
to take a cruise with me.

When he returned from The Hague, he was sent back to
St.Louis where he worked at the Wood River Refinery for
two years.

Don's next move was to Pleasantville, New York, where
he commuted daily to Shell's headquarters on Fifth Avenue in
New York City during this three year tenure. I would tease him
he couldn't claim he lived in New York because Pleasantville
was not THE city and only someone who lived in Manhattan
could say they lived in New York. He finally agreed with me.
Don told me it was while he rode the train into and out of New
York City where he played many hands of bridge as an escape
from the stress of his job which involved refining planning.

In his next career move, he and his family moved to Dan-
ville, California where he was the Assistant Manager at the Shell
Refinery in Martinez, California. This was the closest Don ever
got to fulfilling his ultimate career goal of being a refinery manager. While there, he also spent time at Shell's research facility in
Emeryville, California. Don shared with me many stories of his
weekend trips to Lake Tahoe, only a short three hour drive from
the Bay area, where he and his children learned to ski.

His last career move with Shell Oil Company took him to
Houston, Texas, where he worked in the Head Office once

again, this time as Manager of Manufacturing Operations.

Don was very intrigued with how I had become the care-giver to my grandfather, who everyone in our family called "Pop-Pop," and about his bungalow in Weatherly, Pennsylvania. He was fascinated with my living in "The Big Apple" and with how I had navigated my life from Edgemere, Maryland, to New York City with a year-and-a-half stint with Proctor and Gamble in their Market Research Department.

Graduating from the University of Maryland in 1962 with a Bachelor of Science in Textiles and Clothing, I had first sought a career in Fashion Design in Los Angeles. I lived for four months with my Aunt Irene and her husband in Hollywood. I told my friends I would pick up pins for Edith Head, who was then one of the top costume designers in Hollywood, and indeed, I did have an interview with her. But after countless interviews with other companies and really not liking either my living conditions or LA, I flew to Pittsburg, Pennsylvania for an interview with Proctor & Gamble.

I joined Proctor & Gamble as one of their market researchers. We were a group of mostly young women, who flew from city to city knocking on doors or making phone calls, asking various questions about either P & G products or their competitors. Hence, the question I mentioned to him in an earlier letter, "Do you crumble or do you fold?" was discussed one night in one of these conversations. It was a question asked of households eight weeks after an earlier team of researchers had left several rolls of toilet paper—two different brands—with the participants. Of course, Proctor & Gamble was interested in how much of the product was consumed—folders consume more—but, in the realm of cocktail party conversation, my team mates thought we discovered that it also reflected one's personality. Don was mightily amused.

While at Proctor & Gamble, I met another gal from Baltimore, and we decided to make our mark in New York City.

I told Don how "green" I was. Lois and I had taken the bus from Baltimore to New York. The date of this bus ride—February 10 of 1964. My lucky day! I had sent over fifty letters of inquiry to companies who I thought might hire a Home Economist: fashion magazines, manufacturers, fabric, zipper, thread companies and The Wool Bureau. The Wool Bureau answered my inquiry, and I arrived at my interview wearing demure cotton gloves and a pill box hat.

Don and I laughed at how we might have both been sitting at the exact time at "Zum Zum's," the great German deli restaurant located in the then Pan American building. He would have been there on his lunch break from Shell Oil Company, and I would have walked the few blocks north from 40th and Lexington. The counter made an "L-shape." He would have been sitting on a stool with a buddy from work, and I would have been sitting around the bend with one of my girlfriends. I would have asked him, "Please pass the hot mustard."

I remained at The Wool Bureau the entire time I was in New York City, 1964 until 1975, working my way up the ladder. In 1968, I became the proud owner of my first longhaired standard dachshund; her name, of course—"Park Avenue Gypsy." I told Don the story of how I toyed with the idea of naming her, "Hey You." "Why would you call her that name?" he questioned. "Well," I told him, "If I saw a good looking guy walking up Park Avenue just steps ahead of me, I could let out some slack on Gypsy's leash and say, 'Hey You,' and hopefully the cute guy would turn around thinking I was calling out to him." "Hmm, good logic," Don told me. "A more clever idea than I would have come up with."

In the summer of 1974 my grandfather, who lived alone in his quaint bungalow was not able to continue to live by himself. I was attending a family reunion and had taken a bus from New York City out to Weatherly. Before the weekend was over, I purchased a brand new blue Ford Pinto and drove back to New York City with Gypsy. Friday evenings would come and I would take a cab to the garage where my car was parked. Gypsy and I would make the two hour drive to Weatherly. My devotion and dedication to my grandfather really impressed Don.

Again it might have been fate. Just up the road from my grandfather's bungalow lived a couple, Goldie and Ray, who were his very good friends. In my grandfather's earlier days, he and Ray would go fly fishing together along with my grandfather's younger brother, Sam. Before I started to go to Weatherly, they would invite Pop-Pop for dinner every weekend.

When I started to make the weekend treks to Weatherly, Goldie would marvel at the things I had done for my grand-father. I had converted his coal furnace to gas, painted the rooms of his bungalow and carpeted each room with samples from a home furnishings company where a girlfriend worked. I would cook on Friday, Saturday and Sunday nights and make enough food to last Pop-Pop for the next three nights and then arrange for Meals on Wheels on the off day.

"Something good is going to happen to you," Goldie said. "God is looking down on you and seeing how wonderful you are to your grandfather. One day you will be rewarded."

Years later Don and I would say, "Yes, my reward was the phone call made to me on February 10.

Chapter 6

My Heart Gets Ready

During one of his nightly phone calls, I told Don that waiting for his call reminded me of one of my favorite stories, "The Little Prince." In this famous children's story about a fox and the little prince, the author, Antoine de Saint-Exupéry, intertwines themes of finding love and true friendship. I read Don the chapter where the fox was waiting for the little prince to show up, and the little prince was nonchalant about the time he would appear. The fox told the little prince that it would have been better if the prince had come back at the same hour because then the fox would know what hour his heart would get ready. I told Don that my heart got ready to hear his voice at the same time each night.

The next several letters between us started to become more personal and more exploring of our feelings.

~~~

Friday, March 14
Dear Don –
Your letter really greeted me with a smile tonight when
I came home from a hard day's work. It is a strange feeling
to have someone you've never met yet become part of one's

private and unspoken feelings. But, in many ways, and only through your openness, I feel like I do know you.

You know, Don, I've only known one other man who could express his inner thoughts & feelings like you do in a letter and he was European and I used to think that was why. All kidding aside, either you are a natural born writer & have the gift of expressing yourself in your words, or maybe it's because it's our only—except for phone—mode of communications. But you're right, it's the kind of face-to-face conversation that needs to be continued on a gingham tablecloth at a picnic while sipping wine & eating cheese, or while having a brandy in front of a fire, or while walking through the woods— or really what I'm saying is that it could be anywhere as long as both people are sharing it.

Alas, I've just given myself away. As you can tell, I am an incurable romantic—but the practical type!

Goodnight
Sweet dreams—

I continued my letter to Don two days later—

Sunday 11 PM
Hi again!
I've already taken my car down to the garage so I won't have to get up early tomorrow before they tow it away at 8 AM. I park it at Waterside on 23rd and the East River. It's the cheapest garage around, and then I take a bus back. It's really a drag to have a car in the city.

Yes, you're right. You did mention canoeing in letter #1. I've only been a couple times—but it was fun as I recall. That's the trouble with living in NY, one misses a lot of outdoor type activities.

Also, I should have guessed you were a Libra. Why, my favorite man in the whole world is a Libra—my Dad. I think it's fun—I don't put a whole lot of stock into it, but I do confess, I read my horoscope in Vogue.

I'm just re-reading your letter. You impressed me that when you were talking about your marriage, you didn't put the blame on any one person. A lot of people would.
Take care. April is just around the corner.
Me too!
Diane
PS. Excuse the sun glasses in this picture. Imagine green eyes with a yellow halo around them!

~~~

In one of his letters, Don included a photo of himself standing on the balcony of some hotel.

Don on Balcony - 1975

Chapter 7

Relationships Changing

Don's next letter to me, written on March 19, continued to explore feelings and the possibility of a future relationship.

~~~

Wednesday

Dear Diane

I continue to enjoy your marvelous letters and read them several times. I can appreciate exactly how you feel in anticipation of finding one when you get home

We continually talk about openness, and I guess that is one of the things that gives us meaning to each other. I truly enjoy an open conversation and the expression of my feelings.

There is great beauty in your thoughts on face to face talk—the picnic, brandy before the fire, etc. I can almost feel your presence when I visualize such a situation. I do believe we'll be able to communicate. I could only add that those are also situations that involve touching. I am a toucher.

This week I've been busy getting ready for my ski trip. I leave Friday night and fly to Denver. A friend from Denver will meet me and we drive to Breckenridge

Diane, I've thought about it a few moments here, and I feel a need and desire to be perfectly candid with you. If we are to get anywhere (and I'm not really looking for a pen pal)

that's needed. I'm going to Colo.with a girl I date here.
Diane, I do not explain this out of any sense of defensiveness,
and certainly not guilt, but only the discomfort I would feel
by not telling you

In closing I can only say how touching the "me too"
was. You can imagine that I did not close that letter without
some thought. I did not wish to be trite or off handed, nor
insincere. The word was carefully chosen. Your wonderful
"reaction" showed thought and feeling.

Affectionately
Don

~~~

One night that next week my phone rang. It was Don. I could hear a noise—thump-thump-thump. I asked, "What on earth is that noise?" He told me he was calling from a pay phone outside the lodge, and the noise was the skiers going up and down the steps in their heavy ski boots.

A smile comes across my face now as I think of Don sneaking out to make the calls to me. Did she know? Did she realize she was gradually being replaced by someone he had not yet met? Yes, our relationship was definitely changing.

Chapter 8

Making Plans for My Trip

The question on both of our minds was, "How and when could we meet each other?" I wasn't about to stay with a man, known only through letters and phone calls. I had a small studio apartment, no separate bedroom, so he couldn't even sleep on a couch.

We decided I would fly to Houston in April and stay with my girlfriend and her husband. They lived in the Rice/Museum area and Don lived in Montrose—a short distance.

My next letter to Don was written during my weekend visit to my grandfather.

~~~

March 29, 1975
Dear Don –
I'm writing you from the peace & quiet of the country.
In fact, right now it's 9 PM. I have a pumpkin & an apple pie
in the oven and my Pop-Pop is taking his "Saturday bath"
and while he's in there, I'm sitting here "whiffing" the pies
and "sipping" a Millers. Horrors! What will he say when he
discovers the frig' stocked!! (I'm saying that facetiously,
because he would never say anything to me although he may
be silently thinking—tsk, tsk, tsk!)

Too bad you don't live closer. You could come for Easter dinner. I'm making a country ham and all the fixings.

Today another Aunt & Uncle came up and we dyed Easter eggs. We have a custom in our family where we use a special dye called, "Hinkle's Easter Egg Colors." "It" is 5 bottles of color—red, blue, purple, yellow & green and you dab or dot on colors—maybe 2 or as many as the 5. The eggs become speckled or mottled & very pretty. Anyway, I hadn't done it in a few years, so I thought it would be fun to do with my grandfather.

Monday around 3, a friend called with an extra ticket to the opera," Tosca." I love Lincoln Center anyway. I always feel so inspired when I see those beautiful Chagall's and those chandeliers.

I'm looking forward to mid-April. I think the 19th is starting to look more promising. What will the weather be like then? Is it bathing suit weather? Horrors, can I lose my 5 lbs by then?! I'd like to tack on a couple vacation days. Will you be able to meet me at the airport? I'll wear a yellow rose in my hair so you'll know it's me!

Oh, by the way, I like you in your new glasses! Just a casual observation!

Well, my pies are baked—yummy—oh well, forget those 5 lbs.

So til 3 wks from now or by the time you receive this—2½ wks.

Goodnight, Don. Sleep tight!

Warmly,

Diane

P.S. You too!?

Chapter 9

Gift of Metamorphosis

The excitement began to build. We talked several times a day and continued writing letters to each other. Don had suggested he would take a few days of vacation time. We would get to know each other with no awkwardness, no strangeness, and no hurry.

In one of the last letters I sent to him before my arrival in Houston, I had divulged more feelings including the possibility of feeling a bit nervous when meeting him face to face.

~~~

Tuesday, April 8
Dear Don—
I was a little late for work this morning—9:15—so your letter was waiting for me in my mailbox on my way out. I'll read it as I answer it. It sure was a long letter and I loved sharing some of your rambling thoughts. I think we are very much alike in how we think as we write. I try to write to you as I might be talking to you if you were here sitting beside me.
An important point I'd also like to make...your comment about "single people who are comfortable and settled in their life." As for myself, I consider this period of my life "treading

water." I do not think that what I am doing with my life now is the complete answer. It reminds me of a story by Hesse which—if I can find it I'll send it to you.

I'm sure it is easier for me to fill the loneliness as I've never been in a married state and have nothing to compare it to. But, I certainly do not believe that living alone is the answer. I've been in this apartment now for 6 years and have hesitated in doing any structural changes because maybe I'll find 'the one' and settle down—or even at the house, the things I've done have not really taken that much time and money. I'm sure that's one of the reasons I got Gypsy 6 years ago—for company—to have at least some "almost human" thing here when I come home and face the loneliness.

Sometimes I love the loneliness, like right now as I'm curled up here while writing to you, so I can collect my thoughts. And, I do believe that it is important for couples to allow moments of solitude for the other—because we are still our own individuals.

I think I have only loved deeply twice in my life and maybe that is one of my faults—I take things very intensely. But, again I will say—"but why shouldn't I?" Why should a person do something only half-way, even loving, or especially to love?

Gosh, I've just reread these last few paragraphs. I don't usually open up my inner feelings like this to someone. But, then again—we have been very open with each other.

But, I want to tell you that even though we have been communicating since February, I may still be very shy when I meet you. I have been told by my friends that when they first met me, they thought me "cold" or "snobby"—but actually it was a defense on my unconscious side. I will be nervous in meeting you—but I'm sure it'll only last for a minute or two or three.....

Ah, I'm going to turn into a pumpkin in exactly 5 minutes.

Goodnight, Don—
See you soon—
Fondly—
Diane

Wed—AM
PS—I just found the story in a book called—
C.G. Jung & Herman Hesse
A Record of Two Friendships
By Miguel Serrano
*   Gypsy had found it earlier and had chewed up the*
front cover!

~~~

In this letter, I had included a copy of the story of Piktor's Metamorphosis which was the story of the transformation of a young man called Piktor. Piktor had entered Paradise and found himself standing before a tree which represented both Man and Woman, and then before a tree that represented the Sun and the Moon. Piktor was looking for "The Tree of Life and Happiness" and kept coming into contact with the Serpent. Everything in the forest was changing around him or continuing in their metamorphosis, everything but Piktor since he was still alone. Eventually he was transformed into a tree, but a solitary old tree. A pretty little girl appeared and magically she became one with the tree and was transformed into a new branch on the tree. Piktor was not alone and was happy at last. The moral of the story was that Piktor was happy as a pair. Yes, it was a rather deep story, but I thought I was experiencing these exact thoughts and my own metamorphosis since Don McCormack entered my life.

Chapter 10

Anticipation of April 23rd

In just a few days we would be actually meeting each other face to face. It had been ten and a half weeks from his phone call of February 10. We had traveled far those weeks, had discovered a lot about each other, and hopefully, the best was yet to come. Were we really going to be meeting each other?

~~~

Tuesday, April 15
Dear Diane
I guess it won't be long now—only a few days when you read this. I find myself highly anticipatory of our coming time together. I don't think I am uneasy about it, but I cannot be sure. I have really no fear or concern that we will have a good time and, at a minimum, enjoy each other. Whether we really "hit it off" well is another matter, but it is only a thought to be considered, and nothing to fear. I am very glad that you mentioned your tendency to appear cool (was that the word you used?) on first meetings as my own sensitivity in this area of dealing with females (we discussed this) might cause me some concern if in fact you aren't initially comfortable. Somehow, however, I believe the potential "ice" between us has long since been broken by our very warm and open communications.

*From our first telephone conversations and your letters
I have perceived in you a very warm, sensitive, thoughtful and
deep person. While J___ had mentioned it, your last letter
was a vivid indication of a trait I sensed but hadn't observed
directly—and that's your broad intellectual interests. I had a
tough time with the metamorphosis of Piktor, but certainly
found it beautiful and enjoyable. I had to give it three reading to begin to understand it. So there is a message here—my
depth in this area is not so great. I have always enjoyed some
of the arts, but my experiences are limited and I am not
knowledgeable in them. My music tastes tend to be popular
or light classics. I have only been to a very few operas and
ballets. My knowledge of fine art is strictly on the esthetics—
i.e., I know what I like and I enjoy looking, but don't test me
on artists or history. Maybe you will teach me.*

*This evening I am having dinner with Mary Beth.
I haven't decided where to take her, but maybe I'll let her
decide*

*It is an unusual and uncommon feeling to anticipate
meeting face to face someone whom you have already begun
to know and care for. Diane, I am very anxious for the next
eight days to pass. I'll see you soon and talk to you on Friday
or Saturday.*

*Affectionately
Don*

~~~

Yes, I was anxious for the next eight days to pass as well.
My heart was getting ready.

Chapter 11

April 23rd–First Time Ever

The plane landed and I saw him standing there. "Don McCormack?"—I asked with a questioning lilt to my voice. It was Wednesday, April 23, and it was the first time ever I saw his face.

We went to a small Italian restaurant on Montrose Avenue—Salvatore's, now out of business. I don't remember what we ordered, but I do remember Don reaching over across the table to touch my hand saying, "I'm a toucher." We lingered at the table talking non-stop until the restaurant was closing.

After dinner Don drove me to my friend's house, and I was the one who reached up to kiss him goodnight.

The next morning, Don arrived early for breakfast to discuss some of the things we might do while I was in Houston. He had arranged to take a couple of vacation days from Shell and had planned several events: air races, a bluegrass concert, swimming and a picnic in Hermann Park.

After breakfast, Don took me on a tour around Houston: to downtown Houston where he pointed out One Shell Plaza where he worked, to Memorial and the street where he used to live, and to other areas. We spent the rest of the day at a local pool where we talked and talked. We never ran out of things to talk about. That evening we went back to my friend's house and joined them for dinner. After they went to bed, we sat on their couch and shared more details of our lives, and from time to time Don would reach over and give me a hug or nuzzle my neck or share his soft kisses. It was becoming so easy and natural to be with each other.

D & D – April 24th, 1975 – Taken at home where I stayed in Houston

Weeks before, I sent Don another book I read by Hermann Hesse, "Narcissus and Goldmund." On the inside cover I had written the words.

~~~

*"A language of the soul
had gradually come into being between them."*

~~~

And that evening, this was happening to us. A language of "our" souls was being discovered and was coming into being between us.

Friday was another fun-filled day. That night as Don was dropping me off at my friend's house, he told me he would be late picking me up Saturday morning. He had to go see someone the next morning. He didn't say why and I didn't question him.

When Don arrived Saturday morning, he told me he had gone to see the woman he had been dating. He said he had to let her know their relationship could not continue as it was because of me. (She was the same woman he had gone skiing with earlier in the year.)

It was a beautiful and sunny day, and Don suggested we go on a picnic. We went to this incredible gourmet luxury grocery store, Jamails, and bought a selection of cheeses, hard salami, crusty French bread and other items. I wasn't really paying much attention to what he had been tossing in the shopping cart, but when I saw other items on the conveyer belt, I smiled at him and said, "Hmm, those don't look like picnic items. Let's see—eggs, bacon, English muffins, strawberries. Just what do you have in mind, Don McCormack?" He looked back at me with a sheepish grin on his face and said, "Well, you can't blame a guy for wishful thinking, can you?" We drove to Hermann Park, located in one of the most picturesque areas of Houston and very close to the Rice University/ Museum area where I was staying. We spread out a blanket, drank wine and munched on our array of food. And somewhere between the wine and the cheese, he took me in his arms and looked into my eyes and said, "Diane, I have fallen in love with you."

I was taken aback. I didn't know if I was ready to declare my love for him—yes, I had been writing to him and speaking with him in nightly phone calls for the past several weeks.

I looked into his face, which was so tender and so serious, and answered, "I don't know if I love you or not—but when I do know, I'll let the whole world know."

The wine we shared that blissful day was a 1971 bottle of Louis Martini Cabernet Sauvignon—still one of my most favorite reds. He included the label in one of his letters to me. I had it encased in acrylic and sent it to him as a "happy" a few weeks later. It was the first of the many "happys" (a gift that is unexpected and not for any particular occasion) Don and I would give to each other over the next thirty-two years. Don had written these words on the back of the label.

~~~

Saturday—April 26
Celebrating our love.
You are truly my darling.
My chest throbs for you.
Lovingly, Don

~~~

D & D - Hermann Park – April 27th, 1975

Don told me he loved me several more times that afternoon, and I was blown away with his love and tenderness. When would I know—for sure? Was I already in love with him, but just being cautious?

By the end of that day, I knew I was in love with him.

I was scheduled to fly back to New York on Sunday night, April 28. And, when we said goodbye at the airport, I whispered in his ear, "Yes, my darling Don, I do love you—but, I'm not ready to let the whole world know—YET."

The letter I wrote to him while flying back to New York included some of the thoughts that had started to whirl around in my head.

~~~

Sunday, 10:20 PM
Darling Don—
Just some fast random thoughts to you while aboard
this bumpy flight.
I saw you at the window. You looked so sad. Darling,
don't be sad. It's such a beautiful feeling to know that we
share so many feelings. I'll miss you terribly.
Writing to you helps in the longing—the missing. As
long as I continue to write you're here. I haven't opened the
plane window and yelled out—I love Don McCormack—
YET—but I've said it softly to myself. In fact, I said it about
30 minutes ago when I went to the bathroom and I looked
into the mirror & said—I love Don McCormack.
Goodnight you beautiful man—
Love,
Diane

~~~

I dropped the letter into the mail slot at the airport and
caught a cab back to my apartment in Manhattan.

Monday morning I got up and started on my usual routine. I showered and put on some scruffy clothes, fed and
walked my dog. I dressed for work and was looking for something in my linen closet—when the ring fell from the top shelf
of my closet and landed on the floor at my feet.

Among my closest friends, I was known for starting the
trend of wearing several charms on a long gold chain. The
charms included a locket given to my Aunt Irene upon her
graduation from secretarial school with small photographs of
my Hungarian grandfather and grandmother in it, another
locket with photographs of my mother and father, my grandfather's key bob, a Scorpio charm given to me by Maurine
Antaya, a charm from a business trip to New Zealand and others.

So, on this Monday morning, I slowly bent down, picked up the ring, untied the knot, opened the catch on the chain and added the ring to my collection of favorite charms.

Chain collection - 1975

Chapter 12

Love Letters

Our relationship took on a new meaning, and both of us were reaching out to each other with a new intensity and awareness. We were no longer "pen-pals" but two people trying to build on a long-distance relationship through daily phone calls, letters and cards, and a rendezvous when possible.

Two days after I had returned from my trip to Houston, I received the first of Don's love letters.

~~~

Tuesday, AM
My Dearest Diane,
These thoughts are disjointed and unconnected, except for the common thread of relating my love for you—
I find it necessary each day to express to you the depth and reality of my love. Writing my thoughts to you gives me tremendous internal pleasure, just as I am sure reading them does you.
You cannot (or maybe you can) realize fully the result on me of the knowledge of your love. I have never loved nor been loved this way in my life. The joy it brings me makes me stand more erect, greet people friendlier and just be more of a human being.

Today is today, and lo and behold, I love you, indeed, more than yesterday.

> *I love you.*
> *I need you.*
> *I want you.*
> *I love you …*
> *Forever*
> *Don*

~~~

He penned these thoughts to me later that same day.

~~~

Tuesday, PM
Darling
I have trouble focusing on the page because there are tears of love in my eyes.

I see you in everything—am reminded of you by every-thing and nothing. I feel your presence, and sense your love—oh, do I sense your love. I miss you dreadfully, but I am not sad. Missing you is beautiful and the empty feeling is replaced by the nearness of your love.

I love you, my sweet, beautiful darling, more than anyone else in this world could. You will be mine always.

> *Don*

~~~

An excerpt of his next letter to me.

~~~

Wed
My Darling Diane,
I love you, my darling. It's not going away—it's getting deeper and deeper, better and better. It's funny—talking on the phone saddens me a bit in that hearing your voice makes me want to reach out and touch you.

I just talked to my mother this evening and she was most interested to hear about Diane Young. Of course,

I played it low keyed, but told of all the things "of interest" that we did. I said that we got along fine, and that I was interested. I said I like you and thought you like me. When she asked when I'd see you again, I told her we both planned to be in Chicago. She was pleased that it worked out so well, and hoped that you would care for me if I should develop a love for you. What she doesn't know is that I have and you do.

A thought occurred to me the other day—my life was conceived on Feb 10, but I was born on April 23.

You are the brightest spot in my life. It is such a glorious feeling to love so deeply and completely.

Goodnight, my love.

Te quiero

Don

~~~

I wrote to Don the following morning, and now our letters and phone calls, besides talking about our love, included our upcoming trip to Chicago.

~~~

Wednesday, April 30

8 AM

Good Morning Don darling—

And it is! I feel so good this morning. It was so wonderful talking to you last night. I really missed you yesterday! Today—I miss you more.

You know, honey, it's so beautiful thinking of being with you. In Chicago, Texas, maybe Europe, anywhere—everywhere. Just to have you there so that when I say, "Oh look, isn't that beautiful?" I'll be able to share it with you. It's really beautiful falling in love...with You!

I miss you—but I'm with you, too.

Love You!

Diane

~~~

Our letters and phone calls, within the time frame of only one week from when I left Houston, became stepping stones to our future life together. This was before any phone company had a plan for free long distance calls or before cell phones, so every night Don would drive to downtown Houston, about a twenty minute drive, and use the WATS line at Shell's headquarters. At one point during a telephone conversation, Don asked me to marry him.

Some of the letter I wrote to him later that same night.

~~~

Wednesday PM 11:20
    Dearest Don –
    I just tried to call you. You see how you've affected my heart. It waits for you to call me.
    Just think one week ago I got off the plane and there you were. And 2 weeks from today, I'll be getting off the plane, and there you'll be. But you'll be a different YOU. This time you will be THE man I love and our reunion will be even more beautiful. My heart will really jump!
    I sent the book today, darling. I hope you like it. Well, my darling. I'll close for now. I'll try to call you now—
    Sweet dreams—
    Diane

I added to the letter the next morning.

    Good morning Darling!
    Don dearest, your name was on my mind—on my lips this morning when I opened my eyes. Have no doubts about me, darling. I love you—how could I not love you. You're the most precious man that's ever come into my life—and I mean that sincerely. My love for you is a growing love. And, for me, that's the best kind. Remember I liked you for the first 3 days and loved you on the third night. If I would have loved you right away, then I would be a little unsure—maybe thinking

that it was my readiness to be loved. But, I could feel the love forming, growing. It's just incredible to me that I've found You! It's going to be beautiful growing more and more in love with you. So my dearest, have no doubts about it. That window is open about 1" now. You'll be the first to hear it.

> *What are you doing the rest of your life—*
> *I think I know.*
> *I'll pray on it!*
> *I do love you—*
> *Diane*

~~~

My reference to, "that window is open 1" now," referred to my responding to him at our picnic in Hermann Park, after he had told me that he had fallen in love with me, that when I knew for sure I loved him, I would let the whole world know and shout it from the window.

~~~

Saturday—May 3
11:45 PM—after your call
My darling—
 And you are. I still feel so very close to you so I'll write a few lines to stay closer to you before I go to sleep.
 Don darling. I just swell up with happiness when I think of us being together. It's almost too much to believe that all of this is happening to me. I mean, after all of these years— to finally find you and to be ready to change my past life of 11 years without too much hesitation—of course, there is some of that—mainly because I do like my job. I would have to find something of the same interest, I think. Oh, I don't know—I've never had someone like you in my life at the same time as my job—so maybe that's why I find it so exciting. With you in my life, everything may change. And through you, everything else will take the proper proportion.
 The first time ever I saw your face…
 I love you

~~~

I wrote out the entire lyrics of the song, "The First Time Ever." The words had become so meaningful to us. Our Houston rendezvous was the first time I saw his face.

A letter from Don written Sunday, May 4.

~~~

Dearest Diane
I never tire of talking to you Sweetheart, and this letter is simply a continuation of our talk earlier. How else can I keep telling you that I love you. Oh, but I do.

When we talked tonight I didn't say how much I am enjoying Hesse's novel. It is so beautifully written. So tender, thoughtful and really sensitive.

I really feel good, right now, my love. The thought of spending the rest of my life with you makes me tense with emotion. You are mine, my Love.

Goodnight.
Love

~~~

In a letter Don wrote to me the next day, he wrote the words—"marry me." Parts of this letter.

~~~

Monday
My Dearest—
Oh Sweetheart, if I do not use the words that sound so beautiful as when you use them, do not think I love you any less (I know you don't). I am just overwhelmed by my feeling of love for you. Oh Jesus, how I ache for you. To finally love someone (mutually, too) after all these years, just leaves be breathless and on tender hooks. My Diane, fear not—I'll be good to you forever.

Please marry me Diane. I love you. Don

~~~

Don and I wrote to each other every day, morning and night, and spoke on the phone daily. We were eagerly looking forward to Chicago. There is one more letter I want to include. It's part of a letter I wrote to him on Tuesday, May 6, because in this letter, I talk about God.

~~~

Tuesday night 11:20 PM
Hello my darling—
I'm all ready for bed—make-up off, in my flannel nightgown because it's so cold here, watching the late news— and waiting eagerly for the sound of your voice. I'm sure when the phone rings, I'll grab it on the first ring.

One week from tomorrow. I can hardly believe it. I was excited on April 23rd also—but this time I'll be seeing you differently.

Did I tell you that I have thanked God for bringing you to me? .

Don, I really have faith in us. I have no doubts in us, honey. I really do want to be with you. I need you, I want you, I love you. And…I also "dig" you—you beautiful man, you.

Love You Like Crazy—
Me

~~~

Chicago was waiting for us!

Chapter 13

Chicago

Our first rendezvous after meeting "face to face" in Houston— Chicago! Would we share the same excitement we had shared with each other during the past two weeks through our love letters and phone calls? I felt as excited and nervous as a bride. In fact, the night before I left Manhattan for my flight to Chicago, in my excitement of running around my apartment and packing, I crashed my big toe into the Parson's coffee table that was in front of my sofa bed and actually broke it. I remember telling Don this as I spoke to him that night. He had already arrived in Chicago and I was so upset that my injured toe might put a damper on our being together that I almost cried. What did he do? He laughed. Then I started to laugh as well. How utterly stupid of me!

Don met me at the airport and we took a cab to the hotel. There we were—standing in line at the hotel with him just inches away from me—waiting for our turn to check in at the reservation desk. I was totally nervous. Here were all these business people, mostly men. It was 1975 and I kept thinking they knew Don and I were going to be checking in together and sharing a room with each other. I was being paranoid, of course. As we were standing there, Don reached for my hand. He started to whisper "soft innuendos" in my ears and I know I must have been blushing. I was totally nervous. Oh, I said that already. I was totally nervous. He was actually teasing me and was amused with how nervous I was. "Relax," he said to me reassuringly as he gave me one of his big bear hugs, "Nobody cares." He was right, of course, nobody knew and nobody cared.

When we finally reached the reservation clerk, I asked for a separate bill. No problem, request accepted; see how simple?

The bellhop took our bags—this was before the days of roll-on luggage and escorted us to the hotel elevator. The time the elevator slowly climbed the floors to our floor was excruciating long. We arrived at our floor, the door opened, and the bellhop pointed us in the direction to our room. He followed us and as we stepped aside, he opened the door with the key. I looked up at Don and saw the radiance and gleam in his eyes. The room was quite spacious and had a separate small living area. The bellhop started to tell Don, "Here's the TV control. You click on this. Here's the bar; just help yourself to whatever you want and it will be posted to your bill. Here's the control for the air-conditioning." Here's this and here's that. I looked over at Don, and he had this look on his face that said, "Will he ever leave?"

No. The bellhop also had to show us the sleeping area of the suite. It was when we all moved into that area that Don and I instantly noticed the twin beds—with a small built-in night table in-between the two beds. At this moment, Don reached into his wallet and took out a big bill and started to wave it in front of the bellhop's eyes so he would take a hint and leave.

At last we were alone and all we could do was roar with laughter at the bellhop and the twin beds.

It had been my plan to go over to the window, open the

latch, raise the window and shout to the world, **"I LOVE DON McCORMACK."** After all I said to him, after he proclaimed his love to me, when I knew for sure I loved him, I would let the whole world know.

The window wouldn't open. I tried and tried, but the damn thing wouldn't budge. It was hermetically sealed. I turned around and saw Don with this quizzical look on his face. He probably knew what I had in mind but he didn't let on and my head was already spinning with an alternate plan in mind.

That first evening we discovered this small and quaint Italian restaurant. We didn't have reservations. We had been walking hand in hand down one of the side streets close to our hotel and had just stumbled upon it. What a find! It was dimly lit, had only about twenty or so square tables covered with red and white checkered tablecloths—cloth—not plastic, not with the overlay of white paper found in so many restaurants today. The smells coming out of the kitchen were delicious. The atmosphere was perfect! We sat there with our eyes locked on each other. Once again, Don reached across the table, took my hand in his and said to me, "I'm a toucher."

And, at that very moment, he touched my heart and my soul as well as my hand.

Don reached into his jacket pocket with his other hand and took out a small box. It contained a round heavy gold charm about an inch in diameter, the circumference was a twisted rope of gold, and in the center was a raised Scorpio symbol. It was my astrological symbol. On the back of the charm, he had the words engraved, "Te Quiero—Don." He said it was an engagement gift, and he reached over and took both my hands in his. And, as he squeezed my hands in his, he said, "Diane, I love you. I loved you from the first time I heard your voice on the phone. I loved you from the first letter I received from you. And, I want to continue loving you—forever and

always. Will you marry me?" It was the most magical of moments. I was deliriously happy and my heart was pounding;
I was so very much in love with this man!

Don said he decided on the charm because an engagement
ring would be something special that we could pick out together. He thought I would want it to be an antique because
he knew I loved antique jewelry, and Houston in 1975 wasn't
exactly the Mecca for finding such items.

We sat at the table, oblivious to everyone around us, and
talked about our wedding. If we could wait until August, I
knew most of my relatives, especially my parents, would be in
Weatherly celebrating my grandfather's birthday. The grounds
around his bungalow were so beautiful. Yes, it was decided.
Our wedding would be on Saturday, August 23, and held in
Weatherly, Pennsylvania.

And, my toe stopped hurting.

Chicago – May 16, 1975

Chapter 14

Fourteen Weeks to Go

Daily love letters and phone calls were bringing us closer and closer to the final destination—August 23. Yes, now we had a continuum. We could actually see the fourteen weeks ahead of us as the destination to our wedding day. Our letters now included details of my move and our impending wedding.

An excerpt of my letter written to Don the day after I returned to Manhattan.

~~~

Monday, May 19
Dearest—
I love you, dearest. I really do. I've never felt so complete. Now I know what it means to feel whole. We'll have so many beautiful and complete times together. I can hardly wait for August.

My girlfriends are so excited for me and they can't wait to meet you. They love you already. 'Course I've only told them your good points (now just what are your bad points? I forget.) HA.

Oh, darling, if I would start listing all the qualities I love in you. I'll tell you some of the things that come to mind rapidly—

—when we were touring the science museum and you sensed I was bored, you came up with an alternative.

— asking for the wine label—showed your great sensitivity to our love.

— handling the situation of the noisy man in the Cape Cod Room; some men would have been too weak to raise the issue.

— your stealing glances at me—your love and your understanding of my sore toe.

— when you called Gypsy "our dog"—that was sweet. I love you for realizing my love for her and not being jealous.

— and all the "future" talk about us—i.e.—beds, furniture, doing things, taking a photography course, everything that expressed to me that yes, you did think of us in terms of future and forever.

I'll love you toujours
and
I love you now
Diane

~~~

Parts of a letter he sent the days following Chicago.

~~~

Tuesday
My Darling Diane, My Love,
Whatever the power is that brought you and me together, in the way that it (or He) did, it was certainly done well.

I can only marvel at the complete chain of circumstances and reflect on the key elements of such:

* – A good friend, to each of us, to give such a glowing recommendation to the other in a way to whet the appetite.

* – Over two months of communication, both written and spoken, in an open, caring and searching way, to give us time to begin to care for each other without really meeting. True love does take time.

* – A chance to be together, to really meet and get to know one another, with the wisdom to move carefully, cautiously and yet boldly as the love developed.

* – And then the time apart, seventeen days, to reflect on each other, our love, our experiences together and our future. The many calls, truly beautiful conversations, the many delicate and loving letters!!! Those seventeen days (and nights) are a most important part in the development of our love. Much time to think—to appreciate—to miss—to wonder—to question—and to love. To realize, really fully appreciate and realize, beyond a doubt, what we do and will mean to each other. A seemingly long, but important period to set the stage for—

* – Chicago. After becoming acquainted, meeting, loving tentatively maybe, parting to reflect and realize it's really here. Chicago was a time to love and enjoy each other, and significantly, to commit. And Chicago was also that last little "proof of the pudding," if it was needed. That neither of us remotely doubted the outcome, in looking back in the years ahead we can surely know that Chicago was a chance to prove ourselves, as we did, knowingly, or not.

Oh, my Diane, I love you. I need you. I want you forever. You are undoubtedly the best thing that ever happened to me. Our commitment is complete now, my love, forever.

Te quiero
Don

~~~

In one of his letters that followed, Don wrote he had dinner with his youngest son, Dan, and told him about me. He said he was a little nervous, but Dan's reactions were all positive.

One night as I was in my apartment jotting down some possibilities and ideas for our wedding, my phone rang. I ran to it thinking it was Don. On the other end was my mother who sounded breathless and excited. "You would never guess who we just received a phone call from?" she asked. (The Young family is known for asking questions and making you guess.) "Who?" I asked. And, with even more rapid sentences, she said, "Don—and you would never guess what he just told Daddy and me." Oh my God, I thought. He wants out of the marriage. He's breaking the news to my parents so they can tell me. "He's taken out a life insurance policy on himself and has named you the beneficiary," my mother said. I had just given notice to the Wool Bureau, and Don was concerned that if anything happened to him between the time I formally gave notice and our actual wedding date, that I would be left virtually without a job—or without an apartment. So he was guaranteeing I would be covered. "Yeah, that sounds like Don," I replied. Then my father got on the phone and told me about a phone conversation he had with Don before we had gone to Chicago. Don had called my folks one night, and when my mother answered the phone, as she usually did, he asked if he could speak with my father. Don then asked my father for my hand in marriage, and he wanted to assure my father that he could well provide for "Daddy's little girl." But, that was the kind of man Don was, old fashioned AND always there for me even before we were married.

I was busy making wedding plans and moving plans. When things flustered me, Don knew what to say to me to calm me down. In one letter, it was his humor that lifted me up and made me laugh.

~~~

"It made me feel really good that I was able to cheer you up the other day. Honey, I can only quote the old Latin expression—"Illegitimi non carborundum," which translates "don't let the bastards grind you down."

~~~

In early June, I flew to Houston. Don wanted to take a road trip to show me the Texas hill country. We drove to San Antonio and did the typical tourist stuff and then onto Austin and Aquarena Springs in San Marcos. We picnicked alongside the banks of the Lady Bird Lake after we were kicked off a private spot along the banks of a beautiful and picturesque stream. Well, actually we were "escorted off" by the farmer who had his shot gun pointed at Don the entire time we were making it back to Don's car which had been parked alongside the farmer's property. Of course we saw the "No Trespassing" sign, but we also spotted the beautiful and very private stream. We climbed over the fence and carefully carried our picnic basket while avoiding stepping in cow patties. The spot was perfect! We spread out our picnic blanket with the items from the basket: fresh baked French bread, cheese, pâté, and a bottle of wine. We had only sampled some of our picnic and a glass of wine when the farmer appeared. The first words out of Don's mouth when he saw the farmer approach us —*Oh shit!* We relived this experience many times in our life.

Along the Hempstead Highway, I took my favorite shot of Don. We had been driving with the windows open, and Don was complaining about feeling "all hot and sweaty." I looked over at him and said, "No wonder you are, Honey. You are wearing a

Don in blue polyester -shirt – June 1975

polyester shirt. You might as well be wearing a plastic bag. Remember, my background is in natural fibers and fabrics."

So, at the first decent men's store we came to, I went in and bought him a shirt made of 100% cotton—another *"Happy."*

When we returned to Houston the next week, Don met my parents face-to-face for the first time. They had traveled from Florida days before in their trailer and were staying at a local KOA campsite before heading to Mexico for a few weeks.

Don picked my parents up and brought them to his apartment for dinner. My father immediately liked Don. My mother, however, took more time to warm up to Don—especially after she saw a most familiar suitcase sitting on a luggage rack in his bedroom as Don was giving my parents a tour of his apartment!

Chapter 15

Acceptance & Blessings

After I returned from Houston, I drove to Weatherly every week-end to take care of my grandfather and make preparations for our wedding. Many times one or more of my girlfriends would go with me. It was great to get out of the city in the summer and spend the weekend in the fresh and cool country air of the Poconos. There were always two things my girlfriends wanted to do while we were in Weatherly. One, we had to drive out to one of the farmers and fill our shopping bags with fresh picked vegetables, whatever was in season. And second, we had to stop at the barn on my way from town to my grandfather's bun-galow and get eggs. There was never anyone in sight, and we would drop the coins in a brown paper bag and take our dozen or so of eggs. And, on these weekends, I used little make-up, wore casual clothes and my long hair was pulled back in either a pony tail or braids. Everyone thought I was years younger than I actually was. And, probably so did Pastor Taylor.

One Sunday, I attended church with my grandfather and asked Pastor Taylor if he had some time to talk to me. Most everyone in Weatherly knew me because they knew my grand-father, and they knew I had been taking care of him for the past year, including Pastor Taylor. I met with him after the service and told him I was getting married and asked if he could officiate at our wedding. Yes, he was honored to do so. "Let me know when Don might come with you to Weatherly so I can talk to him," he immediately said to me.

In a letter written to Don, I talked about some of the wedding plans.

~~~

Sunday 12:30 PM

I love the idea about Pastor Taylor not having married anyone before. That will make it special for us even more so. He is a very nice person also. You will like him. He's very young and told me this was his first "charge." I'm sure he'll help make it a beautiful ceremony.

I talked to a liquor store today and he advised me 4 cases of champagne with leftovers for us to celebrate every 23rd for a year, (Ha)

So I'll ask my friends in Balto. He suggested Korbel Brut. He would give me a price of $60 a case—it usually sells for $72 or $71.

~~~

Meanwhile things were progressing. I took my Pinto to a shop where they installed an air-conditioner. I never needed AC in New York or in the Poconos but would definitely need it in Houston.

One weekend I found an old basket in my grandfather's attic. I took it back to the city, lined it in navy and white gingham check cotton, and made matching napkins and a tablecloth appliquéd with a large "M" in the middle. It was one of my wedding gifts to Don.

And, every Sunday I attended church with my grandfather, Pastor Taylor would stop me and ask, "When might Don be coming east? I want to meet him and talk with him."

Don planned a dinner with Mary Beth to tell her about me. He was concerned with how she would react to his getting remarried. Some thoughts I wrote to him.

~~~

Darling, by the time you receive this, you may be ready to tell MB the news about us and I want you to know that my love for you is there to give you the added support just in case you may need it. As we both know—16½ is a rough age. She may take our marriage or more specifically, your re-marriage, as a personal threat to her. Just give her your "papa love" and things will work out. Don't press it—don't press me onto her for she'll resent that. Things will work out—in time. Our love will reflect in her eyes, too, and she'll be happy knowing how happy our love has made you. If not—I'll love you even more to fill the void—just in case there's one there for a while.

~~~

A note I received from Don mentioned he had asked his eldest son, Bruce, to be his "best man" at our wedding.

~~~

My Dearest Diane,

I miss you, Darling. This has been a nice day, but I really need my Baby near me. I think of you so much.

Today was busy enough doing things, and they were fun, too. Read the paper, two hours of tennis (one hour with Dan, and one hour in a pick-up game), a little furniture scraping, and dinner with Bruce. I had a funny feeling when he left—I'll see him in August (he was excited to hear Rainy and Ann are going to come), but it was sort of the last good-bye as my dependent. From now on he's on his own.

You are my Baby.

Love

Don

~~~

I wanted to meet his mother, Rainy, to receive her blessing. Don had told her all about me and that we had set a date for our wedding, but I had to meet her before August 23. We checked our schedules and decided we could meet up in St. Louis the last week in June. I still had vacation time to use. I would fly to St. Louis and Don would drive up in his car so we could camp en-route back to Houston. I could spend a few days with him in Houston and meet some of his friends.

In a letter from Don written on Monday, June 23, some of what he wrote.

~~~

Today really was OK, and I got a lot accomplished.
I got some better maps, fixed the stove (camping, i.e.) got a
tent and cooking pans plus plates from Breckenfelds, fixed up
our symphony seats, got the guy to hold off on my suit until
July 7, fixed my tail light, bought a thermos for coffee while
driving, plus did some work. And you only have three things
to do. (He was teasing me, of course. He had referred to
three things I had to do in an earlier letter—plan a wedding, quit my job and move.) *Oh—and I found my mother*
can fly from St. Louis to Allentown with one stop, no change
arriving at about 3 PM.

~~~

I remember the day I landed in St. Louis as if it were only yesterday. Don's trip from Houston to St. Louis should have included an overnight stop at a motel. But, when I walked down the ramp (no jet way in those days) there he was, lean-ing against the entrance door to the airport. He had this sheep-ish grin on his face. He had driven all night long so that he would be there when I exited the plane.

And, how could I not love Don's mother? She adored her son and she adored me for loving him. Instantly, we both loved each other. There was no pretense. There was just this openness, no aloofness or strangeness. We had tea in her apartment and then took her out to lunch at one of her favorite restaurants, "The Green Parrot." We took her back to her apartment,

Don and Rainy in St. Louis – June 27, 1975

and when Don and I were ready to leave, she hugged me and then squeezed my hand and told me how happy she was that Don had found me.

On our drive back to Houston, we took a leisurely route and camped out at some of the most glorious camp grounds in Missouri and Arkansas. Our time together during these leisurely days seemed like we had known each other for years. Don had packed

Cooking Dinner on Coleman – July 2, 1975

all the gear in his car and I had remembered to pack my travel
Scrabble game. After we had our dinner we sat on a blanket
outside our tent, watched the stars come out, drank wine and
talked and talked and talked.

When we returned to Houston, we hosted a cocktail party
for some of his friends so they could meet me. It had been organized weeks before. It did not go off as we had planned because some of his friends still felt loyal to his ex and they came late
and left early. (In time, though, I did win them over and they
all became some of our best friends later in our married life.)

Things were going 'full steam' ahead. In a letter I wrote
to Don in mid-July, I updated him on some of the plans. Parts
of this letter.

~~~

> First, I picked up the rings. I paid for yours and the
> jeweler will bill you personally for mine. It should be around
> $72 or $75—plus the engraving. I have both rings.
>
> Then I went to the antique place & I really do love THAT
> ring. It fits perfectly and is 18k gold—made in France—is an
> antique—has about 1 carat worth of diamonds—5 diamonds—
> and is $325.00. I put a small deposit of $25 on it and they're
> open Friday, Aug 1 at 10 AM—so I can't wait for you to go
> with me and put the ring on my finger with a kiss.
>
> Don, dearest, how could I have been so lucky in finding
> you & your love.
>
> Love & Love &.....
>
> Diane

~~~

The following weekend I drove to Weatherly, and while I
was there, I worked on some last minute arrangements: the
funeral home would deliver the tent canopies to Pop-Pop's
bungalow, geraniums and hanging baskets of flowers had been
ordered, chairs would be delivered from the fire department,
trays of food had been ordered and the hand-written invita-

tions had been mailed. We had planned on 100 guests. Everything was falling into place. But, then I remembered I was supposed to call Pastor Taylor. I didn't want to discuss wedding details when I would see him in church Sunday with my grandfather, so I called him at his home.

Pastor Taylor seemed very glad I had called, but before I started to tell him details of the wedding, he again asked when Don would be in Weatherly so he could talk with him. Now, I had an answer for him! I told him Don was flying to New York City the first weekend in August because we had to go to Pennsylvania and get our marriage license. I said we could stop for a brief visit after seeing Pop-Pop because we were on a tight schedule to return to New York that night. I didn't give Pastor Taylor a chance to respond and started telling him the details of the wedding—the musicians had been hired, the flowers, the food, etc., and then I added that my niece would be by Maid of Honor and Don's son would be his Best Man. There was a lull on the other end of the phone, and then Pastor Taylor asked me in a quiet voice with a slight stammer, "And…um…um… how old is Don's son, Bruce?" I said, "Well, let's see, he just graduated from college, so he's probably 21 or 22." Then I asked Pastor Taylor again, "So, would you want Don to stop in to see you while we are in Weatherly because this is the only time before the actual wedding when you could have your talk with him." I could hear him clear his throat. Then he said, "No, Diane, that won't be necessary. I didn't realize Don had been married before. No, I don't need to have a talk with him. Actually, Don could probably have a talk with me."

I didn't know how to respond to Pastor Taylor's comment, because up until that moment, I didn't realize what he meant when he kept saying he needed to *talk* with Don. I guess I never mentioned to him Don had been married before.

There was a silence between us. Then Pastor Taylor cleared his throat again and said, "Blessings to you and Don."

Chapter 16

New York City

Only one month to go! I couldn't believe it! One month and I had so much to do, including being fitted for my wedding dress. My niece, Dawn, was flying into New York from Ohio since she was my Maid of Honor and she had to be fitted for her dress as well.

Part of a letter written to Don on Tuesday, July 23.

~~~

My dearest—my love—

It's 12:15 PM. Dawn and I just came back from our measuring and since I have a little while before my 1:00 lunch, I came home with her. And what a beautiful surprise to find another letter waiting for me.

Darling, never have any doubt that your letters are not sensitive. I told you in my letter #1 that you had a beautiful Alma or soul. And, dearest, that was long before I knew you...so you can imagine how much I feel for you NOW. Maybe each anniversary we should sit down with a bottle of Korbel and reread to each other our love letters...to remember our early love and to reflect on how our love will have grown over the years.

*When I stop and think of all the little things we have
in common—the niceties of life—like enjoying a glass of wine,
snacks, driving, discovering, just relaxing together—and
that's so important. Those are the beautiful times I love—
even a scrabble or backgammon game played with you is a
beautiful time together.*

*Dearest, you are my whole world—I can't think of
anything else in the whole world I want or need or love more.*

I do love you—

Diane

~~~

A couple of days later, this letter from Don was in my
mailbox. This is it in its entirety. Even today as I read this, I
have to laugh.

~~~

Hi Love

*Happy Anniversary. I love you, and now let's get down
to business.*

*I want to mail you these folders on places to stay in Va.
so we can talk about them. I probably need to get a reservation in soon. I called them all today and have a little more
information. All are in the same general area.*

*I would expect to drive to Harrisburg or Hagerstown on
Sat. We'd probably get a late start on Sun and arrive in mid
afternoon. We could sightsee along the way and get there
whenever we want.*

~~~

Then he listed five possible honeymoon destinations, but
the only place which took a pet was Bryce Mountains. In his
next letter, he talked about things that might come up in our
marriage.

~~~

Thurs, July 24
9:05 PM
My Dearest
One week from this moment I should be just taking off on my flight to join you. And as I have said so many times, I am more than ready. It has been so long since I really enjoyed my life, overall, that I've forgotten what peace is like. Of course, when I'm with you it is peaceful and beautiful, but there is always the ax ready to fall at the end of the visit. Ah well, it won't be much longer.

Your letter today, as always, was so very beautiful. Your love comes thru so clearly. We just have a dedication to each other that will make the rest of our life beautiful. There is that attitude in each of us that asks "what can I do for the other? how can I show my love? did she/he misunderstand what I said and so be concerned (or hurt)?" These are the things that will carry us on. The four minutes will serve to remind us several times a day.

One of the underlying things in most arguments is "you don't love me." The important arguments aren't over matters of fact. All kinds of things really boil down to "you don't show me you love me." Oh Baby, you are going to have to put up with all kinds of love signs, because I just adore you. Let's be sure that all the "you don't love me's" come up for discussion so we can work them out.

I really loved the thought in your last letter about reading our letters to each other. That's a pretty good idea - sort of a "four minute" experience. Maybe we'll do that during our four minutes from time to time. It also occurs to me just now that I think I will write you a love letter from time to time.

~~~

Years later, Don and I talked about what made our marriage work. For me, I had established my career and knew who I was. I did not have unrealistic expectations. Don had been married before and knew the "pitfalls." Both of us were mature and knew what we wanted in a partner and in a marriage. In one of our phone calls I told him I had read couples need to have four minutes with each other with no other distractions, just four minutes when they could sit and hold hands and connect. This is what Don referred to when he mentioned "four minute" in this letter.

Meanwhile, ever since my aborted attempt to open the window of our hotel room in Chicago to let the whole world know—"I loved Don McCormack"—my brain had been racing with possibilities. How could I accomplish this? One day while walking down Fifth Avenue, I went past one of those funky tourist shops and saw a display of tee-shirts in the store window. The light bulb went off. I knew what I would do! I ordered a bright red tee-shirt with the words, **"I LOVE DON McCORMACK"** in felt iron-on letters centered down the front.

I LOVE
DON McCORMACK –
tee shirt

Don's flight arrived at La Guardia airport on Thursday afternoon before the wedding and I had planned to pick him up in my Pinto. The weather in New York City had been balmy up until that weekend and then it was "Hot as Hades" with the high temperature close to 110°. I put on the tee-shirt and a pair of shorts, but was a little embarrassed to be walking down the terminal aisle (in those days one could go to the gate to meet someone coming in). I also had to walk several blocks to get my car out of the parking garage. I slipped on my raincoat over the tee-shirt and shorts. Thank goodness weeks before I had the air-conditioner installed in my car, but it was barely keeping up. I was tempted to remove the raincoat, but I didn't. I parked the car, located the gate where he would be arriving and waited for him about fifty yards or so away from the actual gate.

I held my raincoat together to cover the tee-shirt. When I saw him step into the aisle, I could see he was searching for me. He probably thought, "Well, this is a fine hello—where the hell are you?" Then he saw me leaning against the wall, and the minute I knew his gaze was focused on me, I flashed open my raincoat. Yes, the whole world now knew that **I LOVE DON McCORMACK.**

Friday morning we drove to Pennsylvania and got our marriage license and stopped off to say a quick hello to my grandfather.

When we returned to the city, we had just enough time to get ready for a party my dear friend, Tom O'Toole, was having for us. Tom and I worked together at The Wool Bureau. I credited him with changing me from "country hick" to New York City girl. When he left The Wool Bureau, he became one of the city's best interior designers and his uptown apartment was very elegant. On this evening it was filled with floral arrangements of white flowers: tall spikes of white gladiolas, calla lilies, roses and even tulips imported from who knew where? He had wonderful appetizers and champagne and all of my New York City friends were there to meet Don.

Saturday morning we went to the antique jewelry store where they were holding the engagement ring I had found weeks before. We walked from my apartment at 34th and Park Avenue to the antique jewelry store which was located in the heart of the diamond district on West 47th Street, just off Fifth Avenue. Instantly the woman recognized me and beamed as I introduced her to Don. When she brought out the ring, Don's eyes sparkled, and he agreed with me that this was the ring. He paid the woman the balance due and I couldn't wait to have him put it on my finger. But, no—he didn't do that. He slipped the ring, by itself and not in the case, inside his blazer pocket. I didn't know what to think, but kept quiet. We walked back to Fifth Avenue, arm in arm, and when we got to the curb Don asked me to wait a minute. He stepped out into the street and looked up to make sure there wasn't any traffic coming. Meanwhile I was baffled. What was this crazy man doing? He turned back for me, took me into the center of Fifth Avenue, knelt down on his knee, and as he took the ring out of his pocket and placed it on my finger, he said, "I can't think of a better place for a New York City girl to get engaged than in the middle of Fifth Avenue." It all happened in a split second and I couldn't help but love this man. He pulled me back to the sidewalk, hailed a cab and told the driver to take us to Little Italy. Don and I would tease each other in years to come that it was Mr. Yost, the New York City taxi cab driver, who was the first one to know that we had just become officially engaged. Talk about a magical moment!

When we arrived back at my apartment, the temperature had reached its high for the day. It was sweltering. My tiny air-conditioning window unit was barely putting out any cold air. Weeks earlier, I had gotten tickets for us to go to the New York Ballet that night, not knowing if Don really appreciated ballet. But, on this hot and humid night, I think we were both glad to be sitting in the air conditioned luxury of Lincoln Center watching a world class ballet performance.

Don flew back to Houston the evening of August 3, and now we only had to wait twenty days until we would be married.

Chapter 17

The Countdown

~

A few days later, Don sent me a card with a note he had written after his weekend in New York City.

~~~

My Darling

There is so little I can say that we have not said to each other over the weekend. The time with you represents another of those most cherished moments together. Not withstanding the heat, I enjoyed every single moment. Your friends are so wonderful and were so warm to me—it is too bad we cannot continue to be as close to them.

I am also so glad that I now have an image of your apartment. I can now see you clearly when I call.

I am very lonely tonight. It is a mixture of a sore back (don't worry about it) and being very tired. I think I can withstand this period easier now—the light is clearly visible at the end of the tunnel, and I can see you waiting at the end for me. Is it a red shirt I see? Is it at La Guardia? I believe it is.

Remember, my love, you have the world's greatest gift— that's all the love that a good person can give. And I give it to you.

I'm off to call you.

Love—your Don

~~~

At 7 Park Avenue, Apartment 14 F, packing boxes were everywhere in sight. There were even four large garment boxes sitting outside in the hallway because there was no room for them in my studio apartment. My life was taking on a new meaning; I was about to close the chapter as a single woman and start a new one as part of a pair. Girlfriends, many of my designer friends from Seventh Avenue, and other friends were taking me to farewell lunches and dinners. The Wool Bureau gave me a going away party, never done before, and presented me with a gold pin in the shape of the Woolmark with sapphires encrusted around the swirls. It had been made by Tiffany's. I was overwhelmed! They also gave us a wedding present, a wine decanter in our crystal pattern, Lismore by Waterford, chosen while Don was in New York City. I already had Wedgwood china and Reed & Barton sterling. Packages started to be delivered to Audubon Avenue in Houston and cards were being delivered to me in New York.

It was also a time of excruciating loneliness for both of us. Don sent me a letter which included photos he had taken using a self-timer, shaving in the morning, making his coffee, sitting at his kitchen table presumably reading a letter from me, playing his banjo, scraping paint off the chair he had been refinishing, chopping up vegetables for dinner, sitting on his kitchen stool with phone in hand as if he were talking to me, and in his bed with his right arm around a pillow—thirteen photos in all, all endearing to me.

The weekend after Don left New York City, I drove to Weatherly. My folks had already arrived from Florida and were staying in their travel trailer, parked next to the bungalow. I had the cases of Korbel Brut loaded in the trunk. It was their wedding gift to us since I insisted on paying for the entire wedding, the correct thing for an independent New York woman to do. Almost the minute I walked in the front door, my mother handed me the wedding license which had arrived at the bungalow days before.

I drove into town to visit with my Great Uncle Sam, my grandfather's brother; his wife, Aunt Florence; her sister, Aunt Nell and another relative, Sam Schaffer. I had become very close to them since the first weekend I drove to Weatherly to take care of my grandfather. They lived together in a big white Victorian house, complete with spindles and scrollwork and a charming front porch with antique white wicker furniture, on a street high above Hazel Creek in downtown Weatherly. They also owned what they called their "country house." It was located midway between Weatherly proper and my grandfather's bungalow, about seven miles out of town on Stagecoach Road, which led directly down to the Lehigh River. This was a huge house with a massive stone fireplace. In fact, it had been the stopping off place for carriages seeking a nights rest on their way to Philadelphia. It was in this home where I spotted the antique oak fainting couch, complete with its original horsehair stuffing, which originally belonged to my great grandfather, Lewis Young, and his wife, Carolyn Flickinger. On this day, Uncle Sam told me they wanted to give the fainting couch to us as their wedding present. I was overwhelmed with joy. Don was overwhelmed with the thought, "Where in the world will we put this monstrosity?" I had already arranged for the moving company to make a stop at my grandfather's bungalow on their way from my apartment to Houston, so what was one more piece of furniture, I asked Don.

When I returned to New York City, there was a letter from Don. Some of what I want to share is what he wrote about really wanting to make our marriage work.

~~~

Tuesday
8-12
My Dearest Diane

I didn't get to write you last night, so I am taking a few minutes after lunch to say hello. My thoughts turn to you so often that I have trouble concentrating on business. I must confess that I am just waiting for the days to pass. This is primarily due to my anticipation of starting a life with you (one week, two hours and 5 min. from this moment when I leave and start for the airport).

Oh, Diane, I just yearn for you so much. I love and love and love you so much. There isn't anything I can do for fun or otherwise that won't be better with you (maybe poker).

I still have a lingering concern (not a doubt) that I'm not quite up to keeping this love as beautiful forever. Mind you, this only stems from my failures of the past, whatever, in fact, they were. I so want to feel this way always and keep the important things in life up front where we can deal with them. Our life together right now has a certain honeymoon quality which one would expect to change to be replaced with a deep continuing love. Darling, I really need the four minutes with your help in keeping me tuned into your love. There really is nothing so beautiful in this world as another person who deeply and honestly loves you (and for all the right reasons).

I guess I'm in a sentimental mood today. The light at the end of the tunnel is there, getting brighter and ever closer, but my anxiety is greater. Oh, Baby, I need you so much. I've just about had it with this courtship business.

I love you, Baby. I can see us together in so many ways, it just fills me up. I see you everywhere. I love you everywhere. I need you everywhere.

You are mine, and I'm yours.
With all the love a mere human is capable of.
Your man

~~~

Don's last card with note was waiting for me in Weatherly.

~~~

Friday
8/15
My Dearest Diane
This is probably the last letter you will receive from me as something other than my wife.

And what more can I say. The day to day news we discuss by phone. So, it's only the expression of love that we transmit by mail. So, all the many letters we have written to each other have been a most important part of the development of our love to where it is today—two 100% dedicated lovers, ready for a permanent commitment.

We can, and will, reread our letters, probably together, and by this they will also serve to sustain our love. But that will really be sustained by other things—a consciousness, a caring, a dedication. Our letters will really be a memory. That we have been apart so much will be a sad memory, but the happiness of the times together is also chronicled in our letters, so there will be happy memories brought forth too.

So my love, I can only say, for the nth time, how beautiful you are and how much I love you and love you and love you. My life begins shortly.

Te quiero
Your Don

~~~

And, my life would begin shortly as well!

Chapter 18

August 23 – Wedding Day

Saying goodbye to "my city" was filled with both sadness and anticipation. The movers were scheduled for later in the day to load the boxes and the few furniture pieces: sofa bed, Victorian dresser, upholstered chair, book cases, round table and chairs and an assortment of other small pieces. I looked

View of Chrysler Building from 7 Park Avenue

around the apartment and took a last glance at my view north to the Chrysler Building.

I carried a small suitcase, Gypsy, and the picnic basket that I had refitted as a wedding gift for Don, down to car. Gypsy settled in her kennel which I had strapped into the passenger seat, and as I entered the Hudson Tunnel, I turned my head and looked back at New York City one more time.

The drive going west along I-80 to Weatherly to my grandfather's bungalow was uneventful until I got closer to the turnoff for Weatherly. There alongside the interstate, placed every mile or so, were signs that read...

YOUNG–McCORMACK WEDDING

My dear sweet father had made these small wooden signs in the shape of a directional arrow and went out that morning to place them along the freeway so my friends driving from New York wouldn't get lost.

All the preparations for our wedding were in place, amazing since all the details were finalized via long distance phone calls to businesses I found by scanning the Yellow Pages of Weatherly and the surrounding towns.

Don and I had chosen the day, August 23, to be "the" wedding day when we were in Chicago. All the Young relatives from my father's side of the family were there, as well as the New Jersey relatives from my mother's side of the family. Most of Don's family was there: Rainy, his mother; his sister Ann and her husband, Tommy; and Don's son, Bruce, as his Best Man.

The actual wedding ceremony was held on the west side of the bungalow by the bank of the creek. Folding wooden chairs had been brought in from the volunteer fireman's hall down the road and were set up along both sides of the pathway. I had ordered potted geraniums from the local nursery and these lined the path from the side walkway down to the creek bank where the minister would be standing. Baskets of cascading summer flowers hung from the many low tree branches along the path. The three musicians, violin, accordion and bass, were waiting beside the minister. All the relatives were escorted to the folding chairs, and my friends, who had driven from New York City and other east coast towns, were sitting on the lawn which meandered in a gentle slope up to the road. On the other side of the bungalow, a huge tent had been erected. I had ordered it from the local funeral home but with specific instructions to please leave off the name, "Jeffries Funeral Home." We had arranged to serve soft drinks to my non-drinking Methodist family members and champagne to others. I had ordered trays of appetizers to be passed around and the reception would culminate with the cutting of the wedding cake and certainly no smashing the cake into our faces—a tradition done at some weddings that both Don and I found to be distasteful.

My mother had a hard time understanding I would not be married in an actual church until I explained to her that outside under the trees and by the side of the creek would be as close to church and God as Don and I could get. And, when she questioned why I wouldn't be walking down the aisle to the tune of the traditional, "Wedding March," I told her, Vivaldi's "Four Seasons—Spring" was more spiritual than Mendelssohn's "Wedding March."

Don, who had arrived two days before, waited with Pastor Taylor as my father beamed with love while he walked me down the grass carpeted aisle. My wedding dress, a long white cotton eyelet sleeveless dress and stole, was designed and made by my special designer friend from New York City, Maurice Antaya. My dress and the dress he made for my niece, Dawn, were his wedding gifts to me.

It was a magical afternoon; we heard thunder booming but it was far away—all was right with the world and God was in His Heaven.

When my father and I reached the minster he asked, *"Who gives this woman away?"* Daddy answered, *"Her mother and I do."* Then he kissed me on my cheek and gave my hand to Don, who was grinning from cheek to cheek.

Pastor Taylor started the ceremony. It was his very first wedding, but his words flowed as if he had performed a hundred wedding ceremonies. Don and I had chosen 1 Corinthians Thirteen, from the English Standard Version, to be recited by the minster.

~~~

If I speak in the tongues of men and of angels, but have not love, I am a noisy gong or a clanging cymbal. And if I have prophetic powers, and understand all mysteries and all knowledge, and if I have all faith, so as to remove mountains, but have not love, I am nothing. If I give away all I have, and if I deliver up my body to be burned, but have not love, I gain nothing.

Love is patient and kind; love does not envy or boast; it is not arrogant or rude. It does not insist on its own way; it is not irritable or resentful; it does not rejoice at wrongdoing, but rejoices with the truth. Love bears all things, believes all things, hopes all things, endures all things.

Love never ends. As for prophecies, they will pass away; as for tongues, they will cease; as for knowledge, it will pass away. For we know in part and we prophesy in part, but when the perfect comes, the partial will pass away. When I was a child, I spoke like a child, I thought like a child, I reasoned like a child. When I became a man, I gave up childish ways. For now we see in a mirror dimly, but then face to face. Now I know in part; then I shall know fully, even as I have been fully known.

So now faith, hope, and love abide, these three; but the greatest of these is love.

~~~

However, in the actual reciting of our vows, we substituted the words—to love, honor and *cherish* instead of—to love, honor and *obey*.

I had hired a friend of mine, a professional fashion photographer in New York City, to take the photos. However, he was having such a good time being a guest; he only took a few shots. As we started to walk away from the minister, someone turned my bouquet around. It had been facing me. One of my friends took this snapshot of us. It was to be our official wedding shot. Don and I laughed about his two-tone brown shoes for years afterwards as did our friends when they spotted his shoes the minute they saw the framed photo.

Don and me coming down aisle – August 23rd, 1975

Earlier in the day, in a private moment between us, Don gave me a box. Inside was a silver bracelet. Included with the bracelet was a small piece of paper, four by six inches, folded in half. He had written.

~~~

My Darling Bride
I love you more than I can tell you. This simple gift,
to me, is beautiful in its simplicity. It can serve as a small,
special reminder of the love I bring to you from this day
forward which, unlike rings, only you and I will share.
Had I been sure of the size, it would be inscribed
"10th, 23rd and Love"
Diane, you are my life.
Don

~~~

The trays of appetizers were served, the cake was cut and then the champagne was popped, Korbel Brut, because as Don had said, "If it is good enough for Henry Kissinger to serve at his wedding, it's good enough for us."

After a few hours, Don and I left the reception and changed into our travel clothes. We carried Gypsy out to the car, turned and waved to everyone, honked the horn several times and departed for our honeymoon destination, Bryce Mountain Resort.

Our life was beginning!

Part Two

Chapter 19

The End of My Life as I Knew It

Now, my Darling Don, I'm brought back to the present. You are lying on the hospital bed and I know that my hours with you are numbered. You are hooked up to so many machines. I know you are comatose—brain dead is what the first surgeon told me. I talk to you because I know you can hear me. I tell you how much I love you, that you mean the world to me and that you are my world. I thank you for all the wonderful memories you have given me over the past thirty-two years. You are on a ventilator, awaiting the arrival of my sister from Ohio. I bury my head in your left arm. It feels so warm to my touch. I stroke your hand, I kiss your fingers. Your eyes are open—those beautiful steel blue eyes. I tell you that soon someone will be lucky enough to receive your corneas—your beautiful blue eyes. I stroke your hair, the hair that hours ago I saw the sun shining through, and I told you how flecked with gold it looked in the setting sun; it looked like gossamer strands of gold.

The attending male nurse comes into the room and asks if I need anything.

"Yes, him," I answer. "He is what I need!"

Then I see the ring on the hand I have been stroking, and I ask him if he can remove it. He does with the utmost gentleness, takes it to a sink and washes it and then comes over to where I am sitting next to you and places it in my hand and squeezes my fingers over it.

I take off my engagement ring and slide your ring up my ring finger to be alongside the matching gold band you had made for me. I put my engagement ring back on my finger to secure the two wedding bands—two bands of gold—two bands of love. And I sit there and stare at the three rings.

Is this a dream?

No. It's a nightmare.

Chapter 20

Nightmare

When did the nightmare begin? Probably when I heard the noise of you tumbling down the stairs hitting the grandfather's clock and then the erratic chiming of the clock as the chimes kept hitting into each other. You were lying at the bottom of the stairs.

The clock stopped at one o'clock.

The weeks preceding this horrific night had been mostly good ones. You had been religious about getting an annual physical, which included a treadmill stress test. All the other years, you had passed with flying colors.

In September of 2006 we were driving down to Nevada City, California to visit Barbara and Buddy Hunt, our friends who had moved there from Truckee. You said to me, "You know, Honey, we just might have to move off the hill one day. It just may be that my shortness of breath is caused by some kind of heart condition and the altitude in Truckee may be all wrong for me. We could move to Nevada City and still be close to our other friends in Truckee."

In October, I had to go to our doctor for some minor ailment. I was sitting on the edge of the examining table when the doctor walked in with both of our charts in his hand. Without any introduction he said, "Tell Don his tests have all come back normal and he's fine." I told him about the conversation we had just days earlier about moving off the hill, and again he repeated to me you were fine. "Write it down so he will believe it," I asked him. And, he tore a page off of his prescription pad and scribbled…

~~~

Don McCormack —
Don
No more Fuddy-Duddy,
Congrats—You are healthy and don't need to move.
J__

~~~

I think you still had doubts and in the spring of 2007, you scheduled another stress test and an EKG (electrocardiogram). Our cardiologist didn't like the results and suspected you might have heart disease. He recommended a heart specialist in Reno who was also a surgeon. You had your first appointment with the specialist on May 3. He recommended a procedure known as a catheterization. While sitting in the surgeon's office, I kept questioning him and wanted to know if the catheterization would be a "piece of cake"—which is the term you liked to use. I had taken out a small note pad and pen to write down notes. I wrote down his words, "I'm the best." He explained that the bad results of your stress test and EKG indicated there might be a problem in one of the heart valves. He told us about the procedure. A long, thin flexible tube called a catheter would be threaded into the blood vessel through your groin and then threaded up to your heart. A dye would be inserted in the catheter. The dye would aid in his viewing x-rays taken of your heart. He explained how the catheterization would not only check the blood flow and blood pressure in the chambers of your heart, but it would also check the blood flow in your coronary arteries. He also told us that if any of the arteries were very tight, he would insert a stent, a small mesh tube that would support the inner artery wall of your heart. This procedure, if necessary, would be performed the same day. I looked over at you and saw the worried look on your face.

We drove back to Reno the next day, and the catheterization was performed. I waited impatiently in the cath lab waiting room. There was another couple in the waiting room. The wife was the one who was scheduled to have a catheterization. Both were so overweight, and I thought, *"Don is going to be just great and will pull through this. Look at the great shape he's in."*

The surgeon came to the waiting room. He told me that the catheterization showed blockage in your main artery. "It was very tight in the main artery," were his exact words. He told me I could soon go in to see you. Very shortly I was ushered into your cubicle. You were still hooked up to the IV. The surgeon came into your cubicle and recommended proceeding with the angioplasty since the "cath" was still in place in the femoral artery. A stent would be placed in your left anterior descending artery. Minutes later someone came in and told us you might have to be moved to a different hospital because of some insurance red-tape. We waited. An hour later the doctor came back and said they would proceed with the angioplasty at his hospital rather than move you by ambulance to another hospital.

Again, I waited. This time I was in a different waiting room; this one was more austere. There were two women also waiting. One was the sister of a man who was undergoing the same procedure and the other was his girlfriend. They talked about how his diet would have to change. "No more Big Macs and Twinkies," I heard them say. They were going to go to his apartment and clean out his refrigerator and pantry. Again, I thought, *"That's not you. We have never had a Twinkie in our house and maybe had one Big Mac in the past twenty years, if that."*

The TV was on and tuned to CNN. Everything seemed beige. I had taken some dog magazines to read. I knew I would not be able to concentrate listening to one of my audio "books

on tapes." The wait seemed so long, longer and more excruciating than the morning wait.

Finally, a nurse came to get me and I was taken to your
bedside. The doctor came back into the room and explained to
us what he had done. He said to me, "He's come through the
procedure with flying colors. There's no need for alarm." I took
copious notes on every word he said to us. I stayed with you
for a few more hours, and then you urged me to drive back to
Truckee to take care of the dogs.

Leaving you in that room was hard—much harder than
when I entered and saw you lying there.

I remember the drive home. The sun was setting and I was
thanking God for you. I was so hopeful, so full of dreams for
our life to go on together, forever. How could I have possibly
known what was lurking in our future?

Saturday morning, May 5, I drove back to Reno to pick
you up after you were discharged from the hospital. You were
very tired, of course, and when we got home, you had to be
careful the two dogs didn't jump up on your tender side. You
stretched out on the sofa with a quilt over you. Vision was on
top on one side and Mirage on the other; that is, until Mirage
could stand it no longer and buried his way under the quilt so
he could be closer to you.

You were given post-operative instructions. You could do
mild exercise; walking would be good for you. The discharge
attendant also gave you some nitroglycerin pills with instructions if you felt any pain or discomfort at all, you were to pop
one of the pills under your tongue and head directly for the ER
at the Truckee Hospital.

We changed our diet immediately. I had stopped at a book-
store in Reno that morning and purchased several books on
heart-healthy cooking. We loved to cook together. We had designed our gourmet kitchen complete with its Wolf range and
oven, and you took such pride in our vast collection of copper
pots and pans which hung from two long copper pot racks

above the center island.

Sunday evening, May 6, was the beginning of our new menus, cooking methods and new diets. Out went the heavy cream, the eggs, and the red meat. I spent several hours that morning studying labels at our local grocery store and at our vastly stocked health food store. I went through our pantry and filled three large shopping bags with all the canned goods that were not going to be in our new regime.

That evening after dinner, we took a short walk down to the end of our street. We took the dogs with us. You had Mirage and I, Vision. But when we neared the end of the long hill at the bottom of Greenleaf Way, you told me you were experiencing some discomfort in your chest. I grabbed hold of both dog's leashes, and we slowly climbed back up the hill. You popped a nitroglycerin pill under your tongue and I took you to our local hospital. You were admitted to the ER. Some tests were run, and the doctor on staff for the night decided to keep you overnight. I stayed with you for several hours, and then went back home to take care of the dogs.

Monday morning, I drove back to the hospital. You were waiting to be discharged. While we waited for the paper work to be completed, we walked around the hospital hallways. You were still attached to the IV. We walked into the solarium and sat down on a couch. You took my hand and tried to reassure me and said you believed everything would be all right. I must have had a worried look on my face.

You seemed to gain some inner strength that next week. The snow had mostly disappeared from our property. You had even raked up several bags of pine needles.

At first you had been very depressed about the entire heart situation. I think you were afraid, and you were not handling it well. I had been shopping in Reno a couple of days after the operation when I received a phone call from my friend, Penny Douglas. "What is wrong with Don?" she asked in a worried tone. "He sounds so depressed. He answered the phone in a voice I hardly recognized." "He is depressed," I told her. We finished our conversation. I hung up and drove home immediately, ignoring the list of errands I had scheduled for that day.

When I arrived home, I found you puttering around the kitchen. "Sit down Darling, we need to talk," I said to you. I told you what Penny had said and that other friends mentioned to me how depressed you had seemed. Your bridge partner's husband had undergone unexpected open-heart surgery on May 16, and I thought his surgery might have been the cause of your state of depression.

The next week seemed to go by as routine. You had your usual meetings: the Truckee Tahoe Airport Community Advisory Team, the Tahoe/Donner Association and other local town strategy committees. You played duplicate bridge. One day you drove to Auburn for an appointment with a dental surgeon, and one day you drove to Reno for an appointment with your dental hygienist.

On May 17, you had another stress test performed. We were back in Reno for a second angiogram on May 21. Again, it was back to our routine life. We picked up the new car, and over the Memorial Day weekend, we drove to one of our favorite restaurants on Lake Tahoe, Sunnyside, for a relaxing brunch out on the deck.

Our life continued as normal. On June 8, we had two of our favorite friends, Lisa Dobey and Debbie Cole, over for bridge and dinner. All of our friends were used to us serving gourmet meals—entrees enhanced with sauces that contained fat and butter and desserts, such as Crème brûlée, made with eggs and heavy cream. This meal was a no-fat dinner and entirely new to all of us, and we graded each course after it was served. We all laughed as we gave the dessert, an ersatz concoction made of fake everything, a minus five. Yuck!

The following week you had another appointment with our local cardiologist and everything seemed great. We were in such good spirits.

On Father's Day, June 17, we awoke with the dogs in bed with us. In our past life, before the heart scare, in honor of Father's Day or a special event, we would have had a Bloody Mary, Eggs Benedict with homemade muffins or biscuits and coffee. But, under our new regime, we opted for coffee, and you had bran cereal while I nibbled on a diet bar of some kind.

Earlier in the week, I was in Reno picking up something for the new car at the dealership and noticed a handyman tool in the showcase. I thought it might cheer you up. I wrapped it and gave it you after breakfast. You opened your "happy," and a big smile came across your face.

You took a short ride on your Harley to Mt. Rose, one of your favorite rides.

We had made plans earlier in the week to attend the Blue Grass Festival in the afternoon with friends. We picked them up and drove to the Nevada County fairgrounds. We sat outside on chairs and listened to the various bands. We walked around the grounds holding hands. We checked out the various vendors selling guitars, banjos, and accessories. Life was perfect. We even found a vendor grilling salmon burgers, and you said to me, "This diet won't be that hard to keep. Look, even at an outdoor festival, there are vendors who serve heart-healthy snacks."

Later that day, our next-door neighbor, Audrey, called. "Why don't you kids come for after-dinner drinks?" she asked. You said to me, "Tell her we'll come over for pre-dinner drinks. It's only 5 PM and we don't eat until 7'ish."

Monday, you and your bridge partner drove to North Lake Tahoe for a day of duplicate bridge. I was happy to stay home in my craft room. I was intent on finishing a project—embroidering colorful dog designs on a denim jacket.

On Tuesday morning, you played a casual game of tennis with your partner. You had given up playing singles the previous year because you found it too strenuous.

Wednesday, you had a Tahoe/Donner committee meeting. You were so dedicated and hardly missed attending a meeting. Before you were elected to the Truckee Town Council in 1994, you were a former director and board president of the Tahoe Donner Association. You also sat on the Tahoe Donner Architectural Standards Committee and their Finance Committee, sharing your experience and skills in operational and fiscal planning acquired years earlier when you were at Shell.

Thursday you played duplicate bridge at the Recreation Center in downtown Truckee.

And, on Friday morning, you had your very first cardiac rehab session. I remember you coming home with the chart the nurse at the rehab clinic had provided. You already had it on a clip board. You were supposed to keep a daily accounting of your diet. You told me, with a smirk on your face, "I've got this beat. You should see some of the people who are there— guys with big, fat stomachs and women who are very out of shape. I'm already ahead of the game since we've been on this new heart-healthy diet for a month."

We were having one of our favorite couples for dinner, Kathleen Eagan and Jim Duffy. In the morning we did some of the preparation for it—of course, low fat or no fat. Then you had a meeting at the airport. I spent over an hour working in the planter boxes on the front deck. The squirrels had dug up many of the plants while trying to bury the peanuts in shells our neighbor would throw out to them. The task was too daunting. Too many plants were ruined. I thought it would be better to replace them. So, I drove down to the local nursery.

While I was looking around for "squirrel-proof" flowers, I noticed all of the sun faces mounted on the outside walls of the nursery, and I remembered the time when we were in Tuscany in September 2000. The highlight of our trip was our stay at Podere Terreno in the village of Radda. We stayed there for several days and that's where we saw the most fabulous collection of sun faces. One of the outside walls of the ancient stone farmhouse was covered with many, many sun faces—in all sizes, colors and mediums. Both of us loved the display.

Thursday, after you returned home from bridge, as we were bringing the deck furniture out of storage and up to the front deck, you had commented to me the side wall of our deck was barren looking. "Maybe we should look for some of those sun faces we saw in Tuscany," you told me. "It might be a fun thing to shop for when we do some traveling. You know how much I hate to shop, but this would be something fun to look for. I wouldn't mind shopping for sun faces, Diane, but just don't make it an all-day project." Hmm.

I looked around at the many sun faces that were on display at the nursery and selected the one with the biggest grin on his face. The salesperson loaded it into the back of the car, along with my new plants, and I drove home.

It was around 4 o'clock when I returned home, and I called up to you, "Honey, come see the 'happy' I've bought for you." I know it was 4 o'clock, because later I came across the email you had been working on, something to do with the ACAT committee, and it was dated 4 o'clock. You hollered you would be down shortly, so in the meantime I planted the new plants and pulled out the hose to water them. It was a beautiful late afternoon, one of those spectacular afternoons that makes us realize how we can endure the hard winters for days and evenings like this. The sun was starting to set, and as I pulled the hose back to the side deck, I said aloud to myself— *"I love this place. I love my house. I love my life."* How could I have known?

You came out to the front deck, and I pointed to the sun face which was leaning on one of the chairs. Your face lit up with happiness, and your smile matched the one on the sun face. You immediately said, "We have to hang him before Kathleen and Jim arrive." So down to your shop you went to look for a hanger. You tried three different kinds of hangers and finally brought up the right one and hammered it to the wall. The sun face was hung. We both smiled at each other—so happy we were with the first of the many sun faces we would surely add to this once barren looking wall.

Kathleen and Jim arrived around 5. We had asked them to come early so we could enjoy cocktails out on the deck before the sun went down and it would become too chilly. You showed them the sun face and recounted the story. You made drinks, and I brought out the low-fat appetizer. We were laughing and telling stories. In fact, one of the stories was about my very first letter to you and how I asked if you smoked, if you hunted and if you liked dogs. We laughed. You were sitting facing south, and the sun was starting to set and the rays were sifting through the pines and shining through your hair. I said, "Oh, Don, you should see how the sun is shining through your hair. It makes your hair look like gossamer strands of gold." And, you replied, "Oh, yeah, Diane, my thinning hair." And, I thought to myself, "*I think you are as handsome as you were the day I first set eyes on you, the first time ever, and I am still in love with you and I am so very, very lucky.*"

When it started to cool, we went inside to the dining room and enjoyed the low-fat dinner. Vino made it more palatable. Such a good and fun evening. You sure did love Kathleen and Jim.

They left around eight-thirty because the next day they had to go somewhere, do something. I can't remember exactly what it was, but I think maybe a trip to San Francisco to visit with Kathleen's mother.

You and I carried the dishes into the kitchen. You scraped the plates while I loaded the dishwasher and put the "leftovers" away. You even washed the crystal, which we would sometimes leave until the next morning when you would wash the glasses by hand. But this night you told me you wanted to clean up the kitchen before we went to bed and started to wash the crystal. As you finished washing each glass, you put it on a towel to air dry during the night.

It was then close to ten o'clock. I put the dogs out for their last pee of the night. I asked you if you wanted them to come upstairs with us. You laughed and said to me as you scratched Mirage's ear, "They've been good doggies. They want to be bed dogs. Let them come up." So, up the stairs they raced. I went into the office to shut down the computer. You were already in bed snuggled with the dogs, one in each arm, when minutes later I came in.

I put on my nightgown and I crawled into bed next to you. "What a great evening that was," I said to you. "They are truly one of the most fun couples we know." You were getting very drowsy, and I turned to face you and gave you a kiss goodnight. You said to me, "Thank you, Honey, for all you have done to help me with my diet." I answered, "Don, Darling, I'm not only doing this for you. I'm doing it for me, for us. I want to take care of you so I will have you with me another ten or fifteen years." "I know, Honey," you replied, "but, I thank you for it anyway. Good night, Darling. I really love you." And, you kissed me ever so tenderly.

"Goodnight, Darling," I replied. "I love you, too, forever and always."

It was shortly after ten o'clock. Little did I know that only a couple of hours later, my life would change forever.

At one o'clock, I heard the terrible banging noise of you tumbling down the stairs. And, then I heard the grandfather clock's tubes hitting together in the most dreadful chorus of chimes. They stopped at one o'clock.

I ran down the stairs and saw you lying there at the foot. "Don, Don," I cried to you, "What have you done, what have you done to yourself?" I saw the blood pooling behind your head and knew it was bad. I frantically dialed 911. The dispatcher was attempting to tell me to turn your head this way and that way and to blow into your mouth. "I can't," I cried back into the phone. "He's bleeding from his mouth."

I ran back upstairs and lifted the dogs off the bed. All the years of trying to train them to not jump off the high bed because of their backs, and tonight they did what they were trained to do. They followed me down the stairs. I had to pull Mirage off of you and finally got them both in the kitchen behind the gate. I knew I had to make room for the paramedics to work on you and somehow managed to push the grandfather's clock to the side by about ten feet. It must have been my adrenaline kicking in, because it's one of the biggest and heaviest clocks that Sligh makes.

I unlocked the front door and left it ajar for the paramedics. Minutes later one of them entered and said, "Oh my God, it's the McCormack residence." He saw me standing at the top of the gallery stairs and asked me, "Oh God, Diane, it's not Don, is it?" He had served on one of the town councils with you. Small town. Small world.

They worked on you as fast and competently as they could and then made a call for the air ambulance. Was it only minutes or was it a lifetime? But, soon they had placed you on a gurney and were rushing you out the front door into the still of the night and into the ambulance and to the helicopter, parked only a couple of streets away in the parking lot of the Tahoe Donner clubhouse.

I was numb. I went down to the laundry room and ran hot water into the scrub bucket and went back upstairs to mop up your blood. I wiped up most of it first with some of my old dog towels and placed them into the garbage bag I had retrieved earlier when one of the paramedics asked me for a garbage bag. I finished wiping up the blood. I know I was in shock. I was trying so hard to make sense of it all. I couldn't. I just couldn't believe this was happening—that "this" had happened. What had happened?

All of a sudden, my senses kicked in, and I became frantic. I ran upstairs, threw on some clothes and started to call our friends.

Chapter 21

The Hospital

My first call was to Kathleen and Jim, who had been with us at our home just hours before. I got their answering machine. Then I called our next door neighbors. No answer. Then I called Lisa and Debby. Again, I got an answering machine and left a message. Minutes later they called back. "Give us a few minutes to get dressed, and we will be there."

Less than twenty minutes later, they were at our house. It was about 2:30 AM. As we drove into Reno, Lisa said, "Oh, we should have grabbed some change of clothes for Don." "I can come back," I said.

We arrived at the hospital, but since it was undergoing major construction of a new parking garage, we drove around for several minutes looking for the right entrance. We parked at one site, walked to what we thought was the door to the ER—no such luck. Back to the car, down another street.

Finally, I said, "Let's just go to the ER entrance. I know they have valet parking." Lisa drove to the ER entrance and left the car with the attendant, and we all went inside. At the receptionist's desk, I gave my name and said my husband had been air-lifted from Truckee about an hour earlier. "I'm here to see him," I said with no urgency in my voice because I thought

I would be taking you home once your head wound healed. The receptionist made a phone call and told me someone would be down to get me.

Within minutes, there was an aide who told me to please come with her. Lisa and Debbie followed. We took the elevator to the third floor. I was trying to remember if this was the floor where you were just weeks earlier when the stent was placed in your artery. It all looked the same.

We were taken to a room—not your hospital room. It was not a typical waiting room, but rather a conference room of sorts: blackboards and bulletin boards all around. A large wooden rectangular table, a conference table, was in the center of the room with many chairs placed all around. I took a seat at one side, and Lisa and Debbie sat across from me. I looked up at the writing on the chalk board and saw where it listed instructions for treating head traumas. *"OK,"* I thought to myself, *"He has had a concussion and will be here for a few days, and then I can take him home."* I opened my handbag and took out a piece of paper and pen and placed them on the table in front of me, waiting to write down any instructions I might be given.

A woman entered the room, dressed in scrubs. Her head was covered with one of those plastic head gears worn during an operation. A male nurse was with her. She introduced herself to me as Doctor—. I didn't catch her last name.

I immediately asked her, "When can I see my husband?"

"We need to talk," she said. I picked up my pen in anticipation to take any notes she would be telling me regarding your care once you came home.

"Your husband has suffered a major head injury. Look, I'm not going to sugar coat this. Your husband is brain dead," she said.

I don't think I was able to focus. My head started to spin. I remember looking over to Debbie and Lisa, and they just sat there with a strange look on their faces. None of us said anything for what seemed minutes—hours.

I knew what brain dead probably meant, but I couldn't grasp the full implications of just what she was trying to tell me. My world was spinning around me. I wanted to run to you. I wanted to tell this doctor she was wrong. You had just hit your head, and they would operate and stitch you up, and in a few days I would take you home. What was she saying to me?

Her words echoed again in my head…your husband is brain dead. "I know what that usually means," I stammered, "but please, I need to know more."

"He is on life support," she said. "He will not recover. He injured his brain stem and there is no hope."

No hope, I thought.

No hope.

No hope for you to get better.

No hope for you to come back home with me.

No hope for our life to continue from where we left off last night at 1 AM.

"There is nothing we can do," she continued.

I don't know if I went in to see you at that point or if I started to make some phone calls. I know I could not cry. I could not focus. I was in shock. I was in denial. "No, no, no," I wanted to scream. My head was spinning. My friends came around the table and put their arms around me.

You were gone from me…

Gone from our dachshunds…

Gone from our home…

Gone from our family…

Gone from our friends…from Truckee…from me.

Your life was over. You were a very young seventy-six and so vital with still so much to share with all of us…so much more to give to all of us.

The landscape of my life was beginning to change.

Chapter 22

Reality Check

The first person I called was my sister, Bev. "I need you. I need you now," I told her. And, then I told her what had happened. "I'll have a ticket waiting for you at the airline's reservation desk," I told her. I was talking to her on my cell phone and using Lisa's to call the airline and give them my credit card information. There was a flight out later in the day from Cleveland with only one stop. They had room. Next I called my friend, Sarah Hill. She and I had been the closest of friends since we lived in Houston. I told her what happened. It was a little past 6 AM in Houston, and Sarah made an 8 AM flight. My dear, dear friend.

They all came directly to the hospital. I don't know how or who, but someone had made arrangements to pick up relatives and friends who were coming in that day. Sarah arrived first. I told the attendants you needed to stay on life support until my sister arrived. I called your kids and told them what had happened. Later I called them again and placed my cell phone to your ear so they could talk to you and say goodbye. I let them have their private moments with you, because I knew they really meant the world to you and how much you loved them. Bev arrived and went in to your room to say good-bye. Other friends came to say goodbye to you—I don't remember who they were. Then I went back into your room and sat quietly with you. I wanted to stay forever. Our entire life together flashed before me. All those magical moments. How could 32 years have passed by so quickly? Then the attending nurse came in, and that's when I asked him for your ring. I kissed you goodbye and slowly walked out of your room.

Bev, Sarah and I drove back up the hill in someone's car. The house seemed so empty, except for the dogs. My salvation—my dogs. Their warm wet kisses covered my face, and I buried my tears in their fur...for not the last time.

The next day was Sunday, June 24. I don't remember what I did that day—probably I spent most of my time lying on one of the chaises on the front deck with a dog or two on my lap. Bev and Sarah made me eat, but I have no recollection of what the food might have been.

For anyone in this situation, busy work is the call of the day. Keep busy and you will forget—or maybe "not" forget but keeping busy will allow the nightmare to be pushed to the farthest recesses of your mind.

On Monday morning I awoke and went into the office looking for some semblance of my life. What do I do first? Who do I call first? What am I looking for?

You had always told me, "If anything happens to me, the first person to call is Tom Rushing." Tom was more than our broker. You both played tennis together when we lived in Houston—those eighteen years ago—that lifetime ago.

I called Tom at his office in Houston. I remember punching in his number on the phone, waiting for the connection to be made, asking his receptionist to speak to him. And, then I heard his voice. I said, "Tom, this is Diane McCormack and I think you probably know why I'm calling you." The tears came again as I retold the story. Tom listened intently, and then said with his voice cracking up, that he would have to call me back. He could not talk through his tears.

I called our lawyer—also a good friend, and he, as well, could not continue the conversation. He told me he would have to call me back.

Everyone I called that morning could not talk without me hearing their voice crack up with emotion—men and woman—you were loved by all.

Before June 23, I had been working tirelessly to defeat an animal rights bill that had been introduced in California in February of 2007. If passed, it would have been so detrimental to purebred dogs. But, I now had to back away from this. Before your death, it had become a full-time job, and I knew that now my next several days and weeks would have to be devoted to putting my affairs in order. I said to myself, *"It sounds so logical, doesn't it—putting one's affairs in order. My affairs were in order, Don, and then you died."*

But, I had to let everyone know I was out of the picture and why, and someone would have to take my place as the Canine Legislative Liaison. So I sent out this email to the list I had compiled to defeat AB 1634—which consisted of breeders, exhibitors and judges alike.

~~~

Sunday, June 24
Hello all -
I don't know if you have heard or not, but I lost my
husband of almost 32 years, Don, yesterday, June 23.
    From what we can piece together - and knowing certain
habits he had like never getting up from bed without his
glasses on - it appears he must have had a stroke, heart attack,
or aneurysm and somehow got to the top of the stairs (just
outside the master bedroom) where he collapsed and then
tumbled down the stairs breaking several bones and landing
at the foot of the steps. He fractured his nose, left cheekbone,

eye socket, and the bone behind his left eye. When he landed at the bottom, he cracked the back of his skull. He had been on blood thinning medications since he had the stent put in— this caused the blood to rush into the brain cavity where it actually smothered the brain tissue and eventually caused his brain to stop functioning.

He had the stent placed in early May and had started his cardio rehab Friday morning. We had been on this diet for over 6 weeks and both of us had lost a lot of weight, and he was feeling very good about his health and future.

He spent Friday afternoon doing odd things around the house and was in good spirits. We had two of his favorite people over for dinner (our new diet regime of low fat, no fat, no salt.) We had cocktails out on the deck and with our friends even relived some antidotes about my very first letter to him (we met as blind dates over the phone more than 32 years ago.) That letter asked him, "Do you smoke, do you hunt, do you like dogs? In Don's wonderful humor he told our friends he had replied back, "Yeah, I smoked as a young man but only a couple of cigarettes a day, yeah I hunted but never sighted the animal, and yeah....I realllly love dogs." I laughed and said, "Yeah, I should have asked him...but do you like dog shows." Don quickly answered, "And I would have said, I especially realllllly love dogs shows."

Our company left around 8:30—we cleaned up the dishes and wandered up to bed around 10ish.

At 1 AM, was when Don got up and somehow got disoriented and was at the top of the steps right outside our bedroom. I think it was there that he collapsed and then started his fall down the steps.

Both dogs were with us in bed, so I know he didn't start his fall first because the dogs would have been right there beside him and he would have hollered out my name or something.

Town folks are planning a memorial/celebration of his life for the general public on Sunday, July 22. Don was the Mayor of Truckee for 2 terms and the first one to die. Place and time will be determined. Kath Eagan is planning this. 530-576-2730.

*In lieu of flowers, Don had an interest in preserving
Truckee.*
Send donations to:

Truckee Donner Land Trust
19069 West River Street
Truckee, CA 96161

Mountain Area Preservation Foundation
PO Box 971
Truckee, CA 96160

*Thank you for your care and concerns. It is the saddest
day of my life.*
Diane Young McCormack

*PS to Dog Friends getting this.... I hope you all can
carry through and pick up the slack because I just cannot do
this right now.*
*WE MUST DEFEAT THIS BILL - YOU ALL MUST PITCH
IN AND HELP.*
*I KNOW YOU UNDERSTAND THAT I JUST CANNOT
DO THIS RIGHT NOW.*

~~~

How I was able to send out this email with so many details and just a day after you died, I still do not know. And,
why I did, I don't know. But, I think I must have been in a state
of suspension. Perhaps I needed to see the words in print as to
what had happened to you to really believe you were gone.
I don't know. I really wasn't cognizant of what had happened,
was I? Were you really gone from my life?

I know I kept telling my sister, "This must be a dream. I
know I'll awaken and he will be here."

She replied, "No, this is not a dream; it's a nightmare."

The phone calls of condolences started to come in, as did

the emails and eventually the hand-written notes and cards of sympathy. You were loved by all. You had made an impact on folks with whom you had come into contact—it didn't matter to you if they were at the highest level of government or were workers paid to plow the streets of Truckee—people were people to you.

I must have received over one hundred emails from my own friends in the dog world. Their words of compassion were mainly for me, because most of them had never met you personally and only knew of you through my bragging on you.

The notes that started to pour in from people who had known you from your involvement with your many committees and offices were overwhelming. Some of their words of compassion included...

~~~

"I always enjoyed working for and with Don, and although a long time ago, 'One Shell Plaza' doesn't seem that long ago."

"I admired him greatly and respected immensely the work he did for our community. He was funny, smart, dedicated...he was someone I learned a great deal from. One of my favorite memories will always be the "Donner Party Chili Party" at your home."

"I do want to say a couple things about Don's ACAT involvement. In my two years as Chairman, Don was always the one who volunteered for extra and was done ahead of time, under budget, and better quality than expected!.... probably sounds like his business days! Don was a corner stone for us and as he took over the Chair from me I think he set a very high new water mark as chair....I am glad I was before him rather that following! ACAT accomplished a lot and he has got us off to a good start in our second

incarnation......and I kind of know he will be looking down over our shoulder going forward to keep us on track!"

"Huge loss to so many people. The entire town of Truckee is in tears."

"People loved Don—how could you not?"

"Don showed love and respect to all folks—from those who had everything material they could ask for to the housekeepers that you all employed. Your housekeepers remain your friends for life. Don always had a hug for everyone."

"Don was doing—vital."

"The town of Truckee has reached their arms around Diane for it is their loss too."

"Don was young at heart—full of life."

"Don lived! — until the very end of his life."

"His free spirit was a treasure and a gift he shared with those of us fortunate enough to have known him."

"Don was a very special friend and ACAT member. Sitting with the two of you the last two Cadillac balls brings very happy memories of you AND Don."

"What a HUGE loss for all of us, for Truckee. I felt it to be such a privilege to work with Don... and I had fun with him."

"I was on ACAT with Don and will miss his experienced guiding light. He was a joy to work with and we appreciate his participation in the aviation community."

"Don was THE man....he could tackle any problem with the utmost balance. He listened to both sides and took everyone into consideration."

"Don was friendly to everyone—he loved everyone and everyone loved Don."

"Don was balanced—he never took sides until he had worked the problem through in his own mind."

"Don taught me how to do the job without telling me how to think about the situation."

"Don was so organized—he always came well prepared to anything in which he was involved."

"Don was people."

"I am so glad he left his mark on the future of Truckee."

"It is a sad day for us all."

"The Celebration of his Life is just a pinnacle, his commitment to the community will be felt for years to come. He was always caring of others and I appreciate his focus and energy/insight/integrity to the community he so loved."

And, some of the notes I received from our mutual friends were the most poignant of all...

~~~

"32 years of joy and love with one man who shared your interests and life. You have so many wonderful memories of days with Don. I know you will treasure them. We will be proud to donate to one of Don's causes, since I truly believe that this is the best way to honor someone's life."

"He lived a long time but he was NEVER OLD. He truly LIVED LIFE to the fullest until the day he died. Don had style...

*he was a wonderful host. Somehow I just can't think that
there will no longer be the fabulous D&D. What a wonderful
life you two have built since Don retired.....always D&D."*

*"It sounds like you and Don had a wonderful, close
marriage...a rare and beautiful blessing."*

*"I never met Don, but to be married to you...to deserve
your love, he must have been a very, very special person."*

*"Don was a wonderful husband who supported her dog
showing hobby 100%."*

*"Pets are supposed to be very good for your heart...and
also 2 Hershey kisses a day."*

*"Don was the life of the party—he lightened up the
room and when he spotted you, his face lit up."*

*"Don was the lifeblood to Truckee—his spirit—his
enthusiasm—his love of life, Truckee, and YOU."*

~~~

The flowers and the plants, and also food, started to arrive
almost daily. Bev and Sarah were busy attending to placing the
plants around the house.

And, I was in a state of disbelief. How could someone who
was so vital, so young at heart, so in love with life and—with
me—have been taken from us...

From your friends...

From your town...

From your family...

From your dogs...

And me?

Chapter 23

The Lost Week

Our friends, Kath, Lisa, Debbie and Kathleen, gather at our home on Sunday, the day after, to help plan a memorial service. We sit around the patio table—furniture we purchased the first summer we were in our new home—on our front deck under the blue and beige umbrella. Each of them has a pad and has already made some notes—names, food possibilities, contacts...whatever.

"Who are they talking about? Whose memorial?" I say aloud to myself.

A part of my mind cannot even contemplate, much less understand, that I am here talking so calmly, so rationally, about your upcoming memorial arrangements.

All I want to do is to roll back the clock and erase this chapter of my life. I want to bring back the chapters where you and I had life—not only the good times, but the bad times as well—if there were truly any really bad times. Every couple has their "pissy fights"—that is, if they are both strong people with minds and thoughts of their own, and we were no exception. I want to bring all those times back. We will argue, then kiss and make-up. We will not have blinders on and we will celebrate the joy and the sadness, as well.

I hear them talking in the background and I know these will be my darkest hours. These will be the moments I will find myself rehashing and remembering. These memories of our friends planning your memorials will endure alongside the memories of Valentine's Day, our anniversaries, your birthday, my birthday, the dog's birthdays and all the holidays we made "our family traditions."

These memories of my saddest hours will become intertwined with the memories of our life—our thirty-two years of life.

Two separate memorials are suggested; one for our immediate family and best of friends. The "Family Memorial Service" will be held this coming Saturday. Another memorial service will be planned for next month; it will be a town of Truckee memorial because, after all, you are the first town dignitary to have died, even though you had been out of office since 2004. Who would have thought "that title" would be bestowed on you?

The other members of our family start to arrive. By the end of the week, they have all arrived: your three children, Bruce, Dan and Mary Beth; our daughter-in-law, Joan; your sister, Ann and two of her daughters; Betsy and Cathy; my sister, Bev and her husband, Art; my nephew, Jeff and his wife, Anita; my Aunt Betty and her new husband, Roger; our son-in-law, Tom and six of our seven grandchildren, Kerri, Davis, Woody, Kristie, Ashley and Lauren. They are sleeping in beds either here at our house, in the motor home parked in the extension of our driveway, or within a stone's throw of our house at various neighbors.

You would love it. You would be in the center of the activity. It would have been a true celebration. I have always had a problem with invitations and announcements that say, "Come and help celebrate so and so's life." How can we mourn a death one day and "celebrate" the same life some days later? How will I ever be able to "celebrate" your death when your life has been taken from me?

Our friends are truly amazing. Stefanie Oliviari came to the house one night with a couple cases of wine—wine you would have approved. Cindy and Herb Chandler, my friends I've known since my New York City days, sent boxes of baked ham with all the trimmings. Other dog friends sent another ham. Penny had our local specialty food store deliver trays and trays of cold cuts and salads. The owner of the specialty store and a former council member, who sat on the council when you did, delivered the trays himself. When Penny called to order the food, he had not yet heard the news and was totally shocked. Then again, everyone was! The entire town of Truckee is still in shock.

On Tuesday, Bev and I drive into Reno to meet with the funeral director. How do I even begin to describe this moment? It takes us a while to find the place even though, when we finally do see the numbers on the building, I know I must have passed it a thousand times on one or more of the many weekly trips I have made to Reno over the past eighteen years. I park the car and say to Bev, "I'm not ready for this. I can't go in there." She takes my arm in hers and steers me toward the front door. Once inside, we hear the solemn music which is being piped throughout every room and hallway. We ask for the name which was given to me days before when we were at the hospital. Someone comes to get us and leads us into a room. There is a long massive wood table in the middle of the room, and there are shelves and shelves on the two long walls holding several containers. "What are these?" I ask my sister with alarm in my voice. I get up and start to examine them closer—there's one with a skier on the front of the container, another with a rod and reel, another with a deer's outline burnt into the wood, marble ones, glass ones....one more ornate and elaborate than the next. "No, no, no," I tell my sister. "These are not Don. This is not what he would want. How can I do this? Oh, God, I can't believe I am in this room with these shelves closing in on me." I look over at her and say, "Gads, Bev, can you imagine if I had to pick out a coffin?" We laugh. It's a soft laugh, but as I laugh, I dry my tears and sit down next to her; she hugs me.

The funeral director finally comes in. He has a folder with him and opens it and starts to ask questions needed for the forms he must fill out. The financial aspects of the arrangements are discussed. "Ah, I should have brought the calculator sitting on the table," I say to Bev. We discuss making these arrangements as if we were planning a party or a celebration. I tell him I want your ashes to be in a simple box. He points out the gray box sitting on the very bottom of one of the shelves. It's the box one gets if nothing more elaborate is desired. I look over at my sister, and she gives me a look that says, "Well, not quite that simple." I settle on a wooden box, a light brown box…probably it's maple. I really don't know, but it will be engraved on the top. It will say—

~~~

Donald C. McCormack
October 1, 1930
June 23, 2007

~~~

That's it. It's done.

I ask him to please separate your ashes into four separate containers. I don't know why I have made this request, but I think maybe I will have need for this down the road, and I surely don't want to be doing this task on the kitchen counter. The thought of my doing that brings a chuckle along with my tears.

Before we leave his office, I order ten copies of your death certificate. Others, who have gone through deaths of family members, have warned me to order more than I think I will need. I say, "Yes, I want ten copies."

The funeral director tells me when I might pick up your ashes to bring home. I hand him my plastic credit card. I thank him for his services, and Bev and I leave. She holds onto my arm as we head for my car.

I am in disbelief.

Chapter 24

The Obituaries

~

A n article on your death appeared in the Sierra Sun on
June 26.

~~~

Former Truckee mayor dies at home

By Greyson Howard
Sierra Sun
June 26, 2007

*Truckee lost a devoted public servant Saturday
with the death of former town council member
Don McCormack, who doctors say may have suffered an
aneurysm.*

*Most recently serving a second term on the Airport
Community Outreach Team, McCormack also served
two terms with Truckee Town Council from 1994 to 2002,
including two years as mayor in 1996 and 2001.*

"For me personally, Don was great council, he was involved in everything," said Town Manager Tony Lashbrook. "Everything he did was well thought out— he demanded that on town council."

Lashbrook said McCormack was involved in many crucial issues for the town during his time on the council from developing the first general plan to bringing the police department into the Town of Truckee.

"His loss is really going to be felt at the airport. He provided leadership and continuity to the team," said Airport General Manager Dave Gotschall. "I'm going to miss him."

Because of McCormack's interest in preserving open space, his family asks that in lieu of flowers people send donations to the Truckee Donner Land Trust or the Mountain Area Preservation Foundation.

Town members are planning a memorial celebration of his life for the general public on Sunday, July 22, the place and time are yet to be determined.

~~~

Two obituaries were printed. The first appeared in the Sierra Sun on Friday, June 29. The second obituary was written by your son, Bruce, who is Editor and Publisher of the Cody Enterprise.

~~~

Donald Charles McCormack, 76, died suddenly June 23, 2007, in his Truckee home.

*He was born Oct. 1, 1930, in St. Louis, Mo., the
son of Royden Charles McCormack and Loraine Powers.
His father was a contractor and his mother one of the
first women to graduate from Northwestern University.
He attended schools in St. Louis and graduated from
the University of Missouri-Rolla in 1951 with a degree
in chemical engineering. He was a Sigma Nu.*

*He took a job with Shell Oil Co.—for which his
parents had to sign their approval because he was not
yet 21—at the St. Louis area Wood River Refinery.
He married Marion Robinson of St. Louis on June 6,
1952; they had three children and later divorced.*

*Don worked for Shell the next 38 years in various
management positions. He married Diane Young
on Aug. 23, 1975, in Weatherly, Pa., and they lived
in Houston, before he retired in 1989, and they
moved to their new house in Truckee.*

*In "retirement" Don turned his considerable
energies toward local government and community
service. He was elected to two terms on the Truckee
Town Council (1994-2002) and was Mayor of
Truckee in 1996 and again in 2001. He served as
board president of the Tahoe Donner Association
and Truckee Donner Land Trust. He was a board member of the Truckee River Watershed Advisory Group,
Nevada County Solid Waste Commission, Nevada
County Local Agency Formation Commission, League
of California Cities Task Force and a number of
other government committees.*

*Typical of Don's resilient, "stick with it" nature
and his continuing desire to give back to his community,
many of his civic contributions came after an unsuccessful*

bid for re-election in 2002. In recognition of his ongoing efforts, in 2003 the Truckee Rotary Club awarded him its "Service Above Self Award." Later taking on one of his more difficult assignments, at the time of his death he was chairman of the Airport Community Advisory Team planning the future of Truckee's busy, contentious airport. He was known for his fair, balanced, prepared and thoughtful ways.

He'd had successful heart stent surgery in May and enjoyed a motorcycle ride up Mount Rose on Father's Day the week before his death. He was a people person with friends from all walks of life, was young at heart, cheerful and a wonderful host. He was proud of his wife and children and happy beyond words with his retirement life in Truckee.

He is survived by his wife Diane of Truckee, children Bruce McCormack of Cody, Wyo., Dan (Joan) McCormack of Austin, Texas, and Mary Beth (Tom) Gear of Keller, Texas, grandchildren Molly Morehouse, Kerri, Davis and Woody McCormack, and Kristi, Ashley and Lauren Gear, sister Ann (Tom) Powell of Charlotte, N.C., sister-in-law Beverly Morgan of Ohio, and many nieces and nephews.

Cremation has taken place and a reception-memorial for family and friends will be at one of Don's favorite places—his home—at 2 p.m. Saturday, June 30. The Town of Truckee is planning a public ceremony to honor him at Town Hall on Sunday, July 22.

Memorial contributions may be made to Truckee Donner Land Trust, 19069 West River St., Truckee, 96161; or Mountain Area Preservation Foundation, P.O. Box 971, Truckee, 96160.

~~~

Chapter 25

Lashing Out

A few days after your death, I decide to tackle some bills. I have been on the phone for over an hour calling a motel in Vallejo. I stayed there in May when I was judging at a local dog show. Bev and Sarah hear me yelling into the phone and come into the office and sit on the sofa without saying a word.

I have started to refer to Sarah as "Saint Sarah," because she is my friend who was on the first plane out of Houston hours after I called her to tell her about you, and it is she who has been so understanding and loving of me. Even now, when she sees how bewildered I am over a stupid misunderstanding with this hotel, she comes up behind me and gives me a hug—no words, just a hug.

My original date of arrival, or whatever they call it, was on a Thursday. But, then I changed the date of arrival to Friday. My Visa bill has just arrived, and the motel had charged me for Thursday. So, I am calling the motel for the third time to try and have this charge taken off.

My anger seems out of control.

Why am I so angry with this poor defenseless clerk? Why am I lashing out at her? She had nothing to do with your death.

After all, when I checked into the motel on that Friday in May, you were still very much alive.

I feel like a ranting maniac.

A ranting widow.

That's it, isn't it? I am a widow, and I'm taking my anger out on this clerk.

I am a widow. I can hardly bear to say those words.

I AM a widow.

Chapter 26

The Family Memorial

B ev and I meet with someone whom we think might be able
to help us with the family memorial. We have not been
church goers during our married life, so we do not have a
family pastor or minister to call upon. The first person with
whom we meet, a woman pastor, seems genuinely interested
in helping us out. But, when talking to one of our friends a
day later, we are persuaded to use a minister who is a friend of
their family. So, we decide to go with their recommendation.

The day of the family memorial is a beautiful and sunny
day, perhaps a bit too sunny because we all will be sitting out
on our front deck. We have borrowed tables and chairs from
friends and have enough for practically everyone to sit. Many
of the flowers are carried outside. The deck looks like a
wonderful party is about to unfurl. You would have been
pleased. But, I don't think you would have been pleased with
the minister of record.

Actually, the memorial service starts out okay. The minister says some comforting words about you and your family.
Then I am introduced and asked to speak. All this week I have
been going through papers up in the office. In one file of yours,

I come across a speech you had given on "Leadership." It seems so fitting for me to use this. It is you.

~~~

DON MCCORMACK'S PHILOSOPHY OF LIFE

October 1, 1930—June 23, 2007

I want to share with you—his family and closest friends—some of Don's Philosophy of Life. But, before I talk about that, all of you know that Don and I were soul mates—he was the love of my life. He used to kid that the dogs were my life...but he knew that he was. How could we not be the love of each other's life—we celebrated our three anniversaries—Feb 10, 1975—when he first called me in New York City—as a blind date over the phone—April 23, 1975—when we first met Face to Face—and August 23, 1975—when we got married at my grandfather's bungalow in Weatherly, PA.

As I was going through some files last week, I came across a paper Don had written for a talk he was going to give on "Leadership in Local Government." As I started to read through his notes, I thought... this is really Don McCormack...this is/was his philosophy of life. And, I know he would want me to share this with you and for all of you to carry these words away with you....

In the first paragraph of his talk, he said that he was going to give his perspective in 15 minutes— for free...so you also, get this in less than 15 minutes and for free.

He started that, "most thoughtful people will come up with at least 2 characteristics of leadership right off the bat....VISION & INITIATIVE."

Vision—*the ability to think outside the lines and see the impact of today's decisions on the future.*

Initiative—*the drive to make things happen.*

Later he mentions, my four keys are as follows:

1—DEVELOP AND USE INTERPERSONAL SKILLS

Hear and evaluate other ideas

Listen carefully and openly

Respect the others (as a side note, he wrote—enough said—that's a week's course in itself)

2—DEVELOP A GOOD WORKING RELATION-SHIP WITH OTHER MEMBERS

Know them as people

Know their basic beliefs

Develop a common respect

3—WAIT FOR THE FACTS

Avoid preconceived decisions

Evaluate, compare, and consider all factors

4—MOST IMPORTANTLY, SEEK COMPROMISE WHERE NECESSARY

There are other valid views

Nobody is right all the time

Adjust your own priorities

Use your VISION and INITIATIVE and reach a consensus.

He closes—with what I think was his own personal philosophy—and one he and I talked about regarding every facet of our lives—be it Don in an official public capacity or me as a judge...standing inside the ring....

"IN ALL YOUR DECISIONS, BE UNCONCERNED FOR YOUR OWN WELFARE.

That's not always easy, but it's pretty basic.

The decision is about what is best for the whole....

IT'S NOT YOUR EGO—YOU CAN CHANGE YOUR POSITION.

IT'S NOT ABOUT YOUR BASIC BELIEF—IT CAN BE MODIFIED.

IT'S NOT THE IMPACT ON YOUR OWN CONSTITUENTS......
        (FRIENDS....FAMILY.....I added that)

IT'S ABOUT MAKING THE RIGHT DECISION FOR THE RIGHT REASON EVERY TIME.

WHEN THE TIME COMES, I HOPE YOU WILL WORK ON IT."

Don't you all agree that the Don McCormack we all knew and loved....lived by those words.

If we can learn something from his death, let's try to remember his philosophy of life. We will be better people for it, we will have better relationships with our friends and with our families...and we will always be true to ourselves.

~ ~ ~

Beverly later tells me that she could not believe how emotionally in control I was—no tears, no wailing. I just stood up and told everyone about your philosophy of life. Of course, I was on auto pilot.

I may appear to be calm and cool, but I know I just have to get through it. The tears, the wailing will happen when I am alone with my memories of you...when I can bury my head in your cotton terry cloth robe—onto which I embroidered a design of a Harley and gave to you one Christmas—and which still hangs on the hook leading to your closet in our bathroom.

But, today I only need to get through this day.

After I speak, Bruce says some words. Dan is next and then Mary Beth. Then Joan adds some of her memories of you.

Up jumps Ann, your sister. Oh, how I do love that woman! She starts off by shouting—

Donald, Charles, Augustus, Sweetbriar, Rosewood, Alginon, Pettingeld, McBelch, McCormack

They are the family names that were given to you when you and Ann were kids. You recited them to me many times during our life together. I added a few of my own—my favorite was, McFart. We used to laugh at that one.

The last person to speak is Ken—Ken, of Ken and Kathleen Ritchie, our wonderful bridge, cooking, hiking and all other activities that we four did together as "best of friends." But, you and Ken shared another activity that you both so enjoyed and that was riding your motorcycles together. You loved the day trips you both took to places like Downieville, Mount Rose, top of Rainbow Bridge, Monitor Pass and other day excursions I'm sure you made up as you rode along.

Ken had asked me if he could speak last, because he wanted to share a story with us and this is what he said.

~~~

Perhaps at some time in his life, every man has had a dream to ride off on a motorcycle. In 1995 Don fulfilled that dream, and he developed a passion to ride...anywhere, anytime. When you feel the wind, there is a freedom for your body, in your mind, and of your spirit.

So this is a poem for Don—

~~~

Can you feel the wind in Heaven?
Are you sleeping on a star?
Are you sliding down a moonbeam?
Do we know just where you are?

Can you feel the wind in Heaven?
Can you hear us call your name?
Do you know how much we miss you?
Life can never be the same.

Can you feel the wind in Heaven?
Can you hear the ladies cry?
Do you know their hearts are broken?
They don't want to say goodbye.

Can you feel the wind in Heaven?
Can the men hold back their tears?
Do you know the way they loved you?
That they wish that you were here.

Can you feel the wind in Heaven?
As we gather here today.
Do you hear our words of worship?
There's so much that we could say.

Yes, you can feel the wind in Heaven.
As you ride along a cloud.
There is freedom of your spirit.
You can smile and laugh out loud.

So there is a Bikers' Heaven.
And I'll meet you there someday.
I'll shake your hand and slap your back.
Then feel the wind our way!

~~~

And, then the minister starts to tell us all a story....and on....and on. I give a pained look to my sister. And he goes on some more. I look at my watch and he has been speaking for what seems an eternity. I cannot stand it any longer. I get up from my seat, go into the house, go through the house and into the powder room and close the door and sit on top of the toilet seat and yell to you, "Get the Hook."

You are laughing. I can hear you. You and I used to use that expression when we were at a play or concert, and it seemed like it would never end. You would lean over to me and whisper in my ear—"Get the Hook."

So, that's what I said for you—since you are not here to say it for yourself....

"GET THE HOOK!"

Chapter 27

Facing Mortality

I am looking for some item I want to remember, and I find our calendar from June 2003. I am struck by a similarity. It was almost four years ago to the date that you had your prostate operation, June 23, 2003.

You were very conscientious about your health and always scheduled a yearly check up at the beginning of the year. It was also customary for you to include having a blood test done to check the PSA levels. You were very aware prostate cancer can often be found early by testing the amount of PSA (Prostate Specific Antigen). And, we both knew that about 2 out of every 3 prostate cancers are found in men over the age of 65, and at what levels we would be concerned. (When prostate cancer develops, the PSA level usually goes above 4.)

In 2001, your PSA levels went above the 4 level. A biopsy was performed, as we were told that about 1 in 4 men at your age and with elevated levels have a chance of having prostate cancer. We met with the urologist for the follow-up, and everything appeared to be fine.

In early 2003 the PSA level had elevated and another biopsy was performed. Cancerous cells were detected.

The level of anxiety we went through before we made the decision to, "just have the damn thing taken out," in your own words, was one of our most stressful times in our married life. You had spoken with so many other men who were diagnosed with prostate cancer. Some had tried radiation, some seeds, some herbs, and some surgery. We discussed each and every option with each other.

You were most concerned you might suffer incontinence. "Well, Spirit wears a 'belly band,'" I said, meaning it to be a joke, and you gave me a glare. (Spirit was neutered and became incontinent after the surgery, and I made a band that went across his body and had little tabs in it so it would hold a small sanitary napkin.) It seemed to solve the problem with Spirit, but you were anxious enough and didn't want me to compare you with our dog.

The other concern was you would be impotent. All one has to do is to watch TV for a few hours, and he will be bombarded with commercials about this blue pill and this white pill. So we both knew there were ways to deal with that issue, if it would become a problem.

Almost overnight, all of those locker room jokes men casually banter around with each other became too poignant. When the thought that you, yourself, have prostate cancer and all the consequences it entails, looms in the very near future, these jokes become classified as insensitive. So, even I curbed my sense of humor. Anything having to do with this particular part of a male's anatomy, I soon discovered, was not to be joked about or discussed with any humor.

In the end, we made the decision to operate and remove the prostate and the cancerous cells. And when the operation was over and you had recovered, there was no incontinence, and there was the blue pill.

Looking back to this time four years ago, I think this was the first time you had to face your mortality. We never discussed the mortality issue. Perhaps we should have. I think the fact you had cancer—the big "C"—and the prospect of the cancer spreading created a level of concern. This "reality-check" changed the focus of your life and might have increased your stress level. You were seventy-two years old but a very young acting and looking seventy-two. But, perhaps the probability that "it" could reoccur lurked in the recesses of your mind.

We all think we are immortal and we will live forever.

Chapter 28

Slowly or Suddenly???

I don't know what is better. Is it better for your loved ones to die suddenly? Yes, better for them, perhaps. But, you were taken away from me so quickly. If you had a long-term terminal illness, we could have stayed awake until the wee hours of the morning re-reading all of our love letters to each other. We could have relived all of our memories that made "D & D." We could have gone down memory lane telling each other what we remembered the most—about us, about our families, about your kids and our grandkids, about our friends, about Gypsy, about Mystic, about Spirit, about Vision, about Mirage—and all the puppies.

We could have held hands—like we always did in the darkness of the movies or across the table in one of our favorite restaurants—and thumped out our secret Morse code system. One of us would go "thump-thump-thump"—which meant *"I Love You."* The other one would "thump-thump" back two times—which meant *"Me Too."* I don't know when we started this, but I do know it must have been during our first year together or maybe even during our courtship.

We could have wrapped each other in our arms and held on for eternity—kissing and hugging until.....Long before you died I had read somewhere hugs need to be held for at least 10 seconds so the endorphins start to work. You would start to pull away after about 5 seconds but finally you acquiesced to me and my desire to hold onto you just a little longer. Did God know? Did the angels know it was your last week?

Would we have talked about death? Would we have shared fears about the unknown in those final moments? Would it have been better for me if I could have told you one more time you were my world?

Is this the first stage of grief the experts talk about—this feeling of numbness and the feeling one is not really living in their life? This is happening to someone else. This surely isn't happening to me. It is someone else's husband who has just died.

Life is a big blur. No one told me to write everything down. But, it was my inner sense, my attention to detail to the point of being referred to as being "anal" that must have prompted me from "minute one" to say to the woman from Shell, to the person from Social Security, to everyone I had to call and talk to about you…to say, "Wait a minute. Will you please repeat that information to me and slowly. I need you to repeat what you just told me. I have to write it down word for word because I know I won't remember it tomorrow and especially hours from now."

The calls I need to make are taking me longer because of the note taking I am doing. But, thank goodness I am doing just that. I will find that out later. I will be thankful I was detail oriented and took notes on everything.

I have started two loose leaf binders, actually, these eventually developed into four. One big one is for your "Medical." I have separate dividers for all the papers from Medicare, another from our secondary insurance. Then I started making separate dividers for all of the health care providers such as the many doctors, the ex-ray techs, the air flight, the ambulance, the doctors in Reno and the doctors in Truckee, the night nurse—yes, I am receiving bills from every one of them. The second big binder is for "Finances." This one includes dividers for all of the Shell information and for our stock accounts. There is a third binder, smaller than these two, and this is for "Tax Information" and the notes you left for me. The fourth binder is for our/my stock accounts after June 23. These details I will now have to do on my own.

I am luckier than many other women who awake one night or day and find out they have gone from the role of "wife" to that of "widow." Unlike other friends, who went from their parent's home to marriage number one, two, etc., I did know how to live alone. I had learned from my twelve years in New York City that if I was to succeed in my solitary life, I had to learn how to fend for myself, how to be competent and how to be a bit assertive.

A theme that would sing its way into some of our "pissy" arguments was when you would say to me, "Diane, you're too assertive," and I would smile and look into those blue eyes of yours and say, "Don, if I didn't learn how to be assertive while I lived by myself in New York City they–would–have–chewed–me–up–and–spit–me–out." You knew I was correct. In fact, that was one of the reasons you told me you fell in love with me; I knew who I was and had my very own identity.

I do know being assertive will help me get through all of this in the long run. I know how to ask questions, I know where to search for answers, I know how to look for details and to act on them. I am not easily intimidated. When I was showing Spirit, and competed against professional handlers, there were five words I would tell myself before I entered the ring, "I Will Not Be Intimidated."

But, my defenses are also down right now. I am more vulnerable. My nerve endings are exposed and raw.

I know I will be going through so many different personal and emotional changes. I know I will be alone and will have to fend for myself as you will not be around the corner to help me out. I know I will not be the same woman I was on June 22. I don't know, yet, who that woman will eventually become, but I know I will be different. All of these things I need to do: all of the bills I need to pay, all the house repairs I have to handle on my own, all of the paper work I need to do—these are only but part of the changes that have happened to my life since June 23. My entire life, as I knew it, has been uprooted. And, you are not here to put me back in the earth, to gently tap down the ground around me, to give me support so I may spring up and become a flower.

Had you not died suddenly, I might have been able to fill in more of the blanks. Yes, you told me you had written down the information I would need to know about our taxes and the stock accounts. But, I would have asked you, "Don, how much insurance have you taken out on you in case you would die suddenly?" I would have asked, "What about our house and the mortgage and re-financing and interest rates. Should I look into doing that now?" I know about the stock accounts because these were started when I came into some family inheritance, but you were the one who was most involved with the day-to-day handling of this. I should have asked, "Is there anything else I need to know?"

I know a lingering and slow death would have been easier for me, but not for you. You loved life! You would not have wanted to linger. I remember every time you took a ride on your Harley, I would tell you to be careful. "Remember, Don, I'm not pushing a wheelchair for the rest of our lives," I would tell you.

The McCormack Family had a thing they used to do—way before I came into your life. When someone at the dinner table had food on their face, one of the other McCormack's would somehow get into the conversation the words, *"Portland Cement."* For instance, the conversation might be about the neighbor down the street planting a new rose garden with a raised rock wall, and one of the McCormack's would say, "I hope she's using *Portland Cement* for the foundation of the wall," and all the other McCormack's sitting at the table would instantly wipe their faces. When you told me that story, and if I saw a bit of food on your face, I would just say, "*Portland Cement*, Don." I wasn't as tactful as the older McCormack's.

That bit of information developed into our own conversation about drool, all in fun, of course. I told you I could take many things in life, but not drool. I said to you, "Don, when you start to drool, it's up to Cocktail Rock." This is the rock formation behind our house where we have taken many of the ashes of our beloved pets.

But, you died suddenly.

Chapter 29

Keeping Time & Dachshunds

On July 2 the family members leave. One by one they go. Of course, the hardest for me to see leave is my sister. I know I will see her again in August since I have a judging assignment in Harrisburg, Pennsylvania. I was hired by the club a year before you died. I could have cancelled the assignment—I have a valid reason to do so, but Bev and I think it will be good for me to get away for a few days. We had planned to do another "sister trip" when I got this assignment, and we tell each other we need to do this now more than before.

Sarah is staying for another week. Thank God for that. I don't know how I could possibly get through these days without another warm two-legged body in the house.

I am remembering how Sarah (and Neil) came into our lives. It was in 1986. We were living in Houston, and I had flown to Florida that December to pick up our sweet puppy—a longhaired standard dachshund. "Gypsy," Park Avenue Gypsy, was my first standard longhaired dachshund. When she died in December 1985, at the ripe age of almost seventeen, you had gently suggested we might want to consider getting another breed of dog. "Why don't you wait for at least six months," you said, "and see if another breed might be of interest to you or to us." After the six months, which I had spent combing through countless dog books and journals and magazines, I told you a standard longhaired dachshund was the only breed of dog I wanted. You agreed. "I'm just giving you options," you had replied.

So the search was on for "the" dachshund. I wanted to go back to the same line of Gypsy—it's human nature to want to recreate the beloved pet one has had, loved and lost. I started my research by contacting the Dachshund Club of America's secretary and was given the name of a woman who was breeding the same line. She lived in Florida, in fact, not too far from where my parents lived. She and her husband had founded the Royaldachs Kennels. I contacted them and arranged a flight to Florida. I stayed with my folks in St. Petersburg and drove down to Venice, where the kennel was located. When I arrived, I was amazed with the number of dachshunds running around the house and yard. They all came running up to me, wagging their tails. The breeder was a jolly sort of woman, dashing here and there in her "moo-moo" dress. She immediately announced I was staying for lunch. She had made a quiche, and we ate outside on her back deck. Of course, I was in heaven, with all the longhaired dachshunds kissing my feet. Alas, she didn't have any puppies at the time, but she did know of a breeder who lived in St. Petersburg and who just had a litter of puppies out of the Royaldachs top male. I drove back to my folks, happy with the thought we may get a puppy. The next day walking through the front door of the breeder to see her litter of beautiful puppies, I was hoping one of them would be going home to live with us. A few days later I was en-route back to Houston with our beautiful new puppy girl who would become Rinac's Mystic Wonderous Star. I remember that first night. We took Mystic up to our TV room and she gave us so many puppy kisses, and then fell fast asleep with her head buried under your arm. Her butt was on my lap—the benefit of having a "long" longhaired dachshund.

We talked about Mystic's future and decided I would show her in conformation since she came from this long line of champion longhaired dachshunds. I really wanted to get my feet wet showing a dog in conformation. You knew the story of when I showed Gypsy. I had no car and had to go to the shows via the local transportation. (Can any of us involved in dogs today imagine going to a dog show with your puppy in a home-made carrying bag—with no kennel, no exercise pen, and no bag of grooming supplies?) I was taking the bus from New York City to Trenton, New Jersey for my very first dog show, when the big and burly bus driver heard Gypsy give out a cry—or, it was probably a big bark that started from a little cry. Over his hand-held mike he announced, "Who on this bus is harboring livestock?" Thank goodness I was young and naïve and innocent looking, and he allowed me to remain on the bus until my stop in Trenton. But, he warned me to never bring a dog on board again. That was the end of my dog showing career while I lived in New York.

When Mystic was almost six months old, I went to a dachshund specialty show being held in Houston and took her along to get her used to other dogs and people. This cute little girl came over and asked me, "Can I hug on your puppy?" That was Sarah Hill's youngest daughter, Elizabeth Sarah—probably only six or seven years old. I later found out she would go around to the owners of many of the puppies to "socialize" them. Many years later, she developed into one of the best handlers in her own right, and many years after that, she pledged Alpha Chi Omega, the same sorority I had pledged back in 1959.

Through this encounter with Elizabeth Sarah and then her older sister, Barbara, you and I became friends with their parents, Sarah and Neil Hill. Sarah and I showed our dogs together on many weekends. But, as couples, we would get together on occasions for dinner and bridge. And, when we re-tired and moved to Truckee, the friendship not only continued but grew stronger.

In the summer of 1991, my litter of puppies was born to Mystic out of Barbara Power's big, red and flashy boy, Shoney. I had already decided I would keep the one and only male puppy, who would become Spirit, but there was also this stun-ning black and tan female. I called Sarah and told her about Jester. Within a few weeks, Sarah came to Truckee to see the litter and fell in love with her. Over the next several summers, Sarah would fly back to Truckee with Jester, and she and I would spend wonderful days together driving to the local dog shows around northern California. After I acquired my first motor home in 1993, Sarah and I would spend weeks during the summer driving throughout the state and to Idaho and Montana to what dog folks called "doing the circuit." Occa-sionally Neil would join Sarah during one of these summer jaunts, and you and he would stay back home in Truckee doing your male bonding. We had lots of fun as couples, and even-tually Sarah and Neil would fly up to Truckee for the week after Christmas through New Year's Eve. Neil would come laden with a cooler on wheels...stocked to the gills with seafood and quail and anything else he could stuff into it. What fun times! We would wake up in the morning and you would ask, "Anyone want to play a game of bridge before breakfast?" Yep, we all did. We didn't mind if we were snow bound—we played bridge, ate, drank, played more bridge—and life couldn't have been better.

One day in that second week after you died, Sarah and I took your chronograph watch to a jeweler in Incline Village, Nevada, to be appraised. I thought I might need to sell it for instant money. He inspected your watch through his loupe and said to me, "It's a bit scratched, it's worn, and probably won't get more than $100 dollars on EBay." No. I won't let your watch sell for that measly amount—not the watch that you wore on your wrist every day for the past 20 or more years. I placed the watch on my left wrist, pulled it tight and asked Sarah, "So, what do you think. Is this too big?" "You can sure see it," she said. "Fine, take out two links," I said to the jeweler as I handed the watch back to him.

It is now on my wrist. I am so thankful I kept it. It felt *your* pulse for all those years, and now it beats on *my* wrist. And every night as I unsnap your watch and take it off before going to bed, I visualize you doing the very same thing. It was the last thing you did at night, before taking off your glasses and placing them on your nightstand and—kissing me goodnight.

Don and Mystic – June 1990 - Nose to Nose

Chapter 30

Fourth of July

Truckee is a small mountain town. When we moved here in 1989, the population was around 8,000. When you died, the population was 14,000 and growing. And, on major holidays and during ski and summer season weekends, the town's population swells upwards by the thousands.

The Fourth of July parade was one of your favorite activities. You believed it to be one of the best old-fashioned celebrations. The day would start with a pancake breakfast, soon to be followed by a one-mile race from the Truckee High School ending in downtown Truckee. Then the hometown parade! Some of our favorite participants included the Bernese Mountain Dogs—over forty of them pulling their decorated carts; the old time cars from the "Cannibal Cruise" car groups; a group of Truckee men, wearing Sorrels (snow boots) who performed synchronized movements with their skis and not rifles, and…of course, one of your personal favorites, the belly dancers. The years you were on the Truckee Town Council, you were asked to be one of the judges. As we drove to downtown Truckee, I would get your attention and say to you with a stern voice, "And, Don McCormack, if I find out you voted for the belly dancers and not the dogs, don't bother to come home." You knew I was teasing you, and answered me, "I won't. I swear to you I won't do it, Honey. I'll vote for the dogs. I promise you, I'll vote for the dogs. I don't care how scruffy or flea-bitten they might look, I'll vote for the dogs." I think you probably did vote for the dogs. In the eighteen years we lived in Truckee, we only missed one parade. The years when you were not one of the judges, you and I would position ourselves in front of the bandstand, set up on Donner Pass Road in the center of Commercial Row in historical downtown Truckee, where one of the town's lawyers was the announcer. His wit and humor as a straight man was priceless. After the parade, we would pile into one of the local establishments for Bloody Marys. Then we would gather with our friends at Donner Lake's West End Beach with a picnic basket to share and wait for evening and the fireworks display.

I didn't think I could be downtown in the center of activities. Your sudden death was still too fresh—too many memories from these festivities that I knew would trigger instant tears. Nonetheless, our friends the Ritchie's, invited Sarah and me to meet them on Commercial Row in front of their medical office which was not located in the downtown area. Sarah dressed in some of my Fourth of July clothes. She looked quite festive in red, white and blue. I don't remember what I wore, black something, and I certainly didn't care. I just wanted to be with friends and watch from afar. It was less raw—less painful.

Years ago when we were discussing President Kennedy's funeral, you said to me, "Diane, I like the touch of the horseless rider. Honey, that's what I want." After you died, I had mentioned this to several town folks, but due to too many regulations, they told me your wishes could not be fulfilled. I was looking down the road towards town when I felt Sarah nudge me, "Diane, look at that," she said. I looked up Donner Pass

Road, and there was our friend, Rusty Pauli, gallantly riding on top of his horse, but his wife, Carol, was walking alongside her horse. Later I learned she had walked the entire route of the parade, from the Truckee high school to downtown Truckee, on the side of her horse. It was her very own personal tribute to you. You got your horseless rider.

When Sarah and I arrived home, the answering machine was filled with messages from our friends who had been downtown. They commented on the remarks delivered by one of Truckee's prominent lawyers who was also one of your good friends, which preceded a moment of silence with the presentation of the national and state colors by the Truckee Civil Air Patrol Cadet Squadron. I told Sarah, "Oh, thank goodness, we didn't go downtown, I don't think I would have been able to hold up." These were his remarks:

~~~

GOODBYE TO A DEAR FRIEND
"Today we pause for a moment of silence in memory of our dear friend and great Truckee citizen, Don McCormack. We lost Don unexpectedly just a few days ago.

Don McCormack was extremely active in the Truckee community; elected to two terms on the Truckee Town Council and served as mayor in 1996 and then again in 2001. Don served on many local boards and was honored with the Truckee Rotary Club's, "Service Above Self Award."

Don loved his wife, Diane, his family, his dachshunds, and enjoyed skiing, playing tennis and cruising on his Harley. Most of all, Don loved the Truckee community and particularly this Fourth of July Parade, which he always attended.

He was a loving, humorous, and dedicated member of our community who will be deeply missed. Even though many of you may not have known or even met Don, please know that he left an indelible mark on our Town. He understood, as you do, what makes Truckee, Truckee, and Don will remain in our memories forever.

Please join me in a moment of silence honoring the late Don McCormack."

~~~

Yes, you were loved!

Chapter 31

Pocket Burrito

~

It has been three weeks since you died and your dog is still waiting at the top of the stairs for you to return. He waits there with his paws crossed in front of him—listening so intently for any sound that might be you.

I had to pull him from your body when you landed at the bottom of the stairs, and Mirage still doesn't understand how you could have gone away and left him.

I don't understand as well.

I look at this sweet dear puppy—I will call him a "puppy" even when he is gray in his muzzle—and remember the day, four years ago.

The six puppies had been whelped in our office on January 16, 2003. We had set up the whelping pen and had enclosed it with several exercise pens to keep them from running all over. I could not decide which of the males I would keep. I knew I couldn't keep the one and only female who would become, "Dazzle." She and her Mama, Vision, were too much alike and would have fought for our attention to the bitter end. And, besides, my days of actually breeding were over now that I was on my way in fulfilling my passion to become a judge. "Blue-

Blue," was the first born and wore the blue lace collar. He was also the best boy puppy, who would become "Sunny" when he was purchased by my dear friend, Polly Savage. He would eventually be shown by handlers and campaigned to be one of the top longhaired dachshunds in the country. One day, when you were typing on the computer, Blue-Blue came over to you, and you leaned over the exercise pen and picked him up and put him in your pocket. How small he was then. I laughed and ran for the camera and took the picture. And, what did you call him when I printed the image of Blue-Blue in your shirt pocket?—A pocket burrito.

But, while all six puppies remained in our home, one other puppy kept coming over to me as I worked away on the computer. The others would be playing together, and he would leave them, and I would hear this little cry. I would look down and there he was. "Pick me up. Keep me. Keep me," he was saying to me.

Pocket Burrito – January 16, 2003

Now in the middle of the night, as I reach out to you, I move my hand over to your side of the bed. You are not there. But, I feel a soft and wet and warm lick on the top of my hand. It is Mirage.

Whoever says that dogs have no soul have never had a dog like Mirage. He has become my "soul dog." He looks into my eyes with those beautiful dark soulful eyes of his, and he knows and feels what emotions I am going through. Mirage now has captured my heart and entwined my soul.

Spirit was my "heart dog," but now I need my "soul dog" since I have lost my soul mate.

Chapter 32

Ashes to Ashes

I was dreading this day. I knew it would happen, but I was not looking forward to what I knew I had to do.

I had received a phone call from the funeral director telling me I could come to Reno to pick up your ashes—the remains, as I think he said. It was in the middle of the week in mid-July, and everyone I knew was either at work or busy with their own lives, and besides, I thought to myself this was something I had to do alone. I had to go and pick up your ashes, because if I were by myself I could cry and grieve over you as much as I wanted to.

A chill came over me as I opened the front door to the funeral home, even though it was quite warm outside. Minutes later I was back in the same room where Bev and I had sat to discuss the financial arrangements and to select the box—the box I knew when I saw it, would make this all be too real.

He came into the room and was carrying a large dark purple cloth bag. He took out the box from within this cloth bag. I don't know why I remembered to ask him, but I did and reminded him I wanted your ashes to be divided in four. He said, "Let me go and check on that," and left the room. He came back in and said something like it's being done now. Good thing I asked, because at that moment I had a mental image of arriving home and opening up the lid and seeing only one big bag. Then what? Would I have had to divide up your ashes on the kitchen butcher block island and weight each bag out on our French scale. *"Oh God, I can't believe I am thinking that thought,"* I said aloud.

He returned with the box. "Inside are four separate bags," he told me and placed the box back into the purple velvet bag. I thanked him and took the velvet bag holding the box and left.

But, once outside, as I approached my car, I didn't know what to do with the velvet bag which held the box and your ashes. I asked myself, *"Where do I put it in my car?"* The two rear seats were down, as they usually were, so that I could easily place dog kennels in the back of the car. I popped up the rear lift gate. Again I asked myself, *"Should I put it in the back?"* But, then I thought it could tip over, and the lid could come ajar and then what? Then I thought I could wedge the bag holding the box in front of the dropped back seats. I tried that and it wouldn't fit. So, I opened up the passenger door and stared inside for a minute contemplating now what. I thought I could put the bag holding the box on the front passenger seat and use the seat belt, but that seemed a bit absurd. So, in the end I placed the velvet bag holding you on the floor in front of the seat and wedged my handbag around it so it couldn't possibly tip over.

I put the car into reverse and slowly edged out of the parking lot and onto the main street leading to the freeway and home to Truckee. *"I'm taking you home, Baby,"* I said as I looked down at the bag.

I didn't know if I should laugh or cry because this entire episode in your life—and now in your death—seemed so ludicrous. It was so unreal.

No one warned me how hard this day would be.

Chapter 33

The Hog in My Life

You sure did love your Harley. Anyone and everyone who met you would eventually know how much you loved that bike.

In fact, it was mentioned by you in each and every one of the Christmas letters you and I would write together and send out—starting in the Christmas letter of 1995.

~~~

Well, I guess there's one thing that's new. After many, many years of wishing, but responding to comments like "your third wife will love it" and "get a soft one, 'cause you're gonna sleep with it," I convinced Diane that I was old enough to have a motorcycle. This Spring I bought a Harley Davidson (is there another kind?) Actually, I bought two— the first was a Sportster model (500 pounds, 883 ccs) the smallest bike HD makes. But after two months, I realized that, while the Sportster is larger than 90% of the non–HD machines on the street, sooner or later I was going to want a "full sized Hog." And, as a Houston friend said, "....and McCormack, you're running out of later." So I upgraded to a Dyna Glide—750 pounds, 1340 ccs, modified with a high-altitude air intake and open pipes (I wanted to HEAR it!!) I must say, traveling the many mountain roads around here is absolutely beautiful, and in seven months I have put 7,000+ miles on the two machines, all in day-trips. Having never (I mean, like NEVER) been on a motorcycle before, there was some fear and trepidation in taking the first step. The smartest thing I did was take a two day resident training course in Sacramento. It provided the machines, small, 150cc Hondas, and started at ground zero—someone pushes you without the motor running. At the end of the course, a test is given on a course layout which qualifies for a license, complete with emergency stops, swerves and weaving in and out of fifteen or so pylons. Had I seen the test before the course, I probably would have thought it not possible. However, after two days, I found I could pass it with a little room to spare, no mean feat. Credit to a really fine course. It was a bit dicey coming home and, for the first time, getting on the big Harley, which was already sitting in the garage."

~~~

Ah, Don—if you only knew. That was "your" take on how you got the Dyna Glide. Now, I'll tell the real story. After Aunt Irene died in March of 1995, we replaced the old twenty-four foot Coachman motor home we bought from my parents in 1993 with the thirty-two foot Aerbus motor home. One night I asked you, "Honey, would you like to use some of the inheritance money and get one of those "putt-putts" that we drove around in when we were in Bermuda?" "Yeah," you said, "I was thinking of that, and, besides that might be a way for me to go to dog shows with you." You came home one day with this two-page glossy brochure and opened it up and said, "Here's the bike I want to buy." Well, to my untrained eye, it WAS the smallest bike on the page. Little did I know that all the bikes were Harleys, and all would be classified as monsters to me. So, one day a few weeks later, I came home and zipped up my garage door. "Oh my God. Yikes," I exclaimed, as this behemoth was parked next to the driver's side of my car. It was the Sportster. Yeah, it was the smallest bike made by

Harley Davidson. And, after a few weeks and several hundred miles, you started to make rumblings it was too small, and if I were really concerned about your safety, you should have a bigger bike. "After all, a bigger bike means bigger and safer tires, it means a bigger handle bar so I can have an additional light added—safety light," you explained, and on and on. I think that's when I first used the phase, "But, Don, I didn't want you to get a bike in the first place," and wife number three, etc. Two weeks went by, and again you brought up the subject that you should have gotten a larger bike. I yawned. Meanwhile, I knew this would eventually happen—you would get the larger bike. But, every time you pressed for a larger motorcycle, a thought kept coming into my mind. If I compromised on your getting the larger bike, would you compromise on something that I really wanted to do involving Spirit? So, one day, as we soaked in the hot tub, you mentioned time was running out—if you were going to trade up the Sportster for a larger model, you had to do it now. I casually asked you, "Just how much extra money are we talking about?" You gave me a dollar amount. I replied, "Well, okay, how about if I take the same amount of money, dollar-for-dollar, and use it to 'special' Spirit next year." You didn't even wait a minute, or a second. You jumped at the chance and said, "Yes, of course you should, Honey." Case closed.

That's how it came about that Spirit was "specialed" the following year. For the non-doggie reader, most show dogs are retired after they earn their American Kennel Club championship. Owners "special" their dogs for different reasons: some want to get their dog into the top rankings so the dog would be more desirable to be used for breeding purposes. For some, it is an "ego game." For me, it was a combination of these reasons, but besides being fun, it was a challenge. Since I was an owner-handler, my only expenses were for travel, entry fees and a handful of advertisements. A dog can also be shown by a professional handler. For handlers, it is their livelihood and their way of life. Their fees may include boarding, travel expenses, entry fees and extra fees if the dog is considered high maintenance and requires special grooming. And, most show dogs are heavily advertised. There is a lot of money involved when a professional handler "specials" a dog. It can easily add up to thousands of dollars.

Little did we know when we decided to "special" Spirit, the next February he would have his big win at Westminster—the Olympics of the sport of showing dogs.

In the end, we both won. You had your beloved Dyna Glide, and I "specialed" my beloved dog.

Shortly after you died, I knew I had to sell your Dyna Glide. Bruce didn't need it, he had his own Harley. "Yeah, my Dad sure did love this bike," he told me one day when he came to Truckee for the town memorial. I knew a local internist who was interested in buying the Harley from you years earlier. You entertained the thought of selling the bike to him after your prostate operation in 2003. In the Christmas letter sent out at the end of 2003, you mentioned.

~~~

After seven years and forty thousand miles, it's sort of "been there, done that"—so it's up for sale. Diane breathes a sigh of relief—at least she will when it's out the door.

~~~

The following year as you had more time on your hands, since you were not as active in the town's civic affairs, and as your fear of spreading cancer cells started to subside, you decided to hold on to the bike. I think even I was okay with that decision. I knew how much pleasure you got from your rides, even if one ride was a short trip to the top of Donner Summit and back.

Now every time I see the Harley in the garage, I am reminded of you, and it is just too painful. I called the internist, who is also a friend, and mentioned I was selling both your Harley and your Chevy Tahoe. He came with his wife and little girl to look at them. That night he drove the Tahoe away. I guess he thought it was the more practical of the two. But, the next morning, I received a call from him, and he asked if he could bring back the Tahoe and take the Harley instead.

He came with his young son and took it for a test drive around the block. When he drove it back up our long driveway, Mirage wailed a sound like I've never heard before. Mirage thought it was you coming home from one of your excursions.

We were standing out in the driveway. He had already decided to take the Harley. "What size shoe do you wear?" I asked. "Ten and a half," he replied. "Wait," I said, and went in the house and got your pair of boots. "Here, try these on." Perfect fit. He was also the perfect fit for your chaps and your heavy black denim jacket. I had given Bruce most of your other Harley clothes and paraphernalia.

You would be pleased that our young doctor friend is now riding your bike—and loving it as much as you did. You would have a smile on your face to see his young son, clinging on to him with his little arms wrapped around his Dad, and wearing his own little boy helmet.

Days later as I was picking up around the house, I started to dust the top of the piano where I had placed several mementos that had been a meaningful part of your life—a sort of shrine to you and your memory—your Truckee mayor pin, the town of Truckee flag that was presented to me during the town's memorial, your Harley sunglasses, the green and white McCormack campaign button when you ran for mayor, the Truckee Tahoe Airport District badge and photographs. And, the silver bell was there, along with the note I had written to you years ago.

After you got the Harley, my hairdresser, Richard, also a Harley rider, suggested I get you a silver bell. "It's a biker tradition," he said, "and Don will really like it." I ordered the bell from my local jeweler, and the bell and this note were in your Christmas stocking that year.

~~~

THE HISTORY OF GOD'S BELL

Sometime during WWII, motorcycle riders started the tradition of hanging a small bell to their cycles.

The bell is supposed to bring good luck to those who believe in God and keep them from ever "going down."

The bell has to be given as a gift—one cannot buy a bell for themselves.

Most hang the bell under the front axle, but it can be hung anywhere.

This bell was hand made especially for you in Sterling Silver—similar to the "forever and always" medal that you wear around your neck. After the Holidays, I will have it engraved....

FOR THE HOG IN MY LIFE

Forever and Always,
Diane

~~~

Chapter 34

The Town of Truckee Memorial Sunday, July 22

This was another difficult day—one I did not want to face. It has been a month since you left me, and I am still living in a fog. Bruce and Mary Beth arrived on Friday. No other family members were here for this "celebration of your life."

There was a concert last night. It was held on the putting green of the Tahoe/Donner golf course as part of the, "Summer Lake Tahoe Concert Series"—which we always loved to attend. Stef once again proved to be that indispensable friend and provided tickets for the three of us. We made it through the evening, sitting out under the stars, listening to the music and enjoying the picnic food. It was a way to encapsulate our private emotions. These are strange and strained times. At one point in the concert, I closed my eyes and allowed my mind to drift back in time, to the memories of all the times we would be on this same hill, listening to the music, talking to our friends and watching for the first star of the night. Whoever saw the first star would point to it and whisper to the other, "There it is, right up there." So, when I opened my eyes last night, I looked for the first star. *"There it is,"* I silently said to you, *"See, darling, it's you."*

Sunday started out early for me. I put a pot of coffee on, and while it was brewing, I walked to the end of our driveway and got the newspaper. The coffee was finished when I got back to the house. I grabbed a cup, tucked the paper under my arm and went outside to try and collect my thoughts and my feelings. I was still in my nightgown and robe.

What were these thoughts and feelings I had? My emotions were like one of those whirlwind tunnels shown on the weather station, going around and around, gaining more fierceness and velocity, until my own head felt like it was spinning out of control. My insides were filled with love, rage, turmoil, questions, despair, more love and hate. I cried out to you, *"Don, I hate you for leaving me as I am the one who is now left to deal with questions from family members about wills and insurance policies and pension funds."*

Light years away from you is how I felt. How will I get on without you?

You are dead.

I wanted to pinch myself to make sure it was me. I told myself, *"It's me, this widow—the widow Mrs. McCormack"*

The Memorial was scheduled for 11 o'clock in the morning.

You would have been so proud of what the town did. They handled the details with such dignity and grace. The invitation they sent out included the photo I took of you when you ran for the Town Council the last time. You were standing outside on our front deck with your best far away look. You hated to stare directly into the camera.

When I arrived, I looked around and saw hardly a dry eye. There must have been close to 300 people there. So many of your friends, my friends, our friends, your bridge gang, my woman's bridge group, members from my dog kennel club and so many people with whom you worked in the past on the "oh so many" committees and boards you were on. And, I was thunder struck! I looked up and saw Anne Katona, the AKC Representative, as she walked towards me. I went up to her and said, "I can't believe you are here." And, she answered me ever so sweetly, "Why wouldn't I be here for you, Diane?" Even Ralph Price, one of the dog show superintendents was there. There were two huge white tents set up with chairs, but many decided to sit on the grass under some trees. It was a beautiful and sunny day.

The current mayor started the ceremony. He said a few words about you and there was the flag ceremony. I had asked two of your favorite people to talk about you—Ted Owens, one of the current Nevada County supervisors, and Kathleen Eagan, the first Mayor of Truckee—and, one of your "favorite" women, besides me. Ted spoke first and gave this tribute to you and your life.

~~~

Don McCormack was my friend and colleague. Today we celebrate his life and his service on behalf of his fellow man. On behalf of the citizens of Truckee and the County of Nevada, I want to thank Don's wife, Diane, and family for having shared Don with us.

I first met Don McCormack in 1996. He was helping a group of us write a skit for the upcoming Truckee Follies. He had ridden his Harley Davidson to the meeting held at the Veterans Building which in some way amazed me ... was Don really a likely "Harley" kind of guy? Perhaps not...it was merely another Don McCormack experience in the freedoms of life.

We went to work, the topic, the Town Council, of which Don was a member and Mayor. He provided the skinny on the inter-workings of the Council and we would tweak it for the sake of maximizing its comedic value. I remember Don several times throwing his head back, looking skyward and letting out that hearty laugh. He loved it. It struck me that Don could laugh at himself and at what was, as he often stated, "very serious business."

Later, it was my honor to serve on that Council with Don McCormack, this time as a colleague. This is where I learned who he really was.

First, Don was a teacher. I'm not sure if he knew that or not, but it certainly did come naturally to him. Don never told me what position to take, he was focused on the facts, the history and the functions of things. He liked to watch minds work and if they worked well enough ... he was not afraid to change his own.

Don was a numbers man. It was Don that always seemed to find the "needle in the haystack." While everyone has a role on a Council, this was clearly Don's hunting grounds. After what any of us might consider exhaustive number crunching, coming away quite sure that there was no "needle" in this haystack, Don would present three ... or four.

Don was locally patriotic. What does that mean? It means he loved that flag on that pole right before us today. The Truckee flag. He was proud of the "little Town that could.." He was a proud representative of his people in the mountains.

Don put his time in. On occasion, he would call and say, "let's go look at that project together." He didn't mean ... on paper, he meant, on foot or four wheel drive. He meant, in the mud if necessary. He had to know where the sun would be, where the view sheds were, where other neighborhoods that might be impacted were. He had to almost physically take the land apart, work the plan in his head, where would the water come from? Where would it go? Traffic ... another set of numbers with which to play. He simply had to understand it. He had to understand it fully.

Don held genuine concern for his community and the people who lived in it. He loved people. A hearty handshake, a hug for the ladies. Always with smile, style

*and enthusiasm. He made it a point to know a little
something about everyone. I cannot recall that he ever
began a conversation about himself, or as we would
part, that he didn't remind me to say hello to my wife
for him. Not occasionally, always.*

*Don could put things away. He didn't carry much, if
any baggage. He was extremely forgiving and understood
clearly that we are all different, came from different
places, held different beliefs, and in the final analysis,
are all just people that inhabit this great place and
love it all the same. Once done with an issue or spirited
debate, Don moved on. He loved his colleagues, man,
and woman....even if he didn't agree with them. He
looked forward, and rarely backward.*

*Don was, in the truest sense, a proud "public ser-
vant". Serving the community of Truckee, whether on
the Council or any of the other countless boards, commis-
sions and committees that Don served on, was truly his
pleasure, his honor and his duty. And while he may now
be gone from us, his dedication to principle, hard work
and to the peoples whose lives were bettered by his
service, Don's place in the history of Truckee is secure.*

~~~

Then Kathleen Eagan went to the podium and began to
talk about you.

~~~

*We are here today to say goodbye to Don McCormack,
and in saying goodbye, we also want to say thank you
for 20 years of service to our community.*

*First, to Diane, Bruce and Mary Beth. Please know
that we cannot speak about Don without having you in
our minds and hearts*

*I see people here today from all aspects of Don's
Truckee Life, both civic and social:*

*TOWN
*COUNTY
*AIRPORT
*LAND TRUST
*TAHOE DONNER
*MAPF
*COMMUNITY AS A WHOLE
*TENNIS
*SKIING
*BRIDGE
*HIKING
*MOTORCYCLES
    AND
*DACHSHUNDS

In reflecting on all that Don has contributed to our community, it's been a challenge to choose what to highlight. There are so many elements of his style and character that we've seen in each of the many leadership roles he played while serving Truckee. Words that come to mind are:

*HIGH ENERGY
*POSITIVE
*ENTHUSIASTIC
*FULL OF LIFE
*YOUNG AT HEART
*BALANCED
*THOUGHTFUL
*OPEN MINDED
*FRIENDLY
*RESPECTFUL
*LAUGHTER
*BAD JOKES
*INITIATIVE
*DEDICATED
*DETAILED
*CURIOUS

*TENACIOUS
*ORGANIZED
*PREPARED
*FOLLOW THROUGH
*RELIABLE

Shortly after his death, Diane, working from his personal notes, shared some of Don's leadership philosophies
with his children and grandchildren. I'd like to relay some
of these philosophies and I know all will see how Don's style
and character are reflected in them.

*Evaluate, compare and consider all facts
*Hear and evaluate other ideas
*Listen carefully and openly
*Avoid preconceived decisions. wait for the facts
*DEVELOP A GOOD WORKING RELATIONSHIP WITH
 OTHERS
*SEEK COMPROMISE WHERE NECESSARY
* be unconcerned for your own welfare

In closing, I must say the one attribute that Don
possessed that I admire the most was the fact that I
never heard him say a negative word about anyone...ever.
Either publicly or privately. He stayed firmly focused on
the issue and no matter how heated the debate, how contentious the issue, he never spoke ill of others. When the
debate was over and the decision made, he moved on.
Ever positive.

This is an extraordinary attribute and, to my mind,
a key indicator of his internal strength. He lived his
philosophy of respecting others and I will forever be in
awe of him in this regard.

The man had character.

Don, we are all here to say our goodbye to you.

We are so grateful that you and Diane came to Truckee.

*We are so grateful that you gave us the benefit
of your curiosity, diligence, good humor and respect
for others.*

*As Jim Simon said in his tribute to Don at this
year's 4th of July parade...*

*"He understood what makes Truckee, Truckee,
and Don will remain in our memories forever."*

*Don, you have left an indelible mark on our
community. We are so grateful.*

Thank you, Don. We will miss you.

~~~

I held up until the Town of Truckee's flag was lowered and presented to me. Someone sitting behind me came and sat next to me and put his arm around me, and I cried softly into my hanky.

Bruce later said to me, "My God, I didn't know my father was loved so much by the folks in this town."

At 3 o'clock, many of our friends met at our home for drinks and snacks. Your "shrine" was on the sofa table we got at an auction a lifetime ago. The photos of you, of you and me, were on the piano. The framed "dedications" from all of the organizations you were once so active in were placed in front of the fireplace. The easel was still up holding favorite photographs of you and our family and friends: you and Mary Beth at her wedding, you and Dan, you and your sister, you and your three kids, the two of us dancing at Pat and Stacey's wedding, you and Polly at your 75th birthday party, and on and on.

It was a potluck and our friends arrived laden with food. There was no "planned" memorial service like the one at the earlier memorial service for the family, no speeches. I didn't have to "get the hook." There were just hugs to me and hugs to each other because they all loved you and felt your loss.

Mayor of Truckee

The kids were not here. Their flights were scheduled for early afternoon, and they left after the town's service.

Our friends stayed for an hour, maybe two. I lost track. But, then they started to leave, one by one, couple by couple. And, then I was alone.

There is no "D & D."

It is a couple's world. As I sat alone on our deck by myself, what started out as a soft sob, became a cry and finally uncontrollable tears.

It is a couple's world, and there is no longer a "D & D."

Part Three

Chapter 35

July–Sunsets

Most nights our routine after dinner would be to either read or watch TV, some show we would have taped, one of our favorite movies on a DVD, or some current program. We both hated sitcoms and the current fad of the reality shows.

You would be sitting on the sofa with your feet on a pillow you had placed on top of the stained glass coffee table and I would be stretched out on the loveseat. Mirage would be on your lap and Vision curled up at my feet.

As the days started to get longer, the evening sky would turn brilliant tones of orange, reds, purples. From out of the side deck window, I could see the sky from where I was and would beckon to you to come and look. We couldn't see the actual sunset, just the brilliant colors of the sky filtered through the trees.

On the Wednesday of the week you died, you suggested we drive to Eagle Rock, the summit of Tahoe Donner's downhill ski hill, where we might be able to see the actual sunset. We piled the dogs in the car in their kennels and drove to the top of Skislope Way. We parked just behind the chair lifts, perhaps the highest point in Tahoe Donner at 7350 feet. However, the trees there were so dense we could not even see the sky let alone the setting sun, so we drove to several other spots, which also proved unsuccessful. Finally, we drove back home. But, I was glad it was your suggestion and not mine. I smiled and thought to myself, *"He still has a sensitive side after all these years."*

Tonight I took the dogs for a walk up Greenleaf Way. There are forest fires in the mountains close to us. The western sky was still ablaze with color, but there was an un-natural glow to the sunset, intensified with added color because of the ash in the air. The image of us driving to see the sunset washed over me. I crumbled to the road and let my emotions be swept by the sorrow I was feeling.

It's those memories that come flooding back to me that catch me off guard. The ache I felt today was as fresh and raw as it was on June 23.

Chapter 36

July–and... The Dogs

To you, going to a dog show was as boring as "watching grass grow." At least, that's what you used to tell our friends when they would ask you why you didn't go to shows with me. You would put your foot down and apply heavy pressure to the brakes and say, "NO," whenever I would ask, "Hey, honey, want to go to such n' such dog show with me next weekend?"

I was going to embroider you a shirt, *"DON DOES THE HOG & DIANE DOES THE DOGS."* I never got around to it. You asked me, "So, honey, you have that fancy sewing machine and make all those quilts for your friends, when are you going to make me a shirt?"

I'm sorry, Don, I never did make you your shirt, did I?

When I ask myself now, why I *didn't* make you a shirt, I recall a time, back in 1956 or so. My father, a Sergeant in the Baltimore County Police Department, came home with his allotment of shirts for the season, twelve long sleeved blue oxford cloth cotton shirts, perfect but with only one pocket. I had been fuming over the buttonhole attachment on my mother's black Singer featherweight sewing machine. It would constantly jam up. My father opened the box of shirts. He told me if I would take one of the twelve shirts and cut it up to make eleven pockets, exactly as the other pocket on each of the remaining eleven shirts, complete with the two rows of stitching and the pocket flaps, he would buy me a brand new buttonhole attachment.

My father did buy me a different buttonhole attachment. But every time you asked, "Where's my shirt?"—*THAT* was the memory I had—making all those pockets for his eleven shirts!

At the beginning of each month, you and I would always get together in our office to check and co-ordinate our schedules. You would add my dog-showing/judging dates to your Palm pilot.

As my schedule would fill with show dates, judging assignments dates, field trials or earthdog tests, you would sometimes moan and groan and complain and say to me, "Our lives have gone to the dogs."

As I continue to go through your many brief cases and "promotional give-away" binders, I find photographs of the dogs: Spirit's winning Best of Variety at Westminster; Spirit and me when he won his Best in Show; Vision standing in front of the photographer's sign that said, "NEW CDX;" me standing next to the owner of the dog I had just put up; Mirage when he completed his Championship title after he won his second "five point major" in Missoula and our litter of six Vision and Casanova puppies when they were just eleven weeks old. Not just in one of your brief cases—but in every one. Yes, I knew you were proud of the dogs or of me and the dogs.

Of course, you loved our dogs. You loved them as much as I did. They were our family. You were the one who coined the word— "hu-mines."

Your wonderful sense of humor came out from time to time when we were discussing dogs. I remember one morning you were driving me into Reno to catch a plane for some judging assignment. The AKC "Gazette" had arrived the day before and I tucked it into my carry-on case to read on the flight. The photograph on the front cover was of the latest dog AKC recognized—the Plott Hound. I showed you the cover and you asked me, "Well, what group is this dog going to be in? He looks like he's a sporting dog." I told you the Plott was the state dog of North Carolina and then explained some other things about the dogs, like they are used to bring to bay big game like bears or wild boars. Before I answered your question as to what group the Plotts would be in, you looked at me and started laughing. "Oh, you said, they're going into the 'Chase and Chew' Group." It was your joke, of course, because we both knew dachshunds do not chase and chew. They scent and chase and scent some more and then chase, but never get the chance to chew.

You proved your love and concern and devotion in the spring and summer of 1992. Mystic's litter was whelped on July 26, 1991. This was the litter sired by Shoney which produced Spirit. When Spirit was about six months old, friends of ours were visiting. Bob Trares had worked with you at Shell Oil Company and Carlene, his wife, was a retired RN. As she was petting Mystic, she felt a tiny and hard lump on Mystic's side. The following day I took her in to see our beloved Truckee vet. An operation was scheduled; the lump was removed, and a sample of the lump was sent to a lab for diagnosis. It turned out to be fibro sarcoma, a deadly form of cancer. Another operation was performed where the area was excised, and our vet recommended taking Mystic to UC Davis for radiation. UC Davis told us we would have to have three treatments on Mystic every week for a total of eleven weeks. You and I worked out a schedule. I would drive down to UC Davis on Friday, take her for a treatment and then stay at the inexpensive dog motel, the one where they always kept the door open. I would show Spirit in local shows over the weekend, even though he was too immature looking to compete with the older dogs. I would stay through Monday and take Mystic for another treatment on Monday and then drive home. You drove down and back with Mystic on Wednesday. We kept up this schedule for the required weeks of treatment. You were a trooper to do this week in and week out, but our Mystic lived to almost seventeen.

The dogs were as important to you as they are to me. You just didn't want me to be away as much. It was one of our "bones" of contention. But, I used to tell my friends, "When I get home after being away for a long weekend, Don treats me like a Queen." You did! I know you worshipped the ground I walked on. You were proud of me, our dogs and all of our accomplishments.

After all—it was D & D DACHS.

Don on Dyna Glide with Mystic and Spirit

Chapter 37

July – Sun Faces

Late in the afternoon of a day in July, just a couple of weeks after you died, there was a knock on the door. When I opened it, there stood Sandy and Darwin Throne carrying an enormous sun face. They had visited with me earlier in the day and heard me tell the story about the sun face I bought you on your last day. Of course, they knew about the sun faces because Sandy and Darwin were our friends who went with us to Tuscany seven years ago.

Our trip to Tuscany was to be our last vacation taken together. You really did not like to travel. Every time I brought up the subject of taking a vacation—somewhere, anywhere together—your response would be, "OK, then Susanville it will be." (Susanville is approximately thirty miles north of Truckee on Highway 89.) It was our standing joke. You would say to me, "Diane, darling. Why should we pay thousands of dollars to go somewhere when people pay that much to come here?" And, then you would add in a more consoling voice, "Really, Diane, we have everything right here. There's no more beautiful spot on the face of the earth than Lake Tahoe and the Sierra."

We did talk about our big anniversaries that were coming up, and you did want to please me, so one night over cocktails you said to me, "Ok, Honey, let's make this special. But, can you plan it?" Of course, you knew I loved to plan and research. So in 2000, when our twenty-fifth wedding anniversary and our significant birthdays, sixty and seventy, were going to coincide, I started planning a trip to Tuscany. After all, we loved Italian food. I used to say I had an Italian stomach but a Hungarian soul.

I started looking through all of my old Gourmet and Bon Appetite magazines and finally pulled up information on Italy on the internet. We left on September 12, and thirteen hours later, picked up our rental car at the airport in Rome. Then we started driving, eating, and drinking our way through Tuscany. From small restaurants, discovered by chance while walking over the cobble-stoned lanes in the non-touristy areas, to the larger well-known and highly advertised restaurants, we never encountered a bad meal or a bad experience. The highlight of the trip for us was when we visited Podere Terreno, a converted 16th century stone farmhouse in the village of Radda. I had discovered Podere Terreno from an article in Bon Appetite and had started an email conversation with the proprietor, Roberto Melosi. It couldn't have been more charming; the walls were made of rustic stone, and in the large gathering room there was a huge fireplace with a wooden mantle. Copper pots and plates adorned the walls and sunflowers were everywhere in straw baskets. There were soft comfy sofas to sink into and a very long wooden dining room table with place settings for 18 guests. The price of our stay included all the wine we could drink. Oh my, the four of us were in heaven! We arrived in late afternoon before any of the other guests had arrived. After a quick tour of the main rooms, you and I followed the wonderful aroma into the kitchen where a rather large man was stirring something on the massive stove. He was the chef, Ben, and was making "Ziti with Tuna, Capers and Raisins." It was the very same recipe that was written up in the issue of Bon Appetite that featured Podere Terreno. And, he was making it in our honor. We started a conversation with Chef Ben and were amazed he had no Italian accent. You asked him, "Where's your Italian accent?" He gave us the biggest dimpled grin and said, "Well, I'm not Italian. I'm from the San Francisco Bay area." After more conversation, we learned he had trained with the legendary Alice Waters of the famous Chez Panisse restaurant in Berkeley, CA, whose culinary philosophy maintains cooking should be based on using organic and locally grown fresh produce and foods that are seasonal. Chef Ben told us that Roberto and his wife, Sylvie, had left for holiday but had left instructions for him to prepare the ziti and tuna pasta dish for our first night. We were literally blown away and knew that we would be well-fed and wined for the next several days!

~~~

ZITI WITH TUNA, CAPER AND RAISINS—

2 to 4 servings

      ½ *cup coarsely chopped carrot*
      ½ *cup coarsely chopped celery*
      ⅓ *cup coarsely chopped shallots*
      ¼ *cup chopped fresh parsley*
      3 tablespoons drained and rinsed capers
      3 tablespoons golden raisins
      3 tablespoons pine nuts
      ½ *teaspoon dried crushed red pepper*

      ¼ *cup olive oil*
      ½ *cup dry white wine*
      1 teaspoon chopped anchovies

1 can solid white tuna packed in oil (6 1/8 ounce)
2 tablespoons chopped fresh basil
1 tablespoon chopped fresh oregano
¼ cup plus ⅔ cup grated Romano cheese
1 teaspoon grated lemon

¾ pound ziti pasta
½ cup bottle clam juice

*Place first 8 ingredients in food processor
and process until finely chopped. Heat olive oil in
heavy skillet over medium heat. Add chopped vegetable mixture, cover and cook until just tender,
stirring occasionally, about 10 minutes. Add
white wine and anchovies. Cover and cook 5 minutes. Uncover, cook until wine evaporates, stirring
occasionally, about 6 minutes. Remove vegetable
mixture from heat.*

*Stir tuna and its oil, basil, oregano and
¼ cup Romano cheese into vegetable mixture in
skillet, flaking tuna into small pieces.*

*Cook ziti in large pot of boiling salted water
until just tender. Drain. Bring tuna mixture
to simmer. Add pasta, clam juice and 2/3 cup
Romano. Toss until heated through. Season with
salt and pepper.*

~~~

One of the photographs from the Bon Appetite article
showed Roberto Melosi sitting in one of the dining room chairs
with his legs outstretched and feet up on another chair holding
a glass of Chianti from his own winery. Before the other guests
had arrived for dinner, you sat in the same chair with your

feet up and holding a glass of Chianti. The photograph of you is in the photo album I made of our trip to Tuscany, next to the one of Roberto.

Don – Tuscany – September 2000

The following day we spotted Sylvie's collection of sun faces mounted on one of the outside walls of the stone farmhouse. "That's what we should do to that bare wall outside our front deck," you said to me. "Let's collect sun faces." Well, we never got around to it until the day you died when I drove down to the Villager Nursery and bought the "happy."

We loved Tuscany with its landscape of rolling hills. I have memories of us walking through ancient stone villages with their streets so narrow we could literally reach out and touch the buildings as we passed by, the Italian women peering down from their balconies to the street below, wrinkled and wrapped in some old sweater, and walking along cobble-stoned streets to a small café where we tasted the best croissants and dark rich espresso, and oh yes, the many accumulated parking tickets.

And the sun faces!

Darwin & Sandy Throne – Diane & Don – Podere Terreno

Chapter 38

August–Sounds of Children Laughing

You had been so looking forward to their visit. It was even programmed into your Palm Pilot—*"Visit from Julie and Girls."* Julie Nielsen and I had known each other since 1997 when I started doing field trials with Spirit. Julie, and her two daughters, Carley and Clair, had been planning a trip to Truckee since late spring after Julie and I had attended the Dachshund Club of America Nationals. She and I had been staying in the motor home during the field trial and earthdog events and then had moved to the hotel's parking lot in downtown Sacramento where the conformation shows were being held. I had left Vision at home and had taken Mirage since only he was participating in the field trials and earthdog test. Vision was entered in the obedience classes and also in the longhaired brace class with Dazzle, Vision's daughter. You made the trip from Truckee to Sacramento to transfer dogs and had taken Julie and me to lunch at the hotel the day you came down. The next week you asked me, "Why don't we have Julie and her daughters come down during the summer? I think they would really enjoy Truckee. I really enjoyed meeting Julie and am sure her daughters would be fun to have around." So, the trip was planned for early August.

You died six weeks before their visit. Julie called me shortly after hearing of your death. She asked me, "Do you still want us to come down next month?" "Do I ever," I replied, "but, can it be for the rest of the summer?" Well, I knew that was out, but it was a good try.

Soon the house was filled with sounds of her two girls laughing and giggling, all the other sounds that little girls, ages eight and ten, make, and, barking! The dogs would race back and forth throughout the house chasing them, and then Carley and Claire would chase the dogs, then all four of them would end up tumbling down on the floor in a pile of dogs and kids. Kisses and wet sloppy tongues were everywhere.

The first day they arrived happened to be Vision's ninth birthday. Naturally, we had to plan a party complete with the typical party fare for a dog's birthday, hotdogs and hamburgers. What was so cute was when the two "two-legged" girls went around to the guests and asked them for their order. They had even written the preferences down on a piece of paper. I was busy on the side deck flipping the burgers and wasn't paying attention to what was happening on the front deck. The girls had wheeled the buffet trolley out to the deck and were passing out the "orders" to our guest. Don, even you could not have carried this off with such finesse.

The next day we did something that I had wanted to do with you since the first summer we were in Truckee; we rafted up, or maybe it was down, the Truckee River. It was the most spectacular day— "JASDIP," for sure. (Truckeeites refer to our fabulous weather in the summer as JASDIP—"Just Another Shitty Day in Paradise.") We drove our car down to the parking area of the rafting company in Tahoe City and were bused to their location alongside the Truckee River. The four of us were loaded into a huge raft, given four orange life vests and handed two oars. Our self-guided raft trip was not like the whitewater raft trip I remember you and I took while vacationing in Wyoming one summer. That was rated a Class Three or Four trip, complete with rapids, many rapids. This was not without its thrills even though it is rated a Class One. (All rivers are rated on a "class" scale to help determine the size and technicality of the whitewater.) We started out at a leisurely pace, casually drifting down the river and enjoying the camaraderie of the other rafters, many of whom were college kids. The girls were getting in and out of the raft to swim alongside us while Julie and I floated along. We maneuvered the raft to the side of a bank, lined with ferns and other rafters, and Julie and I stretched out in the sun while the girls found a high place from where they took turns jumping into the river. Back into the raft and about three miles upriver, the currents started to pick up and we lost one of the oars…and… almost one of the girls. Then we hit a rather big boulder and the raft started to spin around. Other rafters helped us push off and back on track we paddled until we were bumped by other rafts and were caught up on yet, another boulder. When we thought everything was calm we looked up and saw a rather low hanging bridge. One of the girls pointed out to us, "Look, it's covered with bubble gum." We didn't have any. Darn it! We ended our trip at the River Ranch some three hours later, where the rafting company's bus was waiting to take us back to our car. What a spectacular day and what fun! Don, why didn't you and I ever take this raft trip, either with our grandkids or by ourselves? I think you would have loved it.

You and I loved the Tahoe/Donner marina. It's situated on the east side of Donner Lake, which is at 6,000 feet above sea level and has the most spectacular views of Donner Lake with the Sierra Nevada mountains framing it. We used to take our canoe there and paddle around for a few hours. We would pull it ashore and watch the sunset while enjoying a bottle of wine. In fact, in the summer of 2005 we even boarded the canoe at the lake so we wouldn't have to go through the ritual of taking it down from the pulleys in the garage and loading it on top of your Tahoe, a very arduous task. The girls wanted to go paddle boating, so off we went to the marina. It was another gorgeous summer day and the water was so smooth, unlike some of the times. Not quite as adventurous as the rafting, but so much fun. You would have loved it also!

One of the things we did while they were here which was not a planned activity, so to speak, were the nights we would sit out on the front deck in the still of the night, wrapped in the quilts and watch the stars. The dogs would go from one chair or chaise to another, always a welcoming lap would be found. Yes, we saw two shooting stars and several satellites. I told them the story of how you and I sat out on the front deck on an absolutely beautiful night doing this very same thing. We would watch the stars become brighter and brighter as the sky became darker. I told the girls you knew many of them— Cassiopeia, Pegasus, Orion—and others. However, they did not want to go inside and go to bed early as you always did. I think they would have stayed out on the deck all night long, if Julie and I had given the go-ahead, bears and all.

We didn't see any of our famous brown bears, although we looked for them and even drove around looking for one. One of the highlights for the girls was when they saw some deer licking the salt lick on the side of our house. They ran and got their camera and took several shots of them. I love the image of the deer at the salt lick as well. That's one of the reasons we loved living in our little spot of forest. We would put out a new salt lick for the deer almost every year we lived here, replacing the one from the year before which had been licked down to the last inch. The salt licks weighed a ton. You had dragged this salt lick to its location weeks before you died. You

had to use the heavy duty cart and cussed the entire way because the wheels kept getting hung up on one of the many
rocks jutting up on our property. You knew I wanted it there.
You knew how spiritual it made me feel when I looked out the
kitchen window and saw the deer at the salt lick.

I have just returned from taking Julie and her daughters
into Reno to catch their plane home to Vancouver, WA. The
house is so quiet. The dogs keep looking for the two girls. There
are no sounds of children laughing and I miss you.

Chapter 39

August–Coming Back Home

The trip had been planned long before June of 2007. Judging panels for dog shows are put into gear at least one full year before the actual show takes place. I had been invited to judge at the dog shows in Harrisburg, PA, and you had marked the date, Saturday, August 11, down in your calendar and in your Palm. We had even talked about the trip that Bev and I had taken together the year before, and you said to me, "Why don't you and your sister get together for your 'Sister's Vacation' after this show. Take some extra days since you'll already be there. She could drive there from Ohio. It can't be that far. And, don't the Young family relatives live close by?" The gears were put into action. Only, there was a glitch in the gears—you had died.

Bev and I talked about what we should do. Yes, she wanted to see me and spend time with me. Seven weeks before when she flew out to Truckee to be with me after you died, was not the time we had intended for our "Sister's Vacation." That week she was here with me was anything but a "vacation."

I flew into the Harrisburg airport two days before I was scheduled to judge. Bev arrived via car the following day, and we received the grand tour of the Masonic Village where three of my father's siblings live. The Youngs are a family of spry elders. Aunt Florence is 94, Uncle Bill is 85, and Aunt Betty is 83. They all live in this wonderful place in the rolling hills of eastern Pennsylvania. There needs to be one of these establishments in every town and village. They sure do respect their elderly and know how to treat them royally.

I remember a conversation you and I had with some of our friends. It was about this very same subject, long-term care for the aging. One of our friends asked you, "Have you looked into long-term health insurance or long term-housing for the aged, Don?" And, you replied, "No, I don't need it. That's why I married Diane. She's my long-term health insurance. She will look after me."

When I arrived at the show site the next day, the club members greeted me with such loving care. They all knew what had happened to you. The AKC rep also knew and he was most aware of what I was going through. My judging assignment went well. I had 165 entries—that's considered a good "pull" since AKC only allows judges to judge a maximum of 175 dogs per day. I was judging my four provisional breeds and some of my other "regular-status" breeds. Bev sat ringside during my entire judging, and I could feel her support and love and at times when I felt a tear form, I would look over at her, and she was there. You would have been proud. You would have bragged to our friends about my entry—even though you would have missed my being away for a week plus.

On Sunday Bev and I left our relatives and headed for Edgemere, Maryland, the town where I lived from six-months-old until I left for college in 1958. A friend of Bev's from our childhood, and her husband, still live there. When I lived in Edgemere, I would tell friends there was only one road in, and I wanted to get on that road and head out and never come back. Well, these many years later, the town has flourished and it is now the weekend get-away for many of Baltimore's workers. The street where we lived, River Drive Road, has kept its charm. Edgemere, I will admit, is one town that looks better today than it did in 1958.

Bev and I were given the million dollar tour, stopping at Fort Howard. You knew the history of Fort Howard from my sharing stories with you about my childhood. Fort Howard is located on North Point where the Patapsco River joins the Chesapeake. During the War of 1812, it was the major defense and harbor headquarters during this second war to gain independence from Britain and for expansion westward. Fort Howard was the site of the largest invasion in the history of the United States when the British landed about seven thousand men on the "point." Their intent, to capture and burn Baltimore, was halted by the Americans in the Battle of North Point. In fact, Fort Howard was originally known as North Point. It is now a park, acquired as a gift from the United States Government in October of 1973 and is part of the Department of Recreation and Parks. This is where I learned how to swim. Bev, our friends and I walked over to the very same pier, now, of course, rebuilt and sturdy. I remembered wooden planks. We walked past the bunkers, covered with snarling miles of ivy. I remembered playing in them as children; they seemed so mysterious then. I remembered finding a macheté on those very same grounds, so many, many years ago. I walked away from the group; and I wanted to call you on my cell phone and tell you all about this. I wanted to share with you these feelings of melancholy I was having. I wanted to share with you how this visit to my home town was bringing back all of these memories.

During our stay with Bev's friends, we had steamed crabs and soft-shelled crabs. Bev and I were in heaven. Well, we were in "crab heaven." When we were kids living in Edgemere, our Dad used to go down to Miller's Island and buy a bushel basket of blue crabs for about twelve bucks. Once home, he would gingerly take them from the basket when the water was boiling. He would put them in his blue enamel crab steamer. He had made a special rack for the bottom of the pot so the crabs wouldn't sit in the spice concoction he had formulated. Of course, the main ingredient was Old Bay Crab Seasoning. After twenty to thirty minutes, he would check to see if the crabs had turned bright orange. If they were still dark red, he would say, "Nope, not yet." We would line the table with newspaper and the crab orgy would begin. In as much as we never had liquor in our house, we would have Mom's freshly brewed iced tea. Today, I imagine a dozen steamed blue crabs would cost over forty dollars, depending on the size. You heard all of these stories. My sister and I lived an idyllic childhood. Summertime and the living was easy! Mom's cherry pies, using the sour cherries from the trees in our backyard, and crabs, sweet corn and fresh peaches. Ah, the memories. I remember one night, shortly after we were married, telling you about crabs and how to tell the difference between a she crab and a he crab. Only true Baltimore folks know this! I'll let the reader in on a secret. It has to do with the color of their claws. Do men paint their nails red?

The day we left Edgemere, I asked Bev to drive down River Drive Road once more. I asked her to pull over to the side of the street before our house. It now has shutters on it and the side porch is enclosed; the fruit trees in the back yard have been taken out. There are no azaleas in front of the house. The house looks smaller. Then I remember when you would reminisce about how grand your childhood house in Webster Grove, Missouri was. When we went back to St. Louis for my nephew Jeff's wedding, as we drove up in front of your old house, you said to me, "No, this can't be. They must have taken off part of the front porch. It looks so small." Our childhood conceptions! So, I walked over to what once was the grandiose front lawn of my house and took off my sandals and crushed my bare feet into the sod. *"I used to play on this lawn,"* I said to myself and to you.

You had promised me that one day you would go back to Edgemere with me and I would show you all of these sites— my hometown. Now, that will never happen, you aren't here and you aren't back in Truckee either. I hate you for leaving me, and I hate that I can no longer talk to you.

Bev and I headed south and stopped off at the University of Maryland on our way to Williamsburg, Virginia. Since it was summer, classes were not being held, but a student orientation was going on. How young they all looked. How different from when I was going there. Now everyone on campus walks around with their cell phone held up to one of their ears. And, back packs. And, jeans. I am aging myself! When I attended the University of Maryland, 1958 to 1962, even nice tailored slacks were not permitted. Skirts or dresses were the rule of the day. If we wore slacks or jeans, heaven forbid, we wore a raincoat to cover them up until we were outside and past the House Mother's eagle eyes. It was strange to drive through these roads. Bev and I even found Caroline Hall, where I stayed the first two years until I moved into the sorority house. We drove out of the campus proper and parked in the lot behind my old sorority house, Alpha Chi Omega. No one was there, but I peeked into the windows and could imagine my life some forty-seven years ago. Again, I wanted to share this moment with you.

In Williamsburg we stayed with a college friend of mine, Linda, and her husband. She gave us the tour of old Williamsburg and it was fun to catch up on old times. She had also lived in New York City during part of the time I had lived there. You had met her at the engagement party hosted by Tom O'Toole who, at the time, was one of the top interior designers in New York City. Bev and I drove on to Hampton, Virginia, and had dinner one night with my great niece and her family. The next day we headed for Warren, Ohio, and then I flew home.

It was the longest flight I can ever remember. I sat by the window and thought of you almost the entire flight back to Reno. For a good part of the flight home, I looked out the plane's window at the square fields below; fields that look so unreal from so far above. We were flying over the Middle West, the harvest basket. I felt no emotion. Later, when we were flying over the Rockies, clouds started to form, fat and fluffy and white. When rays of the setting sun filtered through the cloud formations, I felt closer to you and prayed you were being watched over by the angels. As I looked at these beautiful, awe-inspiring cloud formations, it was impossible for me to keep my emotions in check.

It was the first time I would be arriving back at the airport and you would not be there waiting for me. I would not be able to call you on my cell phone and tell you, "Honey, we have just landed. I'll see you soon." Before June of 2007, on any trip I had planned, I would pick up my bags and walk outside and you would be standing there alongside one of the cars, wearing your black Harley hat and your enormous grin. I would put my luggage down and run to your arms. You would give me an extra big bear hug. You would get my luggage and toss it into the back of the car. All the while driving the thirty some miles back to our home, one of us would look over at the other and we would start smiling. Our homecomings made the separation worthwhile.

I drove my car out of the long-term parking lot and headed for Truckee. By the time I turned onto Greenleaf Way, the sun was starting to set in the hills around me. The line of crimson colors was diffused against the colors of the dark pines. I couldn't remember when I last came home to an empty house—to no one. I was almost overcome by a sense of bewilderment as I pulled my car into the garage. I retrieved my suitcase from the back of my car, the Hartman wheeled carry-on you bought for me years ago and mounted the steps with the suitcase banging behind me. I entered the house. It was dark and I turned on the lights, one by one. The house seemed deflated and I was carried back to a sense of what I had really lost and of what was once my "normal life."

Even though my absence had been for a short time, I saw things in a new light.

I had come home and it seemed so unreal you were not here.

Chapter 40

August–Christmas Plates

Several days before our anniversary, I sat in the quiet of the breakfast nook and flipped through the August copy of one of my dog magazines that is sent out as a courtesy to all AKC judges.

I looked up and noticed the Royal Copenhagen Christmas plates that were hanging in the soffit area above the cabinets. How many are there— 38—39?

I had started collecting the Royal Copenhagen Christmas plates while I lived in New York City. Walking down Fifth Avenue, I noticed a store front window filled with these plates. The store was one of those "seedy" types that sold imported electronics, embroidered linens, as well as these plates. What attracted me, of course, was the dog on the plate. My first plate is dated 1968 and is of a husky pulling a sled. Can you imagine that—a dog?!

After we were married, I continued buying the current year's anniversary plate. It became one of our traditions for the Christmas holidays—as was the addition of the yearly sterling silver ornaments.

There was a store on Alabama Avenue, not too far from where we lived in Montrose. They had walls and walls of the

Royal Copenhagen Christmas plates, and I remember going in to try and find one from each of our birth years. Yes, they had one of each, but the price was so prohibitive. Later that day, I asked you about it, and you responded, "Honey, are you kidding, that's more than the cost of ten plates. Do you really want them? It's stuff; we don't need them." You were probably correct. A lot of the things were "stuff," but some of the "stuff" we purchased I'm glad to have now because of the memories, of you and of us that are associated with their purchases.

When we designed our kitchen for our mountain home, we purposely designed the soffit area so it would be a gallery of sorts for these plates. We even selected the trim on the counter top tiles to match the blue in the plates.

Last November when the 2006 plate arrived, you got out the ladder, your hammer and tape to measure for the placement of it.

You looked down from the upper rung of the ladder and said to me, "Honey, there is room for only this year's plate, and then we'll have to make a major rearrangement. Maybe this should be our last plate."

No, there won't have to be a rearrangement. There won't be a 2007 plate. There will be no more traditions for us. Because, there is no more "us."

Chapter 41

August–The First Anniversary Without You

I thought the day would slowly creep up on me, but it didn't. August 23, 2007, exploded in front of me because not only is it the first anniversary of our wedding—without you here to celebrate our what-would-have-been thirty-two years—but it is also now two months to the day you died. How could time go by so quickly but yet stand still?

I needed no alarm clock to awaken me on this day. I had given some thought to how I might spend it. My friends, Stef and Debbie, had called earlier for dinner plans. They knew I didn't want to be alone, especially tonight.

This morning as I stood in our master bathroom, ready for my shower, the door to your closet was open. Tears of despair turned to tears of anger. Thoughts went through my mind. *"How could you have left me? How could you leave me to go through this day without you? I am so mad at you, Don, for leaving me."*

I noticed the hose for the central vacuum had not been returned to the laundry room on the first level of our house. I had carried it up last night to suck up some spider webs that were in our bedroom. The thoughts in my mind did a tumble. I turned off the water in the shower, put on some scruffy clothes and started to clean out your closet. The kids had already been through it and I let them take most of your good clothes. *"You left me, damn it, and I'm cleaning out your closet and taking it over for my out-of-season clothes."*

I went downstairs to the laundry room and filled a bucket with hot water and soap, put on some rubber gloves and started to clean. I don't think your closet had been so thoroughly cleaned since we built the house eighteen years ago. I went back downstairs to the garage and brought up several large plastic bags with ties. I started to fill them with your old sweats, jeans, and clothes that were still hanging there as you left them nine weeks ago. One entire bag was filled with shoes. There was a pair of some kind of athletic shoes with cleats on them, probably antique relics from your college days. I had never seen them before.

While I was throwing your old clothes into the plastic bags, I told myself, *"It will be less painful for me when I peer into the open door of your closet and see my clothes hanging there and not yours."*

I thought to myself, *"There are enough remembrances of you and your presence remaining in the bathroom."* I still could not remove the beautiful pastel striped shirt you wore that last night, the one I purchased from Stef at Cabonna's. You told Stef, "I feel like an Easter bunny when I wear it." We both convinced you that Easter bunnies are cuddly and loving. After that, you loved the shirt. It's been hanging over the back of the chair ever since that night of June 23. And the faded red swim trunks you wore when you went down to the hot tub most mornings after you worked out on the treadmill, they are still looped over the faucet in the Jacuzzi bathtub. And the terry cloth robe, that I made for you one Christmas, complete with a Harley embroidered on the pocket, it still hangs on the hook of the door to your, now, my closet.

I gradually carried some clothes over from my closet in our master bedroom to hang. All of my white slacks, capris and colorful tops I never had the chance to wear this summer since I was wearing—black. I carried over some out-of-season shoes. There are still some clothes of yours which I pushed to the back to hang behind the closet door and out of sight.

And, after three hours I finally took my shower and looked into the closet and smiled as I saw the transformation I made happen.

Later in the morning, I swung by the lawyer's office and signed yet more papers. "Hmm," I thought, "that will cost me." Yes, the necessities of life—and, in this case, death—every phone call, meeting, email—the time must be billed to the client....me.

When I left the house, I took the dogs with me, each in their brand new soft-sided kennel, which was bungeed in behind my seat so they were side by side. After I left the lawyer's office, I started driving north on Highway 89. I knew this was one of your favorite rides to take on your Harley. How fitting, I retraced this path today. About thirty miles north was Sierraville. There was a small area which had been made into a scenic overlook. I stopped and got out of the car. There were a couple of benches. The actual rest area was separated from the woods with a small and low rock fence made out of the same natural stones that were scattered all around. I thought to myself, "*You probably stopped here. You would have gotten off your Harley and walked over to this bench, sat down, and looked over and out at the view.*" Did you?

I took Vision out of her kennel and took her over to the woody area and she peed. Then I put her back in her kennel and got Mirage out of his kennel. Of course, the male dog has to cover up the scent. I was not paying attention to what he was doing because my mind was on you. All of a sudden I looked down and there he was—straddling the low stone wall and pooping right on top of it. You see, he also was mad at you for leaving us. This was what HE thought of the whole situation. "Poop on you, Daddy Don, for leaving us!"

Continuing onto Downieville, the road was full of hairpin turns and I told myself, "Yes, this is why you used to love taking this drive. It's a motorcyclist's dream. There's no traffic and the views are breathtaking." By the time I reached the quaint town of Downieville, it was getting late and I had to meet my friends for dinner at six. I knew you used to continue to make the circle and head over to Nevada City, then back to Truckee along I-80, but I checked out both routes on the car's GPS and decided I had to retrace my steps. One day I'll come back to Downieville, I thought, and spend a couple of hours here.

I was a little late in meeting my girlfriends, but they were forgiving. I only half heard the conversation because so many other thoughts were bombarding my memory. We all laughed as I told them what Mirage had done earlier in the day.

At nine o'clock I was back at home. I checked the computer for messages and then when I knew the sky would truly be dark, I went outside and sat on the deck and watched stars. This was one of our most favorite ways to spend the evening. We would turn out the lights in the house, each grab a dog, a quilt and sit on the chaises and look for satellites and falling stars or fast falling meteors, some with kite like tails. The stars in Tahoe Donner are brighter than in downtown Truckee because we are about 6,500 feet in elevation, and there is no light or chemical pollution. We would see many satellites, passing the binoculars back and forth, we would tell each other the path the satellites were taking—north to south over the big tree, south to north over the peak of the house, east to northwest, whatever. You would get tired and say, "Honey, after we see a falling star, then we can go upstairs and to bed," and immediately after you would proclaim you had seen a falling star. Ah, but I was wise to you, Don.

Tonight I had both dogs on my lap. One was under the quilt and one on top. My lap has to be big enough for both dogs now that you are not here to balance out the load.

We stayed outside until eleven o'clock and waited for the magical moment when a shooting star would blaze across the heavens. Yes, there was one. I went inside, put the dogs out on the side deck for their last pee of the night, told them, "Let's go upstairs" and they bounded up the stairs. Mirage can leap onto the bed by himself. I picked up Vision and placed her on top of the bed. I took off my clothes and put on my nightgown and turned on the TV which is housed in an antique mahogany linen press. The dogs and I cuddled under the comforter and watched the news until midnight.

I waited until one minute after midnight. I turned off the TV and then turned off the bedside light. I made it. I got through this day. I know this was—has been—one of the hardest days of my new life, but, I have done it!

I turned the light back on and took one more look at your picture and gathered your pillow to my face and still smelled your scent. I was reminded of something I read long ago...

"In all the very best of loves...one will die and one will live."

Chapter 42

September–Backpacking

I can feel the change in the seasons. It tweaks my memory and I am thinking of our many backpacking trips, one in particular.

In one of our conversations before we married, you told me how much you enjoyed backpacking. You had made several excursions before we were married; one even included a trip to the Wind River Range with your ex-wife. So, in the early months of 1978, when our friends began talking about taking another trip to the Wind River Range in western Wyoming my name was included.

Oh my God, I thought, the city girl is going to meet Mohammed of the mountains.

We started collecting the necessary items we would need. We borrowed a tent and sleeping bags, but I had to get my own backpack. Many improvements have been made to this necessary "item of torture"—but thirty years ago my backpack was advertised as being specially designed for a woman's frame. For weeks before "departure day," you and I would drive the short distance over to Memorial Park, load the backpacks with about a ton of books and off we would go walking the entire loop with my new backpack, weighing about thirty-five pounds. Memorial Park, one of the largest urban parks in the

United States, was the perfect spot for this "practice and shape-up" drill. Joggers, bikers and dog walkers enjoy the more than six miles of trails along the Houston Bayou. Every quarter mile was a marker to remind me of how far I had walked with this heavy backpack on my back and how far I had yet to do—farther and farther as the days clicked by. This was fun?

Very early on the morning of September 1, 1978, we set out for Wyoming and our destination, the Wind River Range—the Rocky Mountain range in Western Wyoming where one would find perhaps the most scenic western wilderness in the upper United States. The "Winds" are known for their huge granite peaks, some over 13,000 feet, thundering waterfalls and spectacular views of cliffs towering over lakes filled with various species of trout ready for the taking.

For the most part, the backpacking trip was wonderful with vistas and views and some of the most majestic wilderness I had ever seen. We even saw wild horses and mountain goats grazing in the far mountains. The one point of this trip that now comes to my mind was called, "Angel Pass." We were about four days into the hike when we came to "Angel Pass." We were above the tree line and west of the Continental Divide and all around was granite. It was a horrendous and tortuous pass to go over. The altitude, around 11,100 feet, made it difficult to breathe and I kept praying I wouldn't fall and bang up my knees or worse. One by one the other wives dropped their packs and crawled over the pass without their heavy load. Their husbands would then double back for their wives' packs. I had refused to drop my pack and climbed on. I had navigated the pass with my entire load on my back. For a moment I was ready to give in, but then the exhilaration took over. As the wind snaked across the top of the pass, I planted my hiking stick into the earth and took a deep and satisfying breath. I was at the top of Angel Pass. I had mastered the climb. When I got to the point on the other side of the pass, about half an hour later where the others were waiting and resting, you came beside me and said, "Honey, why were you being so stubborn? You know I would have gladly carried your pack over the pass." "Don," I whispered in your ear, "I heard some of the women talking about the perils of this pass. One of them made the comment that this was the same pass the group had taken before we were married, when you and your ex were part of the group. Your ex was ready to give up and was the first wife to drop her backpack. I was not going to let that happen to me." You smiled at me and started to rub my hurting shoulders. "Good for you," you said.

When we returned home, I made it my mission to outfit us with the best backpacking equipment I could find. There would be no more borrowed tents and sleeping bags. So, for the next birthdays, Christmases and anniversaries, you would receive a pair of down sleeping bags that would zip together if need be, a Moss tent with canopy, a water filtration unit, an Orvis fly fishing rod that broke apart for easy backpacking and a special compass in its leather case.

Yes, during our backpacking trips and in our married life, you were always by my side to tell me which way was True North. You were my compass in our life.

Backpacking in Wind River Range – September 1-14, 1978

Chapter 43

September–Christmases Past

It was only early September and I was at the mall. Already the stores were beginning to fill their aisles with Christmas items: wrapping paper, gift boxes and all the trimmings one would need to send out early packages. I passed by the game store and felt a smile come across my face as I remembered many of our Christmases.

When I arrived home, I wanted to read our very first Christmas card. It was in the first "D & D" album, mounted on a page before the pages of photographs we had taken that first Christmas. We had come across this card almost by accident and I remembered as I read the verse to you how we both beamed and said almost in unison, "That's the one." Over the years one or more of the verses from this card, taken from "Three Men in a Boat" and dated 1887, would be recited by us because it truly reflected our life.

~~~

Let your boat of life be light.
Packed with only what you need,
a homely home,
and simple pleasures,
one or two friends worth the name.
Someone to love.
Someone to love you,
a cat, a dog and a pipe or two, and
enough to eat, and enough to wear,
and a little more than enough to drink for thirst is a dangerous thing.

~~~

I loved buying you presents. You told me you always had a hard time buying things for me. You used to tell me, with a pained expression, "Diane, when you need or want something, you cannot wait until Christmas. If it's for your sewing or quilting, you need it now. If it's something you need for your dogs, it can't wait for a particular holiday. If it's some article of clothing, you probably saw it on sale, and by the time I would get ready to shop for you, it would be gone." Probably true. But, I would drop hints all year long, but you didn't pay attention to them. We even had a little box sitting on top of your dresser into which I would drop pictures of items I had cut out from catalogues. You were happy when I discovered American Indian jewelry. You could go down to White Buffalo, a wonderful store in downtown Truckee that specialized in American Indian jewelry and always find some goodie for my stocking.

You were easy to buy for, especially the first Christmas. During the many hours we spent on the phone talking to each other the months before we married, you told me about the presents you had gotten for your kids. I decided that this, our first Christmas together as husband and wife, you would be my kid. I bought you so many presents; the pile of beautifully wrapped boxes was almost as high as you were tall. The pic-

ture in our first photo album shows you standing in front of one of the calico stockings I made for you, me and Gypsy—and your pile of goodies. You are beaming in this photograph. What a happy kid!

The one Christmas you did outdo yourself was one of our early Christmases. There were plenty of boxes under the tree for both of us, but there was also this cute little furry dog with long ears with sparkle all over his body. I said, "Oh, he's cute, Honey," and put him aside and started to open the other

Don – First Christmas – December 1975

boxes. You would open one box and then I would open another and so forth. I always wanted to see the expression on your face, so I wouldn't open a box until you were finished. All the packages had been opened and you sat there with a smug grin on your face and said to me, "Well, you totally missed the BEST gift." "But, there are no more boxes," I proclaimed. "It doesn't have to be wrapped," you answered. I looked under the tree and couldn't see another gift, and you hinted about the cute, stuffed dog. I picked him up to give him another look and no-ticed again the sparkles that were on him. Then I noticed two big sparkles that were on his ears, one diamond stud earring attached to each of his ears. You had covered the dog's body with the sparkles and then pierced his ears with the diamond studs. You could be clever when you put your mind to it!

Another Houston Christmas you triumphed was when you surprised me with a Cuisinart food processor. We immediately went to the local grocery store and came home laden with carrots, potatoes, zucchini, any vegetable that we could practice cutting, slicing and shredding with this new gadget. We looked through the paperback cookbook that came with the Cuisinart and were intrigued with the recipe for brioche. We had to set our alarm clock to wake up in the middle of the night in order to punch down the dough. But, in the morning as we sampled our warm brioche, smothered with butter, we both were in heaven.

Chapter 44

September–The Junk Heap

For all of your wonderful qualities and abilities I admired, keeping the garage and your shop clean and orderly was not one of them. For the past few weeks, I've been tackling these two areas.

Your shop was the first on my list. Weeks ago, when one of our friends came over to hang something for me, he had gone into the shop to look for a hook and couldn't find anything because the work bench was piled high with "stuff." This area just had to be cleaned first.

I would pick something up and take a hard look at "it." Well, I certainly wasn't going to be joining two pieces of PVC pipe together with this can of purple goop, so out it went. The metal shelves now contain plastic bins into which I've organized electrical cords, sprinkler parts, whatever. The floor has been vacuumed and scrubbed, and I have even placed a small throw rug on top of the cement, a feminine touch to be sure. And, I can hear you saying to me, "That doesn't cut the mustard, Diane." "Yeah," I answer you back out loud, *"But, I can now see the top of your work bench, Honey,"*

This coming winter may be long and hard and if I'm to survive in this house, without you, I may need to work on some project in your—the—shop.

The garage was the next project. Why on earth did you save all those old snow poles and bits and pieces of parts that I haven't a clue as to their original use or where they would go. I started a pile of discards to be taken to the dump. Next I tackled the storage cabinets on the back wall of the garage. We paid a pricey amount to have them installed. I tossed out items I knew I wouldn't need to make room for the Christmas decorations in the attic. There is no drop-down ladder accessing this attic space. It was a last minute addition to the design of the house when we realized there was empty space above the bathroom. We added a small door, but it can only be accessed with a step-ladder. My plan is to get someone to help me go up the ladder, or at least to hold the ladder for me, as I go into the attic for one last time. I never want to have to go up there again.

The thought process in the back recess of my mind is saying one tumble in this house down any stairs is enough.

Once the shop and garage were cleaned, I continued on my mission to clean out. I started with the space under our front deck. We had it enclosed with redwood boards the second year we were in our house. I found old pieces of hose, dilapidated sprinklers, long pieces of PVC pipe and torn tarps that were once used to cover our firewood, when we burned firewood and before we converted to natural gas. I dragged all of this out and added it to the pile of discards.

To access the area under the front part of the house, I had to go through a locked door. This area contains the furnace system, the hot water tanks and the central vacuum clean out tank. The floor is natural dirt and rocks. As I was dragging out items and adding them to the pile of refuse, like the old Pawley's Island hammock from which the squirrels had pulled yards of the cotton rope to use for their nests, I saw two cloth grocery bags on different sides of the area. In one of the bags were your golf shoes. The other bag contained miscellaneous golf items: three dozen or more golf balls, a handful of tees, your golf gloves, score pads and pencils, a small spiral bound book on "Tips for Golfers" and the rain cover for your golf bag.

The next day I saw one of our friends, a dedicated golfer, at the Post Office and told him what I had found in the space under the house. He said, "Looks like Don came home from having a lousy day out on the course and decided to chuck it all. He probably just took those bags and threw 'em. One landed here and one there. He didn't care. He was through with golf. He had given it his all." "You know what?" I said to him, "I bet you're right. Earlier this year, when I suggested to Don we give golf another try, he nixed the suggestion." As I was walking back to my car, I remembered the moment and could still see the frown form on your face. You said, "Diane, I never want to go out on a golf course again for as long as I live. It's the most frustrating thing I've ever had to do in my entire life."

I didn't add your golf shoes or the other golf accessories to the junk heap that was getting higher and higher. I took the golf gear inside to the garage and added it to the stuff I would eventually give away. But, you probably would have placed your golf shoes and all the accessories on the very top of the junk heap

Chapter 45

September–Major Meltdown

I am so mad at you right now. It's been almost three months since you died and I am still trying to cope.

I can't get the computer to send out any messages. I'm trying to send a reply to one of your sons with attachments on notes I just wrote up on refinancing this house, and I can't get the message to send.

Tonight, for the first time since you died, I decided to stay downstairs and watch TV. I thought the dogs and I could cuddle on the sofa and unwind from this hectic day. The TV had sound but no picture. I kept punching buttons and nothing worked.

You were supposed to be here for me—with me—in *my* old age. We designed and built this house, our dream house, for *our* old age. That's why we put in the elevator. That's why all the handles on the faucets are for the day when we might become arthritic. That's why we installed safety bars in some areas of the bathrooms. You and I were supposed to live in this house for the rest of *both* of our lives.

And someone keeps trying to send a fax, and I run to the phone thinking it's a friend calling me, and all I hear is the beep beep of the fax machine.

I was supposed to drive to Auburn tonight for a dog show committee meeting and I just can't go. I just can't do it.

Questions run through my mind. *"Why did you go and leave me? I hate you for leaving me. Damn you, Don, why did you leave me?"*

I have been distressed all day since meeting with a broker at a mortgage company in Truckee. The meeting was arranged by one of our friends. I am trying to get a handle on our mortgage. Should I refinance or what? It's simply overwhelming. Finance was never one of my areas of expertise. This is probably what triggered this meltdown. Could it have been the final realization and meeting face-to-face with someone to actually discuss how and what I am going to do with the rest of my life—without you? It's up to me to decide what is going to happen. It's up to me how I'm going to forge ahead. I feel overwhelmed. I'm standing in a forest of sorrow and bewilderment and I feel so terribly alone. My life feels frightfully empty. I guess I hadn't anticipated how much it would hurt—physically—to not have you in my life. It's not fair, life's loneliness and the pain one feels when they are alone. I feel lost in this pain and I try to remember you—remember us. This *must* be part of the grieving process. I don't know.

"I hate you. I love you," I call out to you; the Kleenex box is empty.

It has hit me. You are gone.

You are gone!

Chapter 46

September–Street Vibrations

~

It's time again for me to go into Reno for my hair tweaking, a term I had read long ago in a story written by one of my favorite authors, Rosamunde Pilcher.

"Street Vibrations" is starting in Reno. It's one of the largest Nevada motorcycle rallies, always loud and colorful, with vendors set up along the main streets selling every conceivable part for a bike you would want. Several streets are closed off. As I walk down Sierra Street toward the Truckee River where my hairdresser's shop is located, I look over and see a sea of pop-up tents. I can hear the souped-up engines of the Harleys and other bikes as they roar down Sierra Street.

You always came to Reno during "Street Vibrations" to "kick the tires" as you used to say. You loved your Dyna Glide and told me there wasn't a bike you would want in its place.

All those years you had your Harley and I never was on the back of it once. Partly because I had no desire and partly because you told me you would be unsure of having an adult on the back.

You always told me, "Honey, I would buy you your own Harley tomorrow if you wanted one." But, it wasn't my thing, and I had no desire to ride my own Harley.

Now, I remember another time—April of 1997. I was

showing Spirit at the Northern California Dachshund Club specialty in Sacramento. I had driven down on Friday and taken my motor home out of storage where I kept it during the winter months. It was a quick ride from the storage lot at the KOA in West Sacramento to the Red Lion Hotel in Sacramento. You rode down on your Harley that Sunday to see me show Spirit. We were supposed to meet back at the house late that afternoon since we had plans later that evening to get together with some friends for a potluck. As I pulled my car into the garage, and I was always so careful not to get too close to your "baby," I slowly opened my car door and was jolted when I saw the right hand mirror was missing from the bike, and the windshield was scratched.

Your car was gone!

I went inside the house, fed the dogs, put them out and retrieved the potluck dish I had prepared before the weekend. When I arrived at our friend's house, I saw Ken first and asked him in the most casual manner, "If someone had an accident, where would they go?" I told him how I had found your bike. He looked at me in alarm and asked, "My God, Diane, do you think Don had an accident on his bike?"

He immediately dialed the number of the Truckee hospital and then handed me the phone. I heard the receptionist ask if she could help me. "Yes, hello, this is Mrs. McCormack," I said. "Perchance is my husband, Don McCormack, a patient there?" To which she replied, "Yes, he is." And, then I asked, "What are the extent of his injuries?" "His thumb," she answered.

By this time, all of our friends were huddled around me waiting with bated breath to find out what had happened to you. They later told me my face was as white as a sheet, and I was probably in shock. No doubt about my being in shock, especially when I recall my exact words…"Per chance is my husband, Don McCormack, a patient there?" It's a wonder I didn't give her your date of birth and social security number when I said your name!

I drove the short distance to the hospital, saw your car

and parked next to it. I was standing by the side of my car with my arms folded watching for you. When I saw you emerge from the hospital's emergency entrance with your arm in a sling, a smile came to my face as I said to you, "Hi, Honey. Get in. I'll drive us to the party. We can come back for your car later."

You retold this story many, many times and always added how appreciative you were I never once made a comment like, "What a dumb ass thing to do, Don." Yeah, I never said those exact words...but I did think it!

How did the accident happen? You told me later that night as we cuddled on the sofa with dogs underfoot. You had left the Red Lion Hotel and had taken one of your favorite routes which would bring you heading from Nevada City back to Truckee along Highway 20. It's also one of those winding roads that bikers love to ride. You were a cautious and careful rider and noticed a string of cars behind you. So, doing the courteous thing, you pulled into a turn-out to let the cars pass. What you thought was a shadow alongside the road turned out to be a pot hole. Down you went and landed on your thumb. You also cracked your helmet. You did manage to upright your bike with the help of a passerby and drove back to our house and then onto the hospital, your thumb throbbing the entire time. You always said to me, "Honey, can you imagine what would have happened to me had I not been wearing a helmet?"

I always told you, "Be careful, Darling," when you took the bike out for a ride, "Watch out for the other guy." Or, "Remember, Honey, it's a holiday weekend and there will be a lot of traffic on the roads. The other drivers will be anxious to get to their destinations. They have been on the highway for hours. They won't be out for a casual ride as you are." When I would hear the noise of the Harley's engine as you drove back up our driveway, I would breathe a sigh of relief and say a little private prayer, "Thank you, God."

Who would have thought that years later, you would have died from a head trauma that occurred *inside* the house?

Chapter 47

September—Three Months

I awoke with a start. It is pitch black outside still. Did the dogs hear something? Maybe the bear is wandering around outside. Yesterday Audrey told me a bear was up in a tree outside their deck trying to get to her birdfeeder. No, the dogs didn't hear anything. They are still gathered around me under the quilt, Mirage in his favorite spot curled behind my bent knees and Vision closer to my head.

Then my senses take hold and I turn over in my bed and look at the clock. It's 1 o'clock in the morning and it is September 23. Exactly three months ago to this very minute. I pull the covers up over my head and sleep for a few more hours until the dogs start to nudge me. They are anxious to go potty or rather to have their breakfast. Downstairs in the kitchen I click on the coffee pot. I'm getting in the habit like you used to do; that is putting the coffee grinds in and filling the chamber with water the night before. All I have to do is click on the switch in the morning. The dogs are at the back door crying to come inside. They are now doing their circle dance for their breakfast. I put the food bowls down and they inhale it.

Weeks ago I cancelled the delivery of the Sacramento Bee.

I didn't want it sitting out on the driveway with me gone the last several weeks on judging assignments. Then I thought ahead to what the winter might bring and decided I really didn't want to have to tramp through the snow when winter finally comes.

This morning I feel like having my coffee while reading the morning papers. The local deli has several newspaper vending machines located outside their front door. *"I'll drive there and get a copy,"* I say to myself. I head for the garage and then remember the newspaper vending machines take change. My mind races to the top drawer of my dresser where I know for sure there is a lot of loose change.

I think you knew I would take several coins from your pockets each night. One of my pet peeves was when you played with your change in your pants pockets. So, each night I would take out a couple of coins so when you did fiddle with the change, it wouldn't make as much noise. Now, I would give anything to dump all the change back in your pockets and you could play with the coins for as long as you wanted to and you could play with your sideburns, as well.

I am back with the paper in no time at all. I sit at the table and drink my coffee and think of you and think of where these past three months have gone. I look out the back kitchen window and up the hill towards the pines and the firs. Some clumps of them are so intertwined with each other, I can't see through them. I tell you, *"The landscape of my life has changed. I am here and you are distant."*

We had our routines. Our habits were as polished as Truckee's river rocks. Our lives had taken on a pattern of living. You: turning on the coffee in the morning, feeding the dogs their breakfast, driving into town for the mail, playing duplicate bridge, riding your Harley, attending meetings in town. Me: waking an hour after you were up to the smell of the coffee, training the dogs, going to dog shows, quilting, gardening.

As a couple, our life took on its own routine. We had dinner parties, bridge parties, the hot tub at the end of the day when we could unwind, our time with the dogs and all the joy they brought us. Did I take all of this for granted? We would spend the day doing our separate activities. Then in the late afternoon we would start to prepare our dinner together, play a game of gin, cribbage or backgammon, occasionally Scrabble, while enjoying a drink. The intimacy of our marriage, of our thirty-two years together, had allowed us to grow into each other's lives as the branches on the trees outside this window are intertwined with each other and we continued to grow. Your life became my life and my life became your life. Now, I am here and you are not.

Chapter 48

September–Baked Rice Pudding

The field mice have once again taken their fall vacation and have chosen our pantry as their get-away resort. After all, there are lots of handy treats to feed on and soft rags to chew up for their nests.

As I cleaned up the messes they made, I came across a humongous tin. I couldn't remember what I might have stored in it, but when I took it into the kitchen and opened the lid, it was filled with white rice. Ah, one thing the critters couldn't get into and feed upon. I remembered when we purchased the bag of bulk rice last spring and at that time thought how in the world would we ever be able to use up this quantity of rice. You said, "Honey, I have a suggestion. Make one of my favorite desserts, Baked Rice Pudding."

Before I put the tin back in the pantry, I decided to make myself Baked Rice Pudding. My recipe, the one you loved, is a combination of recipes from my sister and a few cookbooks. Now I substituted my heart-healthy ingredients for such things as real eggs, heavy cream and whole milk. I also decided to use organic brown sugar in place of white sugar. The Baked Rice Pudding took a couple of hours to bake and soon the kitchen was filled with the most wondrous smell. No wonder, when I opened the oven door, there was overflow all over the bottom of the oven. Yuck!

Nights are the loneliest of times for me. This is what other widows say, as well. Since I have always loved to cook and create, I am trying to spend more nights in the kitchen cooking. Some widows write about the need to take drugs: Prozac, Lexapro or Celexa among hundreds of those mood-altering and modern day drugs, but so many of them have side effects. I would rather get down my copper pots and pans and be creative. It helps.

Earlier in the day I noticed some cherry tomatoes on the kitchen counter whose skins looked like mine does when I linger too long in the hot tub. In the refrigerator were some sliced mushrooms. I concocted a sauce. I sautéed diced shallots and garlic in olive oil—garlic is always good for the soul. I added the cherry tomatoes and mushrooms and some spices. I sautéed two chicken breasts in a mixture of fake butter and olive oil. I have learned living alone one has to cook for two, one serving for tonight and the second to have a few days later. Then I decided to add some flair and warmed some brandy in one of the small copper pans, poured it over the chicken in the fake butter/olive oil mixture and stood back as I lit the match and flambéed the dish. Yes, I am trying to remain loyal to "our" low-fat diet. I poured some of the sauce over the flambéed chicken breast and voilà—my dinner! I tossed a simple green salad and cooked some gnocchi. God bless the potato gnocchi and the Italians for producing it.

My girlfriend, Penny, called. "Why don't you live closer? I've made this fabulous dinner for two," I told her.

I lingered over my dinner taking in all the subtle flavors. One has to really try hard not to rush through dinner when living alone. I poured a glass of Pinot Grigio into one of the Reidel wine glasses I gave to you as a Christmas present in 2006.

Later, I made a fire, dished out some of my Baked Rice

Pudding, and enjoyed the moment.

Another night, I have made it through. A smile came to my face, as I wondered where the field mice had gone. I wondered, if given a preference, would they enjoy the Baked Rice Pudding or plain old raw rice?

~~~

BAKED RICE PUDDING—HEART HEALTHY

Ingredients:
1 cup short-grained raw white rice
¾ cup organic brown sugar
4½ cups low fat or skimmed milk
1 - 12 ounce can evaporated milk
¾ cup egg substitute - (3 eggs = ¾ cup egg substitute)
1/8 teaspoon freshly grated nutmeg
1 teaspoon pure vanilla extract
½ teaspoon salt
½ cup golden seedless raisins

Directions:
Preheat oven to 325 degrees

Combine all ingredients. Pour into a 3 quart casserole that has been sprayed with non-stick spray.

Place casserole dish in larger pan and pour boiling water half-way up to side of casserole.

Bake in oven for 2 hours, checking to make sure rice is cooked.

~~~

Chapter 49

September–Dismantling of My Life

On a crisp and absolutely pristine day, what we would call Tahoe Blue, the piano movers came to pick up the piano and transport it to Reno to be placed on consignment at a music store. You and I had even discussed selling it months before you died. I had long ago stopped playing it and when I did play, it was with great frustration. When I had spare time and was not involved in any dog related activities, I wanted to be either sewing or quilting—not playing the piano. For the past several years, the piano served as a piece of furniture on which a dozen or more family photographs in silver frames were displayed and for the last two years, the artificial Christmas tree displaced the photographs during the Christmas season.

We purchased the baby grand Knabe when we still lived in Houston. It was something I had always dreamed of doing, sitting down at a piano and playing away. I found the perfect instructor with the perfect name, Lucian Lemieux. He would come to our house faithfully every week and I would groan and moan because I had been too busy and had not had the time to practice the lessons. So, poor Lucian would sit there and witness my struggling through the pieces.

On this day in the last week of September the movers came. There were three of them, all fairly young men, and in no time at all they had removed the legs, strapped the piano to a gurney and slowly guided the piano down the center staircase, out the front door and down the front walkway. They had backed the truck up our driveway and when they hoisted the piano up into the back of the truck, I could feel the tears trickle down my cheeks.

I sold your Chevy Tahoe a few weeks before the piano left the house. Before I left for my dog club's annual Labor Day shows, I posted some flyers around town. I needed to sell it. I needed the money since nothing was coming in yet from your pension and I needed it gone, so that every time I drove into the garage and saw your car, I wouldn't keep saying to myself, "Oh, Don is home."

Tuesday morning the phone rang. It was a man asking if the Tahoe was still for sale. He was a contractor and needed a mountain vehicle. I had asked a neighbor friend of ours to come up and act as the "man-of-the-house." It's one thing we widows need to keep in mind—don't put yourself in a compromising position. Well, all good intentions, as they say. My neighbor was late, the contractor was right on time, and before I knew it, I was sitting in the passenger seat of your car while he drove around Tahoe Donner to show me the town houses he was putting up. When we returned home a half-hour later the neighbor was standing there, very concerned about what had happened to me. The contractor loved your car and within hours he had returned with a cashier's check for the full amount I was asking, no haggling or dickering.

The canoe was sold a few days ago. It was lowered down from the rafters in the garage and placed on top of its new owner's car. We bought it as an anniversary present for each other in 1989. Many happy memories—and some not too happy when we would struggle to lift and heave it onto your car. It stabbed my heart as I watched their car drive out of sight with the bright blue canoe on top.

The next big item I decided to sell was the treadmill. Would I ever use it again? We bought it a few years ago as a way for me to be able to exercise the dogs during winter months if we were snowed in. Vision, Spirit's daughter, was born August 1, 1998. When I began to show her, I talked you into buying the tread mill. We looked for one with an extra wide belt so that I could put my feet alongside the belt, on the stationary part, and Vision would think I was still jogging along with her. What did Vision do? As she jogged along, the movement jiggled her insides. Plop and all the way to the end of the treadmill a poop would go. You doubled over with laughter and renamed the treadmill the "Poop-Mill." Eventually, workouts on the treadmill became one of your ways to exercise. I can close my eyes and see you on it the weeks before you died with your red bandana tied around your head. The treadmill was my albatross after you died. I didn't use it and I wanted it out. I didn't want to be reminded of our mornings, you on the treadmill while I was on the computer. Joan, my daughter-in-law suggested I sell it on Craig's List. I placed an ad on the Reno Craig's List the next weekend. No response. Then she told me I had to keep changing the ad to keep it fresh otherwise it would get shuffled to the end of the listings and get lost. I redid the ad and added, "Perfect for exercising show dogs in the winter months." BINGO! It sold instantly.

The piano is gone from the house and hopefully will be sold. The Tahoe has a new and proud owner. The Harley is being loved by its new owner and his young son. And, the treadmill has found a new home with another show dog.

I still have your red bandana. I dab a tear from my eye with it as I think how my life is being dismantled.

Chapter 50

September–Changing of Seasons

The morning is bright and there is a breeze blowing. The air is filled with the red and yellow and ochre leaves as they detach themselves from the aspens we planted around our house. They spiral down to the ground and blend in with the pine needles that have also started to fall. The leaves left on the branches are almost devoid of color, mostly brown now, not the glorious colors of the reds and yellows and golds. Those brilliant colors are what drew us to plant aspens on our property and the same aspens that would entice you to take your annual fall motorcycle ride with Ken. You would ride down Highway 89 along the Truckee River, then along the western shores of Lake Tahoe, along the hairpin curves about Emerald Lake and then drop down in elevation to Monitor Pass. You would arrive home with a flush on your face. "The leaves were spectacular," you would tell me, "you should have been on the back of my bike so you could experience them with me."

Yes, the days are growing shorter and there is a definite nip in the air. Last night, I stood outside at our side deck waiting for the dogs to have their last pee of the night, and you were so much in my thoughts. It's hard to imagine an entire season has almost come and gone without you here. These last months have been a blur.

One of the reasons we loved Truckee so very much was because of the change of seasons. Even though we knew the winters could be harsh, we still looked forward to the change in the air. You would have your list of chores to get ready for winter: raking up the pine needles, putting up the boards that went alongside the back deck railing so the snow wouldn't cave in on the deck's floor, taking down the yellow jacket traps, disconnecting the sprinkler system and hoses, moving the deck furniture under cover and other chores I was not aware of your doing. I will soon find out because I will be the one who will now have to do all of these chores, or at least find someone to help me do them.

You would come into the house after raking up several bags of pine needles and say, "Diane, it's going to be a hard winter and do you know why I know?" Ah, the bait was there. "No, I don't know why. Why don't you tell me—again?" Then you would tell the story of how the squirrels were gathering up more sugar pine cones than in the previous years. "That's how you know, Honey. The squirrels know more than we do." "Ah," I would reply and give you a poke in your ribs as we laughed.

The aspens are turning color and the leaves are starting to fall. I take a deep breath and give in to the memories of what once was, but can no longer be.

Chapter 51

October–Your Birthday

I'm waiting for Penny to arrive. I need a friend with me during what would have been your seventy-seventh birthday because I'm still going through what another widowed friend of mine referred to as a "Griefquake." She said to me, "California has their earthquakes, but you are having a Griefquake." I asked my friend, "Does it get any easier?" "No, just duller in a way," she answered.

I'm remembering one of the best birthdays you had. I had planned it for weeks. You were turning fifty, the big half of a century. One of our favorite restaurants in Houston was Ninfa's. It was located down in the barrio, away from the touristy restaurants, and our favorite waiter was Roqué. We would always call the restaurant first to make sure he was on duty and would sit at a table in his station. I decided to have a surprise party for you, and I hired Roqué to be the waiter and bartender. I planned an array of Mexican foods with plenty of margaritas and sent out invitations.

All of our friends were there, and your kids had surprised you with a belly dancer. You and I laughed for weeks later when we started to receive the photos our friends had taken and sent to you before the days of digital photography. In every shot of the belly dancer was Roqué ogling at her with a lecherous look in his eyes. You said that Roqué probably had as much fun at your party as any one of the guests. Probably so! But one of the most memorable comments was made to you by one of your co-workers the next week at work. His wife had been ill, so she could not attend the party. When he arrived home she was asking him all about the party and he told her I had probably spent three hundred dollars on it. When he told you this, you said to him, "Hell, Michael, Diane spent *that* much on the margaritas alone."

I gave you a complete darkroom: Beseler enlarger, hypo containers, negative holders, print trays, measuring jugs, beakers, stirrers, a safe light, timers, and developing paper in every size available, the works. I had spent weeks researching to get everything you would need to start up your very own darkroom. I individually wrapped every single item. You sat up for hours after all the guests had left and opened each and every package. Many of our friends later asked me, "How did you know to get Don dark room equipment? I had no idea he was interested in developing his own pictures." You weren't. You and I had already started to talk about taking early retirement and moving away from Houston. I said to myself, "I have my hobbies of sewing and quilting and cooking, all inside hobbies. Wouldn't it be great for Don to have some inside hobby of his own?" When we designed our Truckee home, we included your very own darkroom. When you were not skiing, playing tennis, riding your Harley, raking up the pine needles, or engrossed in a good book, you were in the dark room. You did enjoy it for all those many years!

I'm sure you would rank your "75th" birthday the best. Besides many of our very best friends, all of your children were here and your sister, Ann. Even my sister, Bev, and her husband, Art, flew in. I did the catering myself and spent weeks making various foods and freezing them on big trays. You name it, we served it! The highlight was the cake. The top was an icing image of you, taken from the head shot I took of you in your Harley helmet, goggles and bandana.

This time it was not a surprise party, so you helped plan the invitation. We used part of the verse from our first Christmas card and added, *"Since Don is Like a Fine Old*

75th Birthday Cake

Wine that Keeps Getting Better and Better—No Gifts But—Bring

a Bottle of Fine Old Wine to Share."

There were lots of bottles of fine old wine and some bottles of new wine, as well. Your kids gave you an iPod. There must have been half a dozen of us with digital cameras all snapping away.

Dan, Mary Beth, Don & Bruce

At night, those who were left, bundled up in one of the afghans or quilts from the house, and we all went outside to the front deck. More drinks were poured, and we all swapped stories and laughed and loved. It was the last time

Joan McCormack & Don

Don & Ann Powell

with your family—kids, sister, other relatives—all of us—until the Family Memorial!

Dan took the iPod home and downloaded a video he had put together from all the digital images that were taken along with a DVD. You and I watched this video time after time. We never tired of watching it. Every single shot of you showed you with your radiating, infectious smile. Every single shot of you and me showed us with arms draped over the other's shoulders and smiling at each other. In fact, there is not a person in the video who isn't laughing or smiling.

Your 75th birthday was a love fest. You loved it and you loved us.

It was the best of times!

Chapter 52

October—First Snow

It started as a gentle rain with the drops bouncing off the deck and soon it turned to snow. The sound of the rain became almost silent as the soft flakes started to build up on the front deck. It is the first substantial snow of the season and it is only the first weekend in October. I went outside to retrieve the dog toys and turned my face upward to feel the flakes on my face.

How you and I loved the first snow. Truckee can have snow fall in any month of the year. I can remember a Memorial Day when we were at a friend's home for a party and it started to snow. The snow flurries didn't last long. There was another time in early June when lots of motor homes got stuck going back to Sacramento. They had been to a dog show in Reno, and the weather forecast didn't say anything about the possibility of snow. We were getting phone calls from many of my friends inquiring if they could park their rigs in our driveway because I-80 was closed.

The first snow of the impending winter season was always special to us. It was the first snow that seemed to make everything around us shine with a new beauty. Many winter nights we would go to sleep during a steady rain and awaken in the morning to a white world of soft and fluffy snow. The pines and firs outside our bedroom windows would look like they were covered with white clouds. One winter the snow was so deep it reached to the roof lines of many houses, some fifteen feet deep or more. People spray painted their house numbers on the snow banks so their houses could be found.

Beyond the window through the mist in my eyes, I watched the snow land and start to stick on the deck. If you had been here with me, we would have lit the fire in the fireplace and sat in front of it with a drink.

The dogs jumped in front of the window. They wanted to go out and play in it. They couldn't wait. I opened the door and they raced outside doing their spins and turns. Their antics are the same as they were during our last snow fall, the one last April, and the last one we shared. We would stand by the window and laugh at how silly they were. Just as quickly as they had begged to go outside, they would be anxious to come in and would shake the snow off of their coats in front of us. "Paid us back for laughing at them," you said to me.

I am so glad Penny and I moved all of the deck furniture to the covered side deck. She left a couple of days after your birthday, but I was so thankful for the few days she was here.

We were the owners of two snow blowers. The larger of the two snow blowers was for the front deck, and the smaller one you used for the front path. I do believe you actually enjoyed blowing the snow from the deck and pathway. You would be all bundled up, complete with your ear protectors. You never complained and when you came back inside the warm house, you shook the snow off your jacket the same way the dogs shook the snow from their coats. You would come over to me with your cold face and rub your nose against mine, back and forth several times. "Eskimo style," you would say to me.

I renewed the snow plow service that we used for all the years we lived here. They will blow the snow from the driveway. I told our friends that since your car is gone, when they come to visit, they can park in your old space and come in through the garage, or they can wear their mountain boots and tramp through the snow up the path to the front door. I mentioned this to one of our friends. She said, "Or they can go out and play with Don's toys as he did and blow your deck clear."

Yeah, I liked that idea!

Chapter 53

October–Family Genetics

I am remembering your mother and the time she was in our life as I see her name inked in on the October page of the calendar. At the beginning of each new year, I would write down the birthdays of our family and friends and other special events: marriages, deaths and anniversaries. Rainy's name is written on the square for October 7 and there is a big heart drawn around it. It was the day she died, encased in my arms, as you were driving as fast as you could to the hospital just a few miles away. The last words she heard were me telling her, "Rainy, you are so, so loved." She was eighty-nine years old.

Rainy, as she liked to be called, was one of the most wonderful women I had ever met. It didn't take us long to refer to each other as "daughter-in-love" and "mother-in-love." She was eighty-three years old when she came into my life, born in 1892. Her last year was spent in Houston at a retirement home we found for her.

I now wear one of the rings that belonged to her and to her mother, Garney. It's a beautiful Victorian and diamond shaped with eight smaller diamonds on the sides and a larger diamond in the middle. The night Rainy died, October 7, 1981,

Ann handed this ring to me and said, "Here, this is yours. Mama would want you to have it. She knew how much you loved her."

A few days after Rainy died while cleaning out her apartment, you and I came across the thesis she had written while she was attending college at Northwestern University in Chicago. The title was, "Great Uncle Americus," and it was about his life from 1837 to 1839 when he trekked across the country. Rainy had typed it on onion skin paper. I still have it.

Another one of the memories I have of Rainy is on our wedding day when my grandfather escorted her down our geranium-lined path to her seat of honor in the first row of chairs. I also remember the times she visited us in Houston before she moved there. I would sit on the floor in front of the sofa where she would be sitting and she would run her fingers through my hair—ah, heaven! She would say to you, while shaking her cocktail glass, "Donald, my glass is empty," and you, the dutiful son, would refill her drink, though not as full as she would have liked it to be.

Your father, Royden, known as Roy, was born January 13, 1887, and died December 5, 1956, at the age of seventy. I never had the chance to meet him. He was a contractor for most of his adult life and provided well for his family. He also died of a form of heart disease.

I remember one day when you asked Rainy to tell us about their marriage. "Were you and my father very happy?" you asked, and she practically took your head off. "Of course we were, Donald." She always called you Donald. Later you shared with me that you didn't recall seeing any true affection between them, but I reminded you that in the days when they were married, married couples showed more reserve. "Ah, maybe so," you responded, "but, I still don't think they had the kind of passion that you and I have for each other."

Passion—yes, we had that.

Just a couple of weeks before you died, you sent your sons an email urging them to watch their diets because you felt heart disease was definitely genetic and definitely in the male side of the McCormack Family.

~~~

Wednesday, June 6, 2007
Dear Bruce and Dan,
This is sort of a wake up call. There is nothing like an experience to give one religion.

I am feeling fine and believe that all is well in the old body. I have an appointment with my cardiologist tomorrow, but I know he will tell me everything is going as planned. At this point I am taking a number of medicines to control blood pressure and cholesterol, plus watching what I eat even more than before. The latter will be a way of life from now on. The medicine kind of saps my energy level, but it is coming back.

I am enclosing the front section of a cook book a friend sent me. It is the best thing I have seen to explain heart disease overall, and the need to control one's intake.You are both at the right age to think strongly about what is likely ahead—perhaps still many years off. But keep in mind that your father had heart disease developing around 70 (hyper-tension and high blood pressure) and partial clogging (70%) of the left anterior descending artery (that is the famous widow-maker artery that supplies the blood to the heart muscle that keeps it working) at age 76. Your grandfather died from complications of arteriosclerosis at age 69.

It is a chance to affect the future .
I hope all is well with you both.
Love,
Dad

~~~

The *"widow-maker artery"*...little did we know!

Chapter 54

October–Self-Pity–Maybe

Why does it seem to be harder for me now? I thought it would get easier as it's been almost four months.

Maybe this spell of sadness has been brought on by going through some Christmas catalogues that arrived in the mail today. I am haphazardly turning the pages and thinking I really don't want to face Thanksgiving and Christmas—and New Year's Eve.

Maybe it's because the light outside has turned gray, and that's the mood I am in. I am not depressed and I don't think it is self-pity, but maybe it is. I try to keep my mind from aching, and that also goes for my head and my soul. But, it's hard.

Before I can wallow in more of what might be self-pity, the phone is ringing. I don't get to it in time and the answering machine picks up the message.

It's Penny. I listen to her message. Then I write it down. I will need to read these words again because it's so poignant and this is what I need right now.

~~~

"Hey, honey, it's me. I just wanted to call and say hello. I'm over here in Atlanta, fixing to go to Rio.

And, ah, Diane, I was thinking of you and I love you, and I know how hard this is for you. And, I just wanted to let you know you're always—always in my thoughts, and Ollie and Murphy send their puppy love and all their 'huggies'—they are going around you.

Anyway, I'll be back Tuesday and I will give you a buzz then. Sweetie, you have a good day, and I hope you're off doing something fun.

Anyway, take care.

Bye

~~~

Immediately, I return her call. I tell her what I had just been thinking of when she called, and how much I needed to hear her words. Her timing couldn't have been better. My previous moment of self-pity turns into moments of being grateful for Penny and for my other friends.

Penny talks about Don. She always used to question, "Why can't I meet a Don? Isn't there a 'Don clone' out there somewhere, just waiting for me?" But then again, many of my single girlfriends used to say that to me. "Don was great on the uptake," she says. "You could bounce things off him and he'd be right back at you. He was a great straight man as well as being the object of the joke. No one offended him and never upset him. He always went along with the game." She added, "Don was one of those rare people who was totally at home in his own skin. Everyone was made to feel at ease around him."

Later, after she hung up, I thought about what she said. No translation was necessary for us either. We could almost read each other's thoughts. Then I said, *"Yes, Don, it was so easy to be with you. You were the epitome of an old slipper. Our marriage was like a love affair with an entity of its own."* For a woman who has been fully loved, the loss of a husband is felt ever so more. We used to ask each other, "Honey, how many marriages have lasted as long as ours and how many marriages have lasted as long without either of us having an affair or even the slightest interest in another person?"

I read somewhere that it's worse to live life without a great love than to live your entire life through the pain of expectations crushed. I think of your smile, which was truly encompassing, and of all the wonderful memories of our love affair and fold them into my self-pity and smile.

Chapter 55

October–George II Secretary

While I was searching for something in the bottom drawer of the secretary earlier this month, another memory came to my mind.

We were living in the apartment on Audubon. You had moved there after your divorce and the few furnishings you took with you, I thought, were dreadful. We used part of my pension money from The Wool Bureau towards the purchase of three Oriental rugs, six antique Chippendale style chairs and some other items we picked up while going to antique auctions.

One morning when I went to retrieve our mail, a flyer was included. The photograph on the first page caught my eye. It was of a secretary, one of the most beautiful pieces I had seen in a long time. It was to be auctioned off in a few days from a private antique store located just a few blocks away. Later we learned the owners of the store, York Antiques, were divorcing, and they needed to sell their exquisite pieces for the divorce finalization. I showed you the flyer and you seemed equally as interested in this piece as I was. In the almost six months we had been married, you had come to learn a lot about antiques. At least you could now tell the difference between Chippendale and Sheridan.

The Saturday morning of the auction we were up and out of the house in order to get a good seat. We were sitting in the third row. The auctioneer started on smaller items and then the secretary was rolled up to the stage. It was an original George II piece dated around 1790 and we could hear the swoons of the audience. You and I had discussed what we thought the piece would go for and how much was left of my pension money. We had come up with a price cut-off in case the final bidding would be over our heads. You had wanted to be the one doing the bidding. I can't remember what the starting bid was, but the increments were high, two hundred dollars. When you decided to get in on the bidding, you would raise your numbered paddle so the auctioneer could see it. I was losing track of the bidding. You had placed the paddle on your lap and at that point you were just nodding your head. I could hear a man who was standing several rows behind us calling out actual amounts. The excitement started to mount. Everyone around us knew the bidding had narrowed down to you and this other bidder. A hush fell over the audience. Finally, the auctioneer said, "I have eighteen hundred. Do I hear two hundred more?" I turned in a hurry to you and asked, "Do we have it? Do we have it? Who has the last bid?" I was frantic. You just sat there with a big smile on your face, but I still didn't know. Suddenly the auctioneer pointed to you and said, "Going to the gentleman sitting." I hugged you and hugged you and then the audience started to clap for us.

We walked back to our apartment for a quick lunch, still not believing we had actually won this most beautiful antique secretary. There were some other items we saw earlier we liked; items not featured in the brochure: a planter, a hall tree and some other small things. We decided to return to the auction.

I had noticed in the same brochure an English Sheridan sofa table. I didn't mention I wanted to bid on this table. I thought you would say one antique piece of furniture is enough for now, and I really had no idea how much it would go for.

When we returned to the auction house all of the seats had been taken, so we had to stand in the back of the room. The auctioneer saw us come in the door and go to the back of the room and said into his microphone, "Glad you returned."

The planter and oak hall tree came up for bid. There was not much interest, and you were the highest bidder.

Finally, the sofa table was rolled up on the stage. I couldn't decide if I should suggest to you to bid on it or not. Many of the high bidders had left the auction and several of the larger pieces of furniture had really come down in price. I decided to wait and see how much the sofa table would go for. The opening bidding price started low and I made a hasty decision to get in on the bidding. But, I quickly thought to myself, *"If you can bid quietly and smugly, so can I."* So, I quietly nodded my bids to the auctioneer as you had done when you were bidding on the secretary. Finally, the bidding was over and the auctioneer said, "Sold, to the lady standing." You looked at me and said, *"Are YOU the lady standing?"*—with the emphasis on *YOU*.

I smiled at you and slowly nodded my head, and you simply said, "Shit."

Chapter 56

October–Donnie

❦

On three walls of the ground floor of our home is the family gallery of photographs. The largest wall contains my father's side of the family. On another wall are photographs of my immediate family and on the third wall are your family photographs.

Many of the intimate details of your family I learned during visits from your mother when we lived in Houston. One day she started to tell me about some of the McCormack family history. I said, "Rainy, I need to write this down." I ran upstairs to our office and got eight sheets of legal-size paper which I taped together.

I still have those sheets of paper, now yellow with age, and the tape is not as sticky as it once was. The sheets are filled with the genealogy of both sides of your family. But it is Rainy's side-notes that are priceless. She would tell me the story and I would write it down in the margin of the pages.

This photograph of Emma M. Griffith, your mother's mother, was probably taken when she was around two years old. You and Ann affectionately called her Garney. She was born January 29, 1856. Garney's father, Griffith W. Griffith, was born in Wales in a town called Tinerbren near Chester.

Next to his name I wrote down what Rainy told me, *"He was very musical, played cards, and would say, 'Gentlemen, wouldn't it be nice to start the game with a song.'"*

Garney married Frank Allan Powers on March 14, 1874. Frank was born on January 10, 1853, in Palmyra, Wisconsin

Garney with Parasol - 1858

and died on February 18, 1922. Frank and Garney settled in Chicago after they married. Their first child was George Griffith, born in 1876. The notation next to his name says, *"As a mature man, George smoked a pipe and had a beautiful baritone voice."* Your mother, Loraine Margaret, was the third child born to Frank and Garney. One year, Rainy's brother sent her a book as a Christmas present. The book was entitled, "Powers," and was written by Rainy's uncle, William Penn Powers, who was quite an engineer. In the late 1880's, he invented the "Vapor Disk Thermostat," the precursor of today's room thermostat. Your sister shared with me a wonderful story she remembered about this book. When Rainy got close to the end, as she turned the page, out fell a twenty dollar bill. She immediately called her brother and asked him about the bill. He said, "Well, I'm glad you finally finished the book." Rainy eventually gave the book to Ann who told me, "It was an old red book with a hard cover. And, somehow along the way of several moves and packing and unpacking, the book was tossed out. I always regretted that." Many years ago, Ann was in Salt Lake City and visited the LDS library. She actually found a copy of "Powers." But because it was over an inch thick, she was only able to copy around fifty pages. Years ago, she sent us copies of these pages.

I can't remember if we ever read through all of these pages. I discovered them tucked away in a file we had called, "Family—McCormack." As I was doing research for this chapter of my book, I started to read through these pages and was fascinated with the history of your mother's side of your family. Many of your ancestors served on the judicial bench. One was a member of the State Legislature in New Hampshire. Some were tops in their field of engineering. Perhaps, this is what sparked your interest first in engineering and later in politics.

Along with the photographs from your side of the family, there is a one of your father, Royden, taken in a photographer's

Royden Charles McCormack

studio. Not too much is known about your father's side of the family. Roy's father was Charles B. McCormack and his mother was Marie Dubois.

One of the photos I have always loved is of you as a young boy in a pair of swim trunks. You didn't like this photograph and thought you looked gawky. When I wanted to hang it on the family wall, you just gave me one of your looks and shook your head. I said to you, "But, Honey, it's so cute of you." "Well, if you think it looks cute, then go ahead and hang it," you said.

In conversations with your sister after your death, she gave me additional insights of your childhood. Growing up in Baden, in North St. Louis, you were called Donnie. You once told me you were not athletic as a youth and there was no Little League in those days. However, you did toss a baseball back and forth with Buddy Weller who lived on the same street, Gast Place.

Don

Gast Brewery, which closed many years ago, was located in the area. Whenever we went to flea markets, one of our favorite pastimes, you would comb through boxes of old beer bottles the vendors had, looking for one stamped Gast.

Ann shared with me that you and she did not always get along. You argued about everything and when you played a game together, she would ask you, "Are we going to play the real rules or Donnie's rule." You had to win, she says. Hmm... perhaps an insight to our playing certain games together. Soon after we were married, I mentioned how my Uncle Bill was a fabulous chess player. He taught me how to play chess. So, early in our married life, I got out my chess set I had since I was a teen. "Let's play a game of chess," I asked you. After I beat you at chess a few times, you didn't want to play that game again. Bridge, now that was the game at which you excelled. You had fabulous card sense.

Ann also told me, "At night, we would be in our separate rooms, with only a thin wall between the two rooms and we both wanted to be the last ones to say good-night. It was probably a power thing, perhaps because I was the older sister and I thought I knew everything."

Memories of our childhood give us many insights to our adulthood.

But, I never called you "Donnie."

Chapter 57

October—Widow

I received a book today from a dear friend who became a widow three years ago. The title was in bold black lettering— **"Widow."**

Somewhere I read a description, written by another widow, of what this phase of my life is now, "widow internment camp." How true!

When I opened the package, took out the book and read the title, it was certainly a shock to my system. Not me, no, I'm not a widow. Then I remembered. I am!

I don't believe I've gone through the depression some other widows might have experienced. But, the loneliness, even with countless puppy kisses, catches me and grabs onto my soul when I'm not expecting it.

It is hard to fight the loneliness. Or is it grief? Whatever it is, loneliness or grief, it feels like a bottomless pit. My life, my life as I knew it, is gone. My life is now in a state of limbo. My life's progression is changed forever.

"This is my current husband," I would laughingly say as I introduced you to new friends whom you had never met. They would look at me with a question on their faces and I would laugh, tease and say, "Yeah, well he is my current husband and my last husband."

WIDOW—so that's me.

I don't want a "new" husband. I think it would be so difficult to do the things it took us almost thirty-two years to learn how to do together. So natural and so at ease, it wasn't work for either of us. I could be myself with you. You understood me.

I know some women who have spent their entire lives playing the supporting role, having no part of themselves that wasn't defined by what their husbands did, either in his career days or in his retirement. I've always had my own identity. I never had the role as a mother or a homemaker. I believe it must be harder for those widows whose identity is defined by either their husbands or their children. Yes, their monthly calendar pages will be filled with family oriented activities at least for a while, but then what?

I will not have to totally reinvent myself as some other widows might have to do. My new life will be like an amoeba. I will be expanding on the original shape.

How would a new husband react to an independent woman? Perhaps it will be better not to test the water and just remain this widow, this once again independent woman.

Besides, there are the private and personal customs and traditions that a marriage of 32 years has. Every time I pull the car into the garage, I am reminded of one of ours; the tradition we had of arriving home and kissing each other *before* we got out of the car. If we had a scrap and drove home in silence, we both knew the minute the car was in PARK, and the keys were removed from the ignition, we would have to lean over and kiss each other. Sometimes, it was a quick peck on the lips. At least we knew the minute we walked through the garage door into our house, we would be entering the healing process.

Oh, but I do miss so many of the things we did together as a couple. Especially, after we retired and moved to Truckee we had more time to do things together in a more relaxed mode. We loved going to the movies. I looked forward to these times with you; no phone and no computer, nothing to interfere with us being alone together. Sitting next to you, holding hands, just being close. You were such a mush and I loved you even more for it. You had no inhibition about crying during a touching scene. I would sneak a glance over at you and see you dabbing at your eyes. If we watched a movie where the script called for the couple to split up, at the end you would lean over and ask me in a hushed voice, "They will get back together again, don't you think, honey?"

Now there are the routine chores I have to do by myself. Our house is over-flowing with house plants, and most of these are in self-watering planters that need to be filled only once a month. We took turns doing this task the first of the month, even months I would water the plants and odd months would be your turn. You also helped me groom the dogs. I would grind their nails and trim their coats. You would do the bathing, hand me a dog to dry while you bathed the next one. A "hot dog assembly line," you would say to me and laugh at your own joke.

I certainly don't want to be a "care-giver" to some man. My dear friend Ivy Geiger told me in her most southern drawl, "Honey, at our age they want either a nurse or a purse." No, I could not be a care-giver. You took such great pride in yourself. We would laugh when I would show you one of the ads from a motor home magazine that had just arrived in the mail, the one featuring the man wearing the one-piece polyester jump-suit, complete with super wide suspenders. "When my belly becomes so big and it droops over my belt as a blubbery mass, and I can't button my pants, that's what I'll buy," you would tell me. "It will cover my big, fat belly." "Never," I would answer you. You would look over at me with that Don expression on your face and say to me, "Never—is never going to happen. Because, sweet baby, I would never let myself become unattractive to you."

Yes, you were a treasure. Today is October 23. It's been four months since you died—and I am a widow.

Chapter 58

October–Marriage Retreat

Wwe had only been married for a couple of months when you handed me a brochure you had received from the pastor who was the mediator for your Men's Group. It was about a marriage retreat to be conducted over a long weekend. "Would you want to go to this?" you asked, and I remember my immediate response. "Yes, of course, anything that will help us in our marriage and in our years to come is worth a weekend."

I was not naïve enough to believe we would never have an argument or disagreement in our future life. I had told you when we first married, "*I DO NOT BELIEVE IN THE 'D' WORD.*"— meaning, divorce. I said, "Don, we might have knock down, drag out fights, but we will never divorce." When you approached me with this idea, we both thought what better way to build our foundation and strengthen our relationship. After all, we were both in this for a lifetime.

The retreat was held in an area of Houston that was private and woody. There were some basic "touchy-feely" exercises with the entire group. Most of the other couples had been married for many years. There was one couple with whom we became fast friends. When the course was over, we continued to meet socially for many years. After we moved to Truckee, we learned they eventually divorced. Sad!

In with the piles of cards and letters, I came across the lists of expectations we both had to write during the retreat.

~~~

EXPECTATIONS (Don's)

1) *To love me and show it*

2) *Accept my time for separate pursuits (tennis, poker)*

3) *Share my pleasures (skiing, tennis, camping, bike riding)*

4) *Pull on her half of the oar, but **lead** where she is the most capable*

5) *Tell me when she is unhappy with something and be willing to discuss it*

6) *Understand her own needs, and see that they are served (her own self maturing)*

7) *Act independently under some circumstances (have capability)*

8) *Satisfy my needs (as long as they aren't unreasonable, and then to negotiate)*

9) *Accept my family*

10) *Live within our means*

~~~

EXPECTATIONS (Diane's)

1) *To never lose the loving & tenderness quality that you have now with me*

2) *To be as happy & excited in doing "things" with* **me** *as some men are only with other men*

3) *To keep your sense of humor*

4) *For both of us to keep "working" on our marriage & its growth and not to allow job to ever take a priority*

5) *To be understanding—continue to be 'cause now you are—in my "down" periods*

6) *To always be my best friend—easy for me to discuss anything with you—no matter how silly— trivial—or the other extreme*

7) *To continue to be as "open" throughout our married life and never to feel "I can't with you or you can't with me"—take the open approach*

8) *Never for you to stop telling me you love me*

~~~

Looking back over our past thirty-two years, I can honestly say both of us truly tried to meet these expectations of each other. Perhaps mine were more naïve than yours and pertained to more emotions and feelings. After all, you had been down the "marriage road" before and knew what might occur in the heat of battle. I didn't have the history of a previous marriage or even a serious "live-in" relationship with anyone else. I didn't know the struggles a couple might have such as trying to balance job, family, money—all the other roadblocks that couples might face. All I knew was I loved you so much and wanted our marriage to work.

I'm glad I kept these pieces of paper. They needed to be included in this story about you and about us. They are a living testament to how we both worked at our marriage.

Chapter 59

October–The Motor Home

In the fall of 1993, Spirit and I were on a roll. He was starting to win the dachshund longhaired variety more times than not at dog shows. That meant waiting around the show grounds until late in the afternoon when the group judging would begin. On such long days, it was difficult to keep cool and comfortable. I purchased a tent canopy one weekend and had the vendor load it into the back of my SUV. I had good intentions of taking it to the dog show the following weekend, setting it up under some trees, and stretching out in a chaise lounge until the Hound Group judging would begin.

Wrong! As I was attempting to pull the blasted canopy out from the back of my SUV, I twisted my back. No sooner had I set up the canopy, but a blast of wind came up from out of nowhere and took mine and several others that were set up near me sailing around the show site. Back into the box it went and back to the vendor.

Fate! Two weeks later, my father called from St. Petersburg, FL. He told us his doctor advised him his days of driving his motor home were over. Did I know anyone who would be interested in buying his 24 foot, 1985 Coachman motor home? Did I?" Me.!!!

Before we made the final decision to buy the motor home, you were on a backpacking trip with friends to the Jarbidge Mountains—a beautiful mountain chain east of Reno, NV. I could not go, so you purchased a one-man tent. It rained during most of this trip and you spent hours confined to your small tent. While you were cooped up in these horrid conditions, you wrote down some notes in a 3"x 5" spiral bound memo pad which I came across the other day.

~~~

Buy it	*Tires/Battery*
Air Fare	*Mileage to CA*
License	*Inspection*
Storage	*CD*
Insurance	*Generator*
AAA Club	*Jacks*
Check-up/tune-up	*Phone*

"YES"	*"NO"*
Diane wants it	*Don will have to go to more*
Good for dog shows	*dog shows*
Can travel some	*Don't want to spend much*
Cheap way to start	*time away*
Probably more time together	*Expense*
Don has more time now	*Old Unit (reliability and cost)*

MOTOR HOME RULES

1) Diane does not ask or pressure Don to go to dog shows, (or act in a way to make him feel guilty—pressure)
a) Don will likely volunteer to go to some.

2) *Diane prepares MH before and cleans up MH
   after solo trips.*
      a) *Don may volunteer to help, but maybe not.*
      b) *Both work if Don goes along*
      c) *If you want it, you should be willing to
       take care of it happily*

3) *This is a Dog Show MH. It may **never** go on
   personal trips. Don't pressure or ask Don to
   do so.*

4) *Some things you can't do alone & Don will help*
      a) *Get MH from storage*
      b) *Heavy lifting*

5) *Don't expect to get or start pressuring for a
   longer MH.*
      a) *This may be the only one we ever get,
       as it's for Dog Shows, not travel*

~~~

These memories come flooding into my thoughts as I sit in "my" motor home parked at the Dixon Fairgrounds in Dixon, California. When I left home, I brought with me all of my notes for my manuscript and other miscellaneous letters and materials I had found, but had not had the chance to go through.

This motor home, the Aerbus, was purchased in the spring of 1995. I was at a show in Oakland, CA, in March, March 17, to be exact. We had been storing the Coachman during the winter months at the KOA in West Sacramento. I was just leaving the show, when I heard the most terrible rumble. I quickly looked around for a crumbled car that I might have run into. Nope, no car was in sight. As I got up from the behind the wheel to investigate, I almost fell through a gaping hole in the center of the motor home's floor. Years of Florida weather and probably some help from termites had caused the wooden floor to rot away. The coach battery, which normally was secured under the steps, had fallen through to the road. The door to the outside storage cabinet was ripped from its hinges, and my barbeque equipment—grill, briquettes and some grooming supplies—were bouncing down the road. Somehow, with the help of adrenalin, I managed to get the battery inside the motor home and secured the cabinet door with duct tape. Hours later, I walked in our front door and into your comforting arms. But, something was wrong, I could sense it. As I started to tell you 'my' story, you pulled away from me, looked into my eyes and said, "Wait, Baby, I have some sad news. Your Aunt Irene died today."

Weeks later after her estate was settled, we were sitting in the hot tub and you asked me with a knowing smirk on your face, "So, just what do you want to do with some of your Aunt Irene's inheritance money?" As if you didn't already know. Hence, the name of my motor home— "The Spirit of Irene."

Even though you did not like the motor home or dog shows, you did paste a Harley decal to the back rear window. The few times you did accompany me in the motor home were memorable.

Perhaps one of the best times we both had took place at a dog show that was part of the "Hangtown Kennel Club circuit." It was held at the fairgrounds in Placerville, CA. Placerville is a small town in the California foothills where gold was discovered in the nearby town of Coloma in the mid-1840's. Soon miners were rushing to the site to strike it rich. Locals still refer to the town as "Hangtown" because of the numerous hangings that occurred. I only had the Aerbus for a short time, so I was still trying to get accustomed to it by attending only shows that were close.

My friend, Barbara Cox, and I really wanted our husbands to go with us. She convinced her husband, who also did not like dog shows, to go with her in their motor home since you were going to come with me. You had met Greg once or twice before and liked him. "Ah, come on, Honey, come with me to this show. Greg is coming. We can barbeque outside, and you and Greg can talk about fly fishing and do some male bonding." Reluctantly, you said you would go. Phew! We packed several thick filets, salad fixings for your famous Caesar salad, some potatoes to bake, munchies and, of course, several bottles of wine—because "thirst is a dangerous thing" as we used to say to one another. We arrived at the fairgrounds, which had a high wooden fence around it, early on Friday afternoon and set up. Soon Barbara and Greg arrived in their motor home and parked close to us. It was a beautiful late spring day and the weather promised to co-operate. I was stretched out on the chaise lounge with a book in my hands when I heard this horrible noise that sounded like the roar of many, many engines. I didn't realize the Placerville race track was behind the high fence. The noise seemed to die down as we enjoyed our dinner. Shortly afterwards another couple joined us for dessert. More wine was poured. Suddenly, the noise started up again. Next thing I knew you were at the back of the motor home, climbing up the ladder to the roof, peering over the high fence to see if you could see the race track from the top of the motor home. You climbed back down, looped a camp chair over one hand, and in the other held a glass of wine and back up you went. Then Greg soon followed, carrying a camp chair in one hand and a glass of wine in his free hand. Then the other man followed. Barbara and I looked up to see all three of you in the camp chairs watching the races. Meanwhile, I was in disbelief. My brand new motor home, I thought, and those guys are up on the roof and suppose they crush in the roof. I yelled up to you, "Don, you guys better be careful and don't crash through the roof." You yelled back to me, "Honey, didn't you tell me one of the selling points of the Aerbus was its steel cage roof construction? What we have to be careful of is not falling off the side." Yeah right! I really don't remember too much else about the weekend. Who knows what dogs won? But, as we were driving home you said to me, "Diane, now *that* was a fun dog show."

Now in this new phase of my life, I think I have to simplify my life and there is a "For Sale" sign on the motor home. I have mixed feelings about selling it. It would be a way for the dogs and me to "get off the hill" during gray winter, snowy days and weeks in Truckee. BUT, it could be an added headache without you here to help me drive back to Truckee if it broke down and needed to be taken to the repair shop for an extended period of time.

It's the "speed bumps" I have to get over, slowly, cautiously.

Chapter 60

October–Don's Metamorphosis

In the early days of our marriage, "your" friends gradually came around to being "our" friends, but more importantly for me, they became "my" friends. I had to prove to them I would be worthy of their friendship. For many of them, their loyalties were still with your ex-wife.

Over time, these new women friends would tell me, "Don is changed. You have certainly been good for him. You have changed him. He is more sensitive and caring. And, he certainly is happier. He has a constant grin on his face."

A card you sent to me when you were away on a long business trip in 1982 was a humorous "Snoopy" card, but the words you wrote were from the only Don I knew, the sensitive and caring Don.

~~~

Hello Darling
Well, you're on the home stretch and the end of your isolation is in sight. Again, all is well, I hope.
Did we decide where we would have our anniversary dinner? I believe it was at the new 'Che'. Why don't you go ahead and make a reservation along about mid-week.

*One thought occurred to me just before I left. This is
number 7 and that's when the seven year itch is supposed to
occur. Well, au contrair, I say. Remember how I had some
concerns on being able to sustain my love and appreciation
over time? Well, it has of course worked out. There couldn't
possibly be a 7 year itch—I just don't know how I could do
it. You and I have something so special that few people have.
I really think it is mostly due to you and your makeup but I
suppose you'd argue. Anyway, we are very lucky and I'll be
home to you soon.*

With love —

Don

~~~

I'm glad and thankful we romanced each other with cards
and letters. If we had emailed each other, we probably would
not have printed the messages and saved them. Now, at least,
I can sit here and read your words, in your own handwriting.
I can imagine you sitting in the solitude of your apartment,
before I moved in as your wife, and with each letter, as it pro-
gressed in time, I can see how your love for me grew stronger
and stronger.

Will I remember you? Will I be able to recall the smile on
your face, the twinkle in your eyes when we were out with
friends and you would turn to me and say ever so softly,
"*Later?*" We both knew what that one word meant.

Soon after we moved to Truckee and were trying to figure
out what we would be doing for the rest of our lives, I asked
you if you missed anything we left behind. Your answer gave
me a start. It was so sensitive, so sweet, so caring—probably
unlike the old Don McCormack many of your friends remembered. You looked up at me and said, "Diane, your presence fills
the room, it fills my life. You are my life, and I can't think of
anyplace else I would rather be nor with anyone else." I walked
over to you, put my arms around you and kissed you, and
then walked into the kitchen on the pretense of getting another

cup of coffee. But, what I really did was write down the words you said to me, such beautiful words of love, so I could read them again and again.

Now, as I struggle to go on with my life, I wonder if you will continue to be part of it. My metamorphosis will continue, as yours did after we married, but will you be in it? One lives on as long as they are still remembered. So, my darling Don, will you continue to be remembered? Yes, at least through these pages on which I am inking your legend and our life.

Chapter 61

November–Bunnies & Chickens

It's November and the dates for the field trials for the two local dachshund clubs, Dachshund Club of Northern California and Golden Gate Dachshund Club, have been on my calendar since the first of the year, since before you died. In California, field trials cannot be held until fall, after the wild plants and weeds have finished their life cycles and become dormant and start to die off. If the trials were held in summer months, there is the threat of dogs getting a foxtail in their ear, nose or worse, in their lungs or heart. The fall is also the time when the change in season will bring changes in weather patterns and produce storms. Rain is good for field trials. It holds the scent of the game in the grasses.

All the McCormack dachshunds are both bench champions and field champions. On field trial weekends, I would take my motor home and travel west along I-80 to the site of the field trial where we hoped there would be plenty of jack rabbits. The dogs loved going to field trials. I also looked forward to spending time with my friends who would be there. It would be a continuous weekend of fun, including potluck lunches. For those of us who stayed overnight in our motor homes and trailers, there would be potluck dinners, wine, jokes, and, of course, the companionship of our dogs. What could be better?!

This was another of those doggie activities you really didn't enjoy. The one field trial you did attend occurred because you were going to be in the San Francisco area on a business trip. You suggested you would come to the trial location after your meetings were over on Saturday. These trials were still being held at the Mather Air Force Base, about twelve miles east of Sacramento. It's an area surrounded with grassy ranch lands and vineyards. Today, many housing projects are springing up and the jack rabbits have become scarce. You had planned to come late on Saturday and would spend the night with me and the dogs in the motor home. After the trials on Sunday, you would help take the motor home to the storage lot. Then we would caravan back to Truckee, you in your Tahoe and me in my Jeep.

What a horrible weekend it turned out to be! A storm coming from the Pacific Northwest came through the Sacramento area on Friday night and all night long it rained. On Saturday the rain continued and with it came high winds. Those who were there on Saturday managed to finish the field trials. By the time you arrived, most of us staying on the grounds were snuggled in our motor homes or travel trailers with our dogs, all hunkered down for the night. I had lowered the awning on my motor home to keep the dogs somewhat dry when they had to go outside to potty and had it secured with large lead weights that a friend's husband made for me, especially for this purpose. The lead weights were ingenious and I never had a problem. The rains lashed at the windows and pounded the roof of the motor home and the howling winds caused the awning to creak and groan, but we were safe. The next morning it continued to rain; the temperature dropped and the winds became almost hurricane force. The committee in charge of the trial decided it was too dangerous for us to be out in the fields with our dogs and cancelled Sunday's trial.

The potluck lunches always included an array of tasty food, but one woman was known for her fantastic oven-fried chicken. When the trial was cancelled, she came over to me and asked, "Diane, why don't you take a few pieces of the chicken home with you so you and Don can have it for your dinner when you get home? I know the drive will take a few hours and you're not going to feel like cooking dinner. It will be too late. I've already taken some for me and my husband. Please, take the rest of the chicken." We packed up the gear, the dogs, and the chicken and left the grounds. We arrived at the storage lot within an hour. Equipment, dogs and chicken were transferred to my Jeep and off we went. You followed me in your Tahoe. It continued to rain, and by the time we reached Auburn, some 30 miles east on I-80, the temperature had dropped even more. Now, the rain turned to snow. Road blocks had been put up. All of the cars and trucks were checked for chains or snow tires or four-wheeled vehicles. No vehicle was allowed to proceed east on I-80 towards Truckee since there were white-out conditions closer to Donner Summit; we had to wait in line.

After an hour or so, we were still going nowhere, and by now the snow was really starting to accumulate on the road. I was sitting in my car with the heater on. You got out of your Tahoe and came up to my window and knocked on it. I opened the window and you said, "Hey, Honey, I'm really starting to get hungry. How about a piece of that chicken." So, back to your car you went with a chicken drumstick wrapped in paper towel. Minutes later, there was another knock on my window and you asked me for another piece of chicken. This time you also left with a bottle of water. I was preoccupied in some paperwork, when there was another knock on my window.

I looked up and saw this strange looking man. He was wearing a heavy wool plaid jacket with a hood covering his head, and shivering. I cracked the window a little bit, and he said, "Hey, Lady, I'm in the truck in front of you and I don't know who that other guy is who keeps coming to your car and knocking on your window, but I saw in my rear view mirror that he walked away with some kind of food. It looked like chicken. I'm pretty hungry. Would you mind giving me a piece of chicken like that man just got and how much do I owe you?"

Within minutes you came up to my window with an alarmed look on your face. "Honey, I saw a man come up to your car. Who was he? Are you okay? Was he with the chain control gang? What did he want?"

I told you what he wanted. You just stared at me with this puzzled look on your face. Once you knew I was okay, you stayed and cleared the snow frozen behind the windshield wipers. When the snow started to let up, we were allowed through the barricade. Gradually, we made our way back up the hill to Truckee, arriving around ten o'clock.

These many years later, I can't remember if I gave him a piece of chicken or not. I probably did. Who knows? It made for a fabulous story we shared with our friends.

Chapter 62

November–My Birthday

There was no birthday card from you and none from the dogs because you were the one who gave me the cards from the dogs. Several weeks ago, when I was organizing our history of letters and cards, all kept in the bottom drawer of the secretary, I stacked the cards into piles: Don to Diane on Valentine's Days, Don to Diane on their anniversary, Don to Diane on her birthday, Diane to Don on Valentine's Days, Diane to Don on their anniversary and Diane to Don on his birthday. I had to laugh when I realized that the last stack of cards was from the dogs to either of us on the same holidays and occasions. That stack was twice as high as any of the other piles of cards.

My dear friend, Polly Savage, graciously sent me a plane ticket for my birthday. I flew first to Phoenix, where she lives full-time and spent the night. The next morning, November 2, she and I flew to Chicago and stayed in her condo. She made all kinds of plans for our four-day visit.

Chicago—the name on my lips brings back bitter-sweet memories. Chicago is the town where you proposed to me.

After we arrived at her condo, Polly took me on a tour of Chicago. We talked about my life. "It will never be the same," she said. "And, you will never be the same." I knew that. She reached over and touched my hand. "You were a couple, you were married, and now you're single. Your life will be totally different. Some aspects of it will be the same: more breeds to judge, same friends and new friends," she said to me. "Yes," I told her, as I laughed with my tears about the comment she interjected about more breeds to judge. "I know all of that, and I thank my lucky stars I was single for eleven years in New York City. I knew how to cope when I was alone, and I'm sure I will readjust to being single again," I answered.

We attended a ballroom dance Saturday night. It was held at a club where Polly danced professionally when she lived in Chicago many years ago. We sat at a table with several other people from the local dance club, including a man by himself. He asked me to dance. No, I didn't want to dance. "So, tell me about yourself," he said. No, I especially didn't want to make small talk with the stranger sitting next to me. When tears started to form in my eyes, I tried to stop them and thought to myself, *"Damn it, Polly and I even had our make-up done today at her favorite store, Barney's. Now look at my eyes."* Then I remembered that the make-up artist told me she was using an eye-liner that wouldn't come off. I checked my make-up in my small mirror I had placed in my evening bag. She was right.

The next night we went to a bar, Jilly's Piano Bar, where Frank Sinatra music was played by a most wonderful combo, pianist and bass. The atmosphere was thick with nostalgia. There were photos of the Rat Pack on every wall and I felt like I was stepping into a speakeasy from the 20's. If I hadn't felt so raw about your death, it would have been a fun spot, even with the cigarette and cigar smoke. *"Ah, another trap to stay away from in the future—listening to songs that are romantic or sentimental, especially those songs where the lyrics are sung,"* I thought.

Monday morning I awoke earlier than I usually do. It was November 5, my birthday. I thought to myself, *"Am I starting to grow single as I grow older?"* Who knows? I always used to say, "Age is only a number. If we had no mirror to look into to see our wrinkles or graying hair, how old would we feel?" This morning after I crawled out of bed and went into the guest bathroom and looked into the mirror, I saw a still fairly attractive, but slimmer, mature woman with bright sparkling eyes; even though those eyes cried over you for a little while last night.

This was certainly not the way I had thought I would be "celebrating" my birthday. I thought I would have slept in a little late and gone downstairs to where you would be sitting on the sofa reading the newspaper. The coffee would have been made. I would grab a cup and go into the living room. You might have made a fire. You would get up, come over to me and then give me a warm hug and a kiss. I would open a small gift from you and my cards: several from friends and family, one from you and, of course, one from the dogs.

When I arrived back home in Truckee late that night, I reflected on the past events as I looked at the notes I had scribbled down during the past four days.

My birthday is past. I know I am being repetitious when I write the words once more—*thank goodness for my friends.* But, it is true. "Thank you, Polly. You were there for me."

Chapter 63

November–Children vs Career?

~

In 1975 when I was in my early thirties, the norm for most women was to have had their babies before they reached forty.

You and I talked about children, to have or not to have them. "I have given to the world," you told me. "But, if the day ever comes you feel the need to have a baby, then we'll discuss it." Yes, you had your three children who ranged between the ages of 17 and 22 when we married. Would I want to have a child or children of my own?

I had always believed a marriage needed a year or more to grow on its own, like planting a flower, a time for the seed to germinate and then become a plant and then time for the blossoms to appear.

So, the first year of our marriage was not the time to have a baby. These early marriage days were blissful except for me not being able to find a job for seven months. I had gone on countless job interviews where one interviewer after the other, would look over my portfolio with a look of amazement in his eyes. Yes, they had been impressive projects. Then they would ask, "How much did you make at your last job?" I would answer, "My salary in New York should not correlate to the salary scale here in Houston." But, they would press on. When I finally gave in and answered, the look of amazement on their face told me I would never be hired by "that" one person.

One sunny Sunday morning, as I was reading the news-paper's classified ads, I noticed this advertisement. When you came home from playing tennis, I showed you this ad—

~~~

WANTED:
Experienced Man.
Marketing Director for Small Boutique Company

~~~

"See. It's 1976, and this town is still living in the dark ages. It's a man's world," I said to you with disgust in my voice. You looked at the ad and said to me, "Honey, call them tomorrow and make an appointment to apply for the position." You knew I was capable. The next morning I did apply and I did get the job. Of course, I was probably making much less than their de-sired "man" would be making, but at least I was now gainfully employed.

It was a shoddy company, selling fashion wigs, doing business in a store front building and owned by a man who ill-treated his employees. He made himself feel important by walking around checking on everybody, all the while smoking a big cigar. The job did have its perks. He sent me to Como, Italy, to buy Italian scarves and jewelry. He hoped he could change the company's image by adding high quality acces-sories. It didn't.

Monica was my Italian translator. She and her husband became fast friends although he did not speak a word of English and I not a word of Italian. But through gestures, we managed to get by. I came home from Italy with an Italian espresso machine and many of Monica's recipes. One of our favorites was taking a whole eggplant and grilling it over the coals, turning it frequently until the eggplant was black. We would mash the insides, add garlic and herbs and serve it on bread that had been sliced and grilled. We also grilled chicken the way Monica did and continued to use her special marinade. You laughed when I told you they fed their dog pasta for his nightly meal. "What, they don't feed kibble dog food," you asked. "Nope," I answered, "It's leftover pasta, sometimes noodles and sometimes risotto, but never dog food as we know it." Lucky dog.

During this first year of our marriage, we moved into our home in the Montrose area of Houston, an area known as "artsy." It was an old Victorian home built in 1905 and had the original glass door knobs and hand-blown windows. We found antique stained glass windows at flea markets and auctions that we hung in front of the dining room windows. The interior of the house had already been modernized. The kitchen had brand new appliances, new oak cabinets and a Mexican tile floor. We bought a small John Boos butcher block table for the center of the kitchen and spent many hours cooking our meals together. The living room, dining room and foyer had mahogany beams in the ceiling and a mahogany carved staircase gently curved up to the second floor. There was only one bathroom upstairs, complete with its original claw-footed iron bathtub. We added a small bathroom onto our master bedroom. Down the hall, at the back of the house, was a very small room. We purchased two narrow daybeds, which were positioned to form an "L", and a console television. This is where we curled up with Gypsy, and later Mystic, and either read or watched TV. Another room, slightly larger than the TV room, had a twin bed and the table you had refinished before we were married, and this was set up as my sewing room. There had to be a swimming pool to make living in Houston tolerable, so we installed a kidney shaped pool. Was the house suitable for a baby? No.

I had been at this boutique company a little over a year. My letter of resignation was written and in my desk drawer. All I was waiting for was your phone call to tell me your former

Mount Vernon Avenue - Houston

house had sold. There had been road blocks to closing the sale for one reason or another. When that day finally came, I handed in my resignation.

My next career move was a brief stint with Neiman Marcus. I had known Mr. Stanley because their flagship store in Dallas was one of my accounts during my career with The Wool Bureau. I was interviewed by him and offered a position as Clientel Director of their Houston store in the Galleria. After six months I realized I did not enjoy retail.

My next job was with Schey Advertising and it opened up new doors to me. I loved the exciting world of advertising and this was the closest to what I had been doing in New York City. I was making good money and had some very interesting accounts. You were amused at my story pertaining to one of my accounts, a pest exterminator. They had hired a termite sniffing dog, a beagle. They named him Tommy the Termite Dog, and it was my job to promote this dog. I got him an interview on one of the leading TV shows. We had hidden petri dishes around the studio, some containing actual termites. Tommy went to work. The camera man had all he could do to keep up with Tommy who went running around the studio, searching for the termites. Tommy was a hit and I earned a raise. The company wanted to test Tommy in an old Victorian home, so I arranged for him to come to our house. Sure enough, he alerted to termites in our upstairs back closet. Thank goodness they were subterranean termites and not the kind where our entire house would have had to be tented.

So, three years had passed and what to do, what to do? It was 1978. If we had a baby now, you would be in your late 60's when "she" would be getting ready for college. Would that be fair to you?

My gynecologist told us in her most frank tone, "When you're forty, one of you will have to bite the bullet and either have your tubes tied or be snipped." Your hand went flying up in the air without the slightest hesitation. "I will, I will."

Now, without you, was this the wrong decision? Did I sacrifice by NOT having a child? I made the choice or rather we made the decision. But, what if? Would "our" child be here for me now?

This was not to be and I do have my seven step-grandchildren. Years ago I told you, "Any child who is either born or brought into our life during our married life is also my grandchild."

Another memory flashes across my mind. We were in Houston visiting your daughter and her husband. She had married a man who came to their marriage with three beautiful young daughters from his first marriage. It was Thanksgiving and we had been having a great visit. You were at the sink peeling potatoes when one of the girls said, "Grandpa, you have to cut the eyes out of the potatoes. You can't leave them in. They look yucky." Later that day, the older granddaughter looked at me and your daughter and said to us, "We have something in common. Mary Beth has the best step-mom and so do we." Out of the mouths of babes, as they say.

I know that people who do have children are often alone in their old age. "When I'm old and alone, they will be there for me," is not a good safety hedge. I also think that those of us who have never had children know how to be alone. To be alone means we must look within our own beings. We must develop interests that are specifically ours. We must create our own self first.

Having children for one's later life is no insurance policy to not being alone.

But, what if?

Chapter 64

November—Thanksgiving Day

Several weeks before Thanksgiving, I received a phone call from Julie. "Hey, I'm searching the internet and just pulled up a flight from Portland to Reno. It arrives the Monday before Thanksgiving in the late afternoon and leaves the Friday after, again in the late afternoon so we won't have to get up at the crack of dawn to make the flight just in case there's bad weather. Are you ready for this, for the three of us, round trip, it's around $400 total." "Book it," I said, without the slightest hesitation. "I'll pay for all the food and whatever else we decide to do."

How could I have possibly gotten through my first Thanksgiving Day with you not being here without my friends to help? How could I ever start to look forward to this holiday, one that was so special in our lives, without my friends?

I can remember the first Thanksgiving we had in our new Truckee home. My sister and her husband and my Aunt Irene all flew in. For four days it seemed all we did was cook and eat and drink. What fun we all had. We were burning real wood in our fireplace back in those days and we would spend the evenings after dinner in front of the fire sipping brandy in the wedding present you loved the most—the Lismore brandy snifters from Cindy and Herb.

It snowed on one of the days and Bev and I decided to go down to the hot tub. We had on our bathing suits, were giggling and having a great time when I said to her, "You know, Bev, in the Scandinavian countries, after they are in the hot tub for a few minutes, they run out and roll in the snow." Before I realized, she bolted out of the hot tub, ran to the back of the house and jumped in the snow. I followed her. We were laughing so hard we didn't hear you come out of the house with the camera. You captured the moment of our "sister delirium." Good thing we had on our bathing suits!

Now, some eighteen years later, I am celebrating Thanksgiving Day with my friend Julie and her daughters, Carley and Claire. Our two very good friends, Debbie and Lisa joined us and brought lots of dishes to go with the turkey. As we were laughing someone said, "Hey. It's a turkey-hen party."

After Debbie and Lisa left, Julie and I were cleaning up the kitchen. I started thinking of you. Julie could sense my mood changing as I started to talk about you and some of our past Thanksgiving Days. Julie is such a good listener. One needs a good listener going through these stages of grief. She said to me, "I know this is very, very hard for you. You and Don had something so special. You have told me how much the holidays meant to the both of you. You know what, Diane, you will start to make your own very special traditions. They won't include Don, but they will be yours and they will be special."

Chapter 65

November—Lifelines

~

Five months after your death, my sister sent me a book on being widowed. It was written by a renowned psychologist. She, too, had lost her husband. After reading the book, I thought the only thing we had in common was that we were both widows. Her husband suffered a slow and long illness; whereas, you died suddenly. She spoke of having no real friends. I do have friends, good ones, and many. They are more than *friends*—they are my lifelines.

I am blessed to have these friends in my life. Not only do I call them, but they call me. They send me funny but meaningful cards and emails. They come to Truckee to visit me. Many of these friends were our friends; many of them are mine. I cherish each of them for their desire to help mend and heal my broken heart. They allow me to talk about you, not talk about you, to cry over you, or to cry with me over you. I think it's because you had touched their lives, as well. Why wouldn't they want to be here in our home and to feel your presence still? I guess it's all part of the process.

I remember years ago when you told me, "I marvel, Diane, at how many friends from your past you've kept in touch with, from when you were a small girl living in

Edgemere, to college days, to your time in New York City."
I answered, "Don, one has to work at friendships, the same
way you and I work at our marriage."

If I had forgotten my friends on their birthdays, on their
anniversaries, or on their holidays, the friendships would have
started to die. If I didn't call them out of the blue to just say,
"Hey, it's Diane, I'm thinking of you," the friendships would
have died some more. Over the years, and especially since
many of these friends were separated from me by distance,
these friendships have been cultivated and nourished and they
have survived.

A needlepoint pillow Penny sent me years ago sits amongst
my collection of other needlepoint pillows I have made over
the years. The pillow is rectangular, blue and cream, with a
simple geometric border and simply says, *"IT'S THE FRIENDS
YOU CAN CALL AT 4 AM THAT REALLY MATTER."* And, I *have*
called Penny in the wee small hours of the morning.

We met Penny, who is a flight attendant, when we lived in
Houston. Our vet was also her vet. Penny had two old standard

Good-bye Houston – Hello Truckee

"What's This For?"

longhaired dachshunds and was looking for another. We three became fast friends. Over the years Penny has owned many puppies from my line, all relatives of Spirit. Penny, you and I were not only friends, but family, dog family. Our last day in Houston was a whirlwind. On the very same day you retired from Shell Oil Company, we closed on our house and the movers came. That last night in Houston we stayed with Penny, and she threw us the biggest and best "Goodbye Houston—Hello Truckee" party.

During one of Penny's many visits to our new home, she brought us a cappuccino/ espresso machine. We were all standing around in our kitchen, enjoying the camaraderie and anxious to try out the new toy. Penny read the instructions, "word for word," that came with the machine. She filled the machine with ground coffee and water and it started to hiss. You, being the typical engineer, pointed to one of the knobs and asked her,

"What's this for?" "Don, please, leave it alone. Don't touch it," she yelled. Too late! You had already unscrewed the knob. Coffee and grinds came gushing out—over the counter, on the walls, and even on the ceiling. I quickly grabbed the camera. The picture of Penny watching you, with bewilderment, as the coffee spewed out everywhere, is priceless.

A quick phone call is made to my girlfriend, Lory, who lives in Reno, just to touch base. We met years ago after you and I moved to Truckee. Mystic had become an AKC Champion and I was ready to start working her in obedience. In 1989 I went to an all-breed show in Carson City and was looking for a trainer in obedience. Someone pointed to this woman who was about thirty feet away and said, "There, go talk to Lory. She's the best." I started driving into Reno for private lessons with Lory and in fall of 1990 Mystic received her obedience title. Lory and I became the best of friends. She is so prophetic. We meet for lunch many times throughout the month. You and I spent many holidays with Lory, her family and other friends of hers. Lory was one of our first friends I called on that Saturday in June after you had been air-lifted to the hospital.

Lory now tells me, "You are doing so great. Everyone is so proud of you and how you are coping and handling all of this. Friends are doing what they can do, but they can't replace what you're feeling. We all have memories of feelings. The feelings can be called up in a month, a year—and it's a blessing and a curse." Yes, Lory and I can wrap our arms around each other. We do not need to talk. We speak to each other without having to utter a spoken word.

Ivy is one of my dearest friends who calls me frequently. We four were good friends when we lived in Texas, Bud &Ivy and "D & D." We loved going to their ranch in Brenham, Texas, a small town located halfway between Houston and Austin. During the days, we would go on hay rides on their property or drive into the quaint town where we explored the many antique stores. Many happy nights were spent playing liar's dice or sitting around the piano while Ivy played old tunes and we would sing along. This photo I took of you and Bud Geiger is a treasure. I love the big smile on your face. I cropped the original to only your face and printed an 8 x 10 which I have above my desk.

Bud and Don

After you died, I called to tell her and all she could say was that it was always going to be "D & D"—"D & D" forever. Ivy and I are old souls. One morning she called and told me I was on her mind. She needed to connect with me. She had gone to the movies to see a rerun of, "Gone With the Wind" and she compared me with Scarlet. "You both have spirit," she told me. "Scarlet did what she had to do to put food on her family's table. And, Diane, you won't let a whole lot of grass grow under your feet. You are a fighter. You are strong. You will get through this," she said. I told Ivy, "Yes, I know I'm strong, and

I know I will get through this, but Don was my hopes and my dreams. He was my world, but, yes, my world has now changed, maybe like Scarlet's world did."

"*I know, I know, it's gone—gone with the wind,*" I say softly to myself.

Days later, I received an email from Ivy which simply said, "*Good friends are like stars. You don't always see them, but you know they are always there.*"

My friends are a blessing to me. They are my lifeline.

Chapter 66

December–Christmas Blues

⌒

One December afternoon, during a blizzard, I sat in the Queen Ann chair in front of the secretary and just stared out the glass doors. Snowflakes spiraled down to the deck, and I felt myself spiraling down along with them. As the flakes descended, I too descended into a feeling of self-pity. We, who are suddenly alone, can be hit with this sense of self-pity, especially during the holidays when everything around us is festive—children dressed in their colorful holiday outfits—couples walking arm in arm through the malls shopping for friends, family, their children or each other—catalogues arriving with "the perfect gift for her and for him." The songs, each word, each verse talking about joy and love—all of these images bombard us, *The Alone.*

I felt my aloneness watching the snow descend. Sometimes this feeling is so overwhelming. The most ordinary kind of a past memory can bring grief into focus and set it off. I remember something I read about grief. The experts tell us that missing someone is the simple part—it's the journey *through* the grief. That is the hardest.

To break this spell, I played with the dogs, fed them, poured a glass of wine and started to make my dinner. Everything has become methodical. I'm on autopilot. It helps to do something, anything, just stay busy.

After dinner, I sat on the sofa with the remaining wine in my glass. In a distance I heard the coyotes up on the hill. The dogs were curled up beside me and I smiled to myself as I thought how you used to gather Vision up on your lap when we heard the coyotes. You would bring her paws up onto your shoulders and look into her eyes and say, "You better watch out Vision, the coyotes are on the prowl for Loin of Vision."

As I thought of you, I also heard the sound of the wet snow as it slid from the roof and landed outside the sliding glass doors. I opened the doors and stared into the murk beyond. It was completely dark outside. The night was so chilled. But, it wasn't the cold that caused me to shudder. I knew that. I closed the doors and returned to the couch and briefly surrendered myself into memories of what once was but can be no longer. *"I will be okay,"* I said to the dogs and to myself. *"I must make an effort to avoid both the thoughts of the future and the memories of the past. I know I will find my new normal."*

It would be hours before I would be ready for bed. I decided to sort through the many boxes of Christmas decorations. Several of my friends asked me, "Will you be decorating for Christmas?" This was one of the topics of conversation over Thanksgiving dinner a few days ago. Our house was always decorated to the hilt, mostly with items I had made over the years: a nativity scene I needle-pointed that included the holy family, the three wise men, donkeys, a cow, several lambs, the shepherd and two camels painted on canvas by my dear friend, Audrey. There are also stockings made out of calico; a tree skirt to match; swags of holly leaves made out of various fabric and the yo-yo garlands.

Everyone loved the yo-yo garlands. But, not our mothers! It was the Christmas of 1979. We were living in Houston, and my folks had driven from St. Petersburg and your mother had flown from St. Louis. What fun times we all had together. At night after dinner we all sat around in the living room in front of the fire, playing rack rummy or some other game.

I had taken a couple of vacation days to spend with our parents and during the daytime, when you were still at work, it was up to me to "entertain" our family. My father was usually tinkering around the rambling old house, finding some project to do, but our mothers sat twiddling their thumbs. For our very first Christmas, I made stockings out of various calicos: one for you, one for me and one for Gypsy—with our names embroidered in red embroidery floss. I had lots of the same calico fabric left over from this project—what to do with it and what to do with our mothers? I came up with the idea of making a yo-yo garland. Yo-yo's were popular in the 1930s and 1940s and many were used to make quilt tops. But, I thought a garland made of yo-yo's to drape over the carved mahogany

Christmas 1979 – Making Yo-Yo Garland

banister would add charm. So, I showed our mothers how to cut out 9" circles, gather the edges, and fill the circles with fiber-fill stuffing which created a puffed circle. As they finished one yo-yo, I would string them together on a long red narrow ribbon. Our mothers were still at this project when you arrived home and came into the kitchen nook, where we were sitting around the antique claw-footed table. You picked up the camera and snapped their picture. The look of concentration or probably disgust on their faces is priceless.

When we moved into our Truckee home, we needed an additional garland to cover our second banister. Of course, I was now the one who had to do all the cutting, gathering, stuffing and stringing. Oh, where were our mothers?

Another Christmas while in Houston, I cut branches off of our holly trees. I carefully laid the branches out on the floor and strung them together with heavy string and made boughs for over the archways in the living and dining rooms. Within days the leaves turned brittle and the spiny teeth became weapons that would puncture our skin if we brushed against them. Down came the real holly boughs, dried up and brittle, and up went swags of hand-crafted holly leaves, each cut out of various holly printed fabric and sewn to look like a holly leaf. Tiny red balls, sewn on by hand, completed the look. These also were altered to use in our Truckee home. Each year you were the one who got out the step ladder and tacked them above the door frames.

This year I will have to change some of our traditions. I can't bring myself to crown our small pre-lit tree with the same tree topper we had used for the past thirty-one years. We were trying to watch our budget that first Christmas and I went down to the local craft store and bought five fake reindeer on stakes, the kind that florists use in a holiday floral arrangement. I wrapped an empty toilet paper holder with metallic paper and entwined the reindeer around it. Voila! Our Christmas tree topper. Each year as you climbed up the ladder to place the reindeer on top of our tree, we would open a bottle of Korbel Brut Champagne and relive our humble beginnings and thank the stars for our good fortune, good marriage and good life. This year I will replace the reindeer with an antique hand-blown crystal topper, complete with hanging teardrops, which my Aunt Irene had given us years ago.

I also have to rethink the Christmas stockings. I know it would be too painful for me to hang the calico ones I made that very first Christmas. Both of our stockings would now be empty. Yours usually would be filled with a few DVD's of your favorite movies, fishing flies and Harley gadgets and mine with another wooden spoon, a pair of warm socks and at the bottom of the stocking, some trinket.

By the end of the evening, I felt invigorated. During the night, I did not have visions of sugar-plums dancing in my head but rather images of how I would decorate the house.

The next morning I started to sew. I made three stockings: one for Vision, Mirage and Santa and a new tree skirt from fabric I had in my stash. The following day, after the tree was decorated, I hung the yo-yo garlands on the banisters, tacked the fabric holly leaves swags around the door frames and then went outside to put lights up around the front door. I couldn't put the lights around the outside of the perimeter of the house the way you used to, although it was not your favorite thing to do. You used the big lights and followed my father's pattern of placing the lights, red/blue, green/blue, red/blue, green/blue and so on.

The house does look beautiful and the inside is made brighter with the various Dachshund items given to us over the years by Polly: the Dachshund tree, the sleigh and the train, and the small ceramic tree with tiny lighted candles at the end of each branch my mother made when they lived in Baltimore. The stained glass wise men and gnomes I made are hanging in their usual places in the windows.

This Christmas season, love and grief will be as entwined as the strings of lights are on my Christmas tree.

Chapter 67

December–Don's Christmas Almonds

I was looking for a tin or some kind of container in which to store ground coffee. We would buy several bags of whole coffee beans: one Decaffeinated, one Espresso, one Columbian, and you would systematically blend them together. It was one of the things you liked to do. Each night you would grind the coffee beans, fill the coffee pot with water and have it ready to click on in the morning as you entered the kitchen.

The day after you died, the coffee grinder, which had been a wedding present, also died. So, in another of my decisions to "simplify my life," I decided I would not replace the coffee grinder but would buy coffee already ground.

Mirage had chewed up a corner of the bag of ground coffee I had just purchased. To preserve the coffee, I needed to transfer it to a tin. Most of the tins were stored in one of the cabinets above the refrigerator, so I got the step-ladder out of the pantry and looked in those cabinets first.

A small pain took me by surprise when I spotted the bag of small tins I bought for you last year at one of the after Christmas sales. The tins were to be used for "Don's Christmas Almonds." Giving these small tins of almonds to your list of special friends at Christmas was your very own tradition.

The process would take an entire day. You started by blanching the almonds and then would rub them in a towel to remove the skins. You had researched all of my cookbooks to create your very own recipe and to find the best way to roast the nuts. You made test batches for us to sample. In the end, you decided the best way was to simply toast the blanched almonds in butter in one of the heaviest skillets. You stirred them continuously. When they turned a rich, buttery brown, you would remove them from the skillet, dump them out onto clean cloth towels and sprinkle them with kosher salt until the nuts were thoroughly dried. Many times, we simply could not wait for the nuts to cool completely before we sampled them and ended up burning our tongues.

You had such fun in giving out these tins of almonds to your special friends. I know they'll miss receiving "Don's Christmas Almonds" this Christmas.

As I know they're already missing you!

~~~

DON'S CHRISTMAS ALMONDS

To blanch raw almonds –
Place the almonds in a large bowl and cover with boiling water. Let the almonds sit for only one minute—no longer or they will become soggy and lose their crispness. Drain in a sieve. Place the almonds on a course terry cloth towel and rub vigorously. The almonds should pop right out of their skins, but if not, pop the skins off with your fingers.

Method One

Place the blanched almonds in a heavy skillet and dot with 1 to 2 teaspoons butter. Stir continuously until they turn a rich, buttery brown.

Remove them from the skillet. Dump them out onto clean cloth towels. Sprinkle them with kosher salt and let them dry thoroughly.

Method Two

Preheat oven to 350°.

Spread the blanched almonds onto a shallow baking tray. Bake for approximately 20 minutes, stirring occasionally until they start to turn a light golden brown. Sprinkle with 1½ teaspoon of kosher salt. Bake for another 3 minutes.

For each cup of almonds, toss with 1 to 2 teaspoons butter.

Spread on paper towels and cool completely.

~~~

Chapter 68

December—
The Answering Machine

Your voice is still on our answering machine. I can't erase your voice from the recording—not quite yet.

~~~

"This is 555-3148.
To leave a message for Don, hit number one.
For Diane number two.
For D & D number three."

~~~

Our neighbor just called. He didn't leave a message, but before he hung up, I could hear him bellow to his wife before the connection was severed, "Oh for Christ's sake. She still has Don's voice on her answering machine."

I remember mentioning to my friend Barbara Cox after her husband had died following a lengthy illness that her husband's voice was still on her answering machine. She told me she knew it was and added, "If it ever happens to you, you'll understand." Now, I do understand. It was her last connection to him. Hearing your voice is my lifeline to you and I'm not ready to let go of it.

I always would call you before I would leave my dog club meeting in Nevada City. The meetings usually went on until after nine, and I had the hour drive ahead of me. Highway 20 was full of curves and turns and there were always herds of deer waiting to spring across the narrow two-lane highway. I would call you the minute I was leaving, and you would then expect me home in an hour. The first meeting I attended after your death, as I got into my car and turned on the ignition, I called our number without thinking. I was still on auto-pilot. I heard your voice as the answering machine came on. I sat in my car for a long moment, almost in disbelief, trying to get a grip on my emotions when I realized you would not be there for me in an hour. In a way, it was reassuring to hear your voice. Maybe your angel was sitting on my shoulder keeping me out of harm's way along that treacherous road as I drove back home. I believe so.

I remember when we purchased this new phone with the four incoming boxes. After you had programmed box one through three, I laughed and said to you, "Hey, Don, you should have added, 'For bitches in season who want to breed to Spirit, hit number four.'" You looked at me and answered in a dry tone, "Now really, Diane, don't you think that might be going a little too far." I shrugged my shoulders. Then you added, "Because, Honey, we have to be very selective as to what bitch we allow to breed to Spirit. She can't be just any tramp."

The essence of you is now gone. Tonight as I wrote down these notes on the pad by the phone on the secretary, I decided it was time for a new message. The one I just recorded simply says, *"This is 555-3148. Please leave a message."* As I played back and listened to this new message, I recalled your comment about not any tramp and laughed.

Chapter 69

December–Ten Hounds

~

This is the day I've been waiting for. I received the letter from AKC that my application for ten additional hounds has been accepted.

Don, you would have been so proud of me, even though you protested about my going away on weekends to do my doggy things, you would tell everyone you knew, "Hey, Diane now has a total of eight hounds she can judge. She'll have the entire Hound Group yet." You appreciated the dedication I gave to being a judge, even though it was also one of our "bones of contention."

When I returned home, the snow was coming down. Yes, I say to myself, *"My own hounds deserve a walk through the snow."* By the time we came back home, their coats were coated with snow. They ran into the house and started to play with each other and, of course, I could only laugh. Why is it dogs seem to be much more animated when they are wet? As they each came over to me and gave me a wet lick, I thought of how they have comforted me. Yes, they do require attention, even though you said to me many times, "You are right, Diane. Having two dogs is better than one. After all, if they were not down there on the floor rolling around with each other, I would have to do it." They do make it hard when I need to look for puppy sitters. I can't just pick up and go like some of my other widow friends who are pet-less. I also know that having pets leaves their owners open for heartache when the pets become ill. I can't imagine being in this big house all by myself without my dogs.

Years ago, I made a pillow for a friend and embroidered on it, "Dogs Are Not a Part of My Life. They Are My Whole Life." I thought of these words as I curled up on the couch with my dogs.

Why are dogs such a part of my life? Like today, dogs and humans just need to be near each other. We need the presence of another soul. Dogs understand the healing power of touch. Perhaps that is why after we rub their ears then stop, they will raise their heads towards our hands.

The memories of former dogs have the power to take us back in time to places that are comforting. No matter how many decades might have passed, my dog's presence makes me recall the other dogs that went before.

Dogs are not selfish. They are loyal. They never doubt. They stand beside us as the world spins and as it darkens and even as the winds howl, they are here for us. Devotion is their mantra. Devotion—and to be loved in return. They are with us when we need to have someone there, when the dark hours come, to warm us when we feel a chill go down our backs.

Dogs elicit a feeling of bearing and strength and support.

Dogs do not scrimp with their affections. People sometimes do. Dogs are by our sides no matter the reason. When we step into uncertainty, they step with us and quite often they are the ones to take the first step. My dachshunds are big dogs in a small dog's body. Don't tell them that. They think they are big dogs, because no matter their size, they will always be there for me—safeguarding me and listening for any signs of danger and then moving in to protect me.

Dogs live in the present. They don't worry about the future. If they worried about their next meal or the next bone, then I guess they would not enjoy the meal they are gobbling down now. You used to say to the dogs as you placed their food bowls down on the floor, "Isn't this the best meal you've ever had in your whole life." It was the same old food they always ate, but they didn't know and wagged their tails at you as they devoured it.

I remember reading a poem to you. It was called, *"If I Didn't Have Dogs."* When I finished, you said to me, "Honey, those words are so true. We are so intertwined with our dogs." It's too long to include here, but I'm sure it can be found on the internet.

Yes, how empty my life would be now without my dogs since you are not here! My dogs are sitting beside me as I scribble down these thoughts. Their *raison d'être* is sharing life with me.

Chapter 70

December–Time To Go Forward

O n a rather cold and bleak day in December before we
had any major snow dumps in the Sierra, the handymen
arrived to attack my "to-do" list.

First on the list was to re-plaster the hole and paint the
wall board by the staircase, the hole you made with your
elbow as you tumbled down the stairs that horrible night
last June.

While they had the bucket of goop in one hand and the
paint can in the other, I had them go around the house and
touch up the other fine cracks in the walls made by the settling
of the house over the past eighteen years.

When they left, I made a drink, lit the logs in the fireplace
and started our Sligh grandfather's clock. It had not chimed
since *the* night. It seemed only fitting. Moving forward is my
metamorphosis; I want to be reminded now of your life, not
of your death.

I remembered a poem I wrote down in a notebook long
ago. I don't know who the author is, but I think the message
is so true.

~~~

"The clock of life is wound but once, and no man has the power.
To tell just when the hands will stop…at late or early hour.
Now is the time you own - live, love, toil with a will.
Place no faith in tomorrow, for the clock may then be still."

~~~

As the clock strikes out six times, I raise my glass to you, wherever you are, and say out loud, *"I can do this. You would want me to do this. Time needs to go forward."*

Chapter 71

December–New Year's Eve

~~

For many New Year's Eves, it was our tradition to have a dinner and bridge evening. We were four couples: Sal and Frank Bulkley, Kathleen and Ken Ritchie, Pat and Bob Breckenfeld and us. We would start the evening with appetizers, play some bridge, then have the soup course, play more bridge, then a salad, play more bridge, and a few hours later would have the entrée, and then more bridge. The dessert course would be served close to midnight. As the clock neared midnight, we would be glued to the TV set to watch the ball descend in Times Square while holding a glass of champagne and waiting to bring in the New Year with a toast of love, joy, hope and health for the year ahead.

The menus were planned to be spectacular—no limit on expenses or preparation time. We were dedicated to make it a "Menu to Remember."

The first New Year's Eve was 1997. Memorable dishes from that night included: a sweet potato soup with lobster and orange crème fraîche; a beef tenderloin with roasted shallots, bacon and port for the entrée; and a white chocolate cheesecake glazed with a cranberry sauce. For the 1998 menu, we paid tribute to California vineyards and chefs. Some of the menu for that year included: appetizer of crab cakes with basil aioli from a restaurant in the Sonoma wine country; a duet of roast pork loin and tenderloin of beef with three peppercorn sauce from the Ahwahnee, the fabulous resort in Yosemite; and a chocolate pecan torte from a winery in the Napa Valley area.

Our friends from Houston, Sarah and Neil, heard us rave about our New Year's Eve dinners and bridge. In 1999, when the Breckenfelds moved from Truckee, they joined the tradition. They were a part of our New Year's Eve every year for the next eight years and would arrive with a humongous cooler on wheels, stocked with all kinds of seafood, ducks, and meats. You name it, Neil had packed it. The first year, Sarah's carry-on included a chocolate cake, carried on her lap the entire way.

Sarah & Neil Hill – New Year's Eve - 2004

One year they brought eight lobster tails. When someone asked me what size they were, I held up my very long and narrow foot and said, "Larger than this."

This year the tradition stopped with your death. All of us made other plans. Polly had invited me to join her in Phoenix

Debbie Cole, Diane, Sarah Hill, Lisa Dobey, Kathleen Ritchie – New Year's Eve - 2004

while we were in Chicago over my birthday. In mid-December, Sarah called to tell me Neil wanted to go hunting with his brother over New Year's. She would also be alone. Of course, Polly invited her to join us. I drove with my two dogs, and left Truckee three days before Christmas. The almost fourteen-hour drive would have been too hard on both me and the dogs, so I drove as far as Riverside, California, where a friend was playing in a jazz quartet at the Mission Inn. The next day was an easy six hour drive to Phoenix. Sarah arrived from Houston a few days after Christmas.

Polly planned several parties for us at her home, including one where all six of our dachshunds were in a dog fashion show. Friends of hers had parties as well and invited the three of us. At one of the parties, one of Polly's friends spoke with me about your death and said to me, "Remember, Diane, you are the chosen one. You were left to carry on." When I told Polly about this conversation, she said, "All of these people you've met during the past few days did not know Don. They have met you in a new light. They were not thinking of him when they told you how sorry they were. They cared for you."

Sarah's plans were to help me drive back to Truckee. On the last night we were in Phoenix, we were watching the weather forecast for the Sierra Nevada and made the decision to leave earlier than originally planned. They forecasted a blizzard for Truckee and the Sierra Nevada. "A blizzard is coming and we have to drive straight through and not spend a night on the road," I told Sarah. To which Sarah asked, "What's a blizzard?" "We don't want to be driving in it, Sarah. We need to get back to Truckee before it comes and we don't have an extra day to spare." Sarah and I decided to tackle the nearly 1,000 mile drive in one day.

We left at 5 o'clock in the morning. Sarah and I shared the driving which certainly helped. The dogs were gems, hardly a whimper out of them. We decided to take a different route than the boring interstate and drove west on I-10 until the turn off for U.S. 395 north.

The first section of this route was rather depressing. I remember when I was campaigning Spirit and would make this trip between Truckee and San Bernardino. It wasn't as built-up then; there was much more open space. Now tract houses and even new towns have sprung up.

Once we passed the Ridgecrest area, the scenery changed drastically. We were climbing higher in elevation. Passing the small towns where signs pointed to the beginning of hiking trails, I was again reminded of the many backpacking trips you and I took with our friends into the Desolation Wilderness area.

We pulled into Truckee at 7 o'clock at night, some fourteen hours later. Our first stop was the grocery store to stock up for groceries before the impending storms. It seemed everyone else had the same thoughts. I had never seen such long lines.

Walking into our home was easier with Sarah there. I knew there would be no you and my mind knew there would be no you. My heart was not ready. If I had been all alone, without a friend by my side. If?...

Word got out I was back in Truckee and the phone started to ring. *"How are you?" "How was Phoenix?" "Tell us about your holiday." "How is Sarah?" "We have been thinking about you and you have been on our minds."*

Then the snow started to fall and it didn't stop until there was over three feet on the front deck. I watched as it gradually began to build. It stopped just below the smiling cheeks of the sun face that Sandy and Darwin had mounted on your memorial "sun face wall." Was it serendipity that the sun face was not entirely covered up? Its smile was still beaming at me.

We were luckier than many. The snow continued through the night but we did not lose our electric power except for two minor glitches. Once I knocked the snow from the satellite dish, we had television to catch up on the latest news. The next few days that Sarah stayed with me were spent taking down the Christmas decorations, playing cards, and watching some movies from our collection.

Sarah was scheduled to fly back to Houston on the Tuesday after we returned to Truckee. The snow was still falling as I drove her to catch the limo service between Truckee and the Reno airport. She kept telling me, "Oh, I hate to leave you," but she had to return to her husband, her house, her life, and I had to get on with mine.

I drove back up the hill and entered my house, our house. It was so still, so silent, even with the dogs.

Even the snow was quiet.

Chapter 72

January–Don's Tree House

~

Sarah helped me take down the Christmas decorations, all stored in plastic boxes, before she returned home. We carried all of the boxes down to the garage and into the built-in cabinets.

Years ago, we had this wall of built-ins installed by a closet company. I had drawn up the specifications which included separate and specific cabinets, all with doors. There was a long cabinet for skis, a wide one for your Harley equipment, another wide one for dog kennels and equipment. Several cabinets of the same size were designed for the many plastic boxes of Christmas decorations. At the very end was a cabinet that was much deeper and broader than all of the others. It was for the Christmas tree!

It reminded me of our first Christmas in this house, January of 1990. We were taking down Christmas, and the ornaments were stored in the attic storage space in the craft room. It was a painstaking and treacherous task to carry the boxes up the stairs of the fold-down ladder. I was always so afraid you would slip and fall. "Be careful, Honey," I would say as you carefully carried up the boxes, one at a time. You would cuss and mumble under your breath, "Next year, Diane, we're cutting down on the decorating." After all the boxes were stored and you relaxed with a glass of wine, you would say, "Honey, I really did love the way you decorated the house. I know Christmas is an important holiday for you and you make everything look so special. I'm sorry I fume and fuss, and I really do like the end results." With emphasis you would add, "It's just that there are so many, many damn boxes."

We stored all the Christmas decorations in the attic except the Christmas tree. It was too big and too heavy to lug up the steps of that rickety ladder. It was the same artificial Christmas tree we had in Houston, seven feet tall, and still in its original box which was starting to fall apart. You had tried to secure the sides of the box with a couple of bungee cords and many feet of masking tape. You were not about to carry this humongous box up the ladder, so we dragged the box down to the gallery level of our house with the intention of storing it somewhere in the garage.

As I was cleaning up the kitchen the next morning, I heard banging and hammering and sawing and an occasional cuss word here and there and went down to your shop to see what was going on. It looked like you were assembling some kind of container or shelf. "Don, whatever is that?" I asked you and there was an expression of desperation on your face. "I'm making a shelf for that damn Christmas tree," you told me. You had moved both of the cars out to the driveway to give you room and you were assembling this shelf, or whatever it was, at the rear of the garage next to some inexpensive metal shelves. You had used pieces of wood and lumber that happened to be lying around your shop, under the house in the crawl space, or in the garage. There was heart redwood left over from the siding on our house, some old pieces of shelving the contractor used for the pantry shelves, and some plywood you used for covering up the back windows during snow season. In other words, if a piece of wood happened to be in your line of sight that morning, you probably used it. You also used nails, screws and fasteners of all sizes and shapes to hold the damn thing together. For most of the morning, you continued to hammer away.

I checked on your progress several times until you called for me to come and take a look. I had to cover my mouth to keep from laughing and said to you, "Hey, I know. Let's call it "Don's Tree House. " Not only would it house the Christmas tree, but it looked like some kind of tree house that a little kid and his father would have built in their big old oak tree in their backyard. You looked at me and said, "Well, we could call it *cattywampus*, but that's a mouthful."

The shelf did the job for which it was intended until ten years of gravity caused it to shift. One day we heard this horrible noise coming from the direction of the garage. We had been sitting in the living room reading the newspaper and having a last cup of coffee and immediately looked at each other and shouted at the same time, "Earthquake!" No, it couldn't be. Nothing else was rumbling in our house. We immediately thought that possibly a raccoon or worse yet, a bear, had entered our garage foraging for something to eat. We both took off running down the steps and into the garage. When we saw what actually happened, we both laughed so hard, we had tears running down our faces. "Don's Tree House" was a pile of lumber and nails and screws, and the cardboard box had broken apart and there was the Christmas tree—branches broken and spread in all directions on top of the mess.

We stood there looking at this pile of wood and artificial tree branches and laughed ourselves silly. You looked at me and said, "Honey, I think it's time for us to get a new tree next year. This one has literally just bitten the dust."

Weeks later the cabinet company came and installed the solid bank of built-in cabinets in our garage, all lined up in an even row until the very end where the cabinet was custom designed to house our new Christmas tree.

Chapter 73

January—Six-Month-Old Ham

B esides the books I've read on widowhood telling me the days
will get better, some of my friends who are widows also
say the same thing, "Diane, of course you will still have your
bad days, but for the most part, they do get better." The days
do seem less raw. Maybe not less raw, but the nerve endings are
not as close to the surface. They are correct. The days are getting
a tad better. It's also because of plowing ahead—trying to make
this new life for myself without you.

A few days after Sarah left, I looked into the freezer and
I saw this mound. I couldn't quite figure out what it was. Then
I remembered it was the ham. It was the spiral ham some of
my friends sent right after your death. I thought, well it's been
six months and you're not supposed to keep things in your
freezer past six months.

I emailed a few friends and invited them to come over for
dinner. They immediately asked if they could help and bring a
side dish. You and I liked to prepare most of the courses ourselves, usually based on an international theme. We would
have everything prepared beforehand. The kitchen would be
semi-cleaned and the food placed in the warming drawer by
the time our guests arrived. Without you, my "sous chef," to

help me, I decided to let my friends help out.

I looked in my recipe collection for dishes that would go well with ham. For an appetizer, I prepared Artichoke Dip. For side dishes, I prepared Corn Chive Pudding and Brandied Fruits. Penny Fink, a new friend I met at Stefanie Oliviari's house the weekend after your death, brought a delicious sauce to serve with the ham. Sandy and Tom Combs brought Green Beans with Water Chestnuts. Penny also brought loaves of home-made bread because she is the ultimate bread maker. Lisa and Debbie brought the dessert. Bob Fink is one of the best wine connoisseurs I know. He brought two bottles of wine, Pinot Blanc from the Alsace region in France produced by Meyer-Fonné and a Pinot Noir from Raptor Ridge in the Willamette Valley of Oregon. I served the six-month-old ham. It was fun entertaining in our dining room, again.

I have to admit it sure was easier on me, and with every-one pitching in to help it became *our* party, not just *my* dinner party. I think this is what I will try to do in the future, unless I decide to make a totally Hungarian dinner using some of my grandmother's and grandfather's favorite recipes. I've made these dishes—Chicken Paprikás, Spätzle, Székely Gulyás (Sauerkraut and Pork,) Stuffed Cabbage and Peppers, Creamed Cucumber Salad, and Palacsintas (Hungarian Rolled Crepes with Jam)—so many times in the past years, I can practically make them with my eyes shut. You loved all of my Hungarian dishes and used to say to me that you must have been part Hungarian.

The next day after the six-month-old ham dinner, I received thank you emails from all my friends who were there. It was the message from Penny and Bob Fink that made me smile.

"Good Friends, Good Food—Truckee Rocks."

Chapter 74

January–Sous Chef

As I was writing about the six-month-old ham, I was reminded of the times we spent cooking in the kitchen. This book about my special remembrances would not be complete if I didn't elaborate about my "sous chef"— you.

I recall one of the first meals you and I made as husband and wife. It was a Chinese dish, probably including some dried red peppers and other spices since we both preferred Hunan or Sichuan. We were still living in the apartment on Audubon. You came into the kitchen and asked if you could help. I said, "Sure, Honey, would you like to chop up the scallions?" When I looked at the small dish of scallions which you had just chopped, they were one inch in length. Oh dear, he's an engineer, my brain said to me. So the next time you asked, I replied, "Sure, Honey, would you like to chop up the scallions? I want them about ¼" in length and on the diagonal, and please separate the green section from the bottom white part." That worked!

Over the years, you learned how to make several dishes from each of the various courses: Appetizer, Salad, Dessert, whatever. Recipes that called for "scant" or "pinch" were enigmas to you. In our early days of cooking together, you would ask me, "Why don't they just tell the reader how much they want to use?" Later, of course, as you became more experienced, you didn't even have to measure at all.

I mentioned to one of our friends, who was sharing a meal with us, that you were the sous chef de cuisine. You immediately got out the dictionary to see what this meant. "Ah, second in command. That's me, for sure," you told us.

When we married, my collection of cookbooks included bound copies of Gourmet magazine from the years 1968 to 1974. We continued to subscribe to Gourmet, along with several other cooking magazines. You and I enjoyed looking through them searching for recipes to make together.

We had our favorite cookbooks. The one we particularly liked was, "Mamie & Ike." It is now worn with age and several of the pages are sticking together. I found this cookbook on sale at a major department store in Houston soon after we were married. It has been used a lot over the years and besides the sticky pages, the spine has lost its rigidity.

There are the "Black Books" that line one entire shelf in our kitchen nook bookcases, leather binders 5½" x 8" that are actually black. It started with one book when I lived in New York City. Now, there are ten of them, containing our favorite tried-and-true recipes. Another black binder contains actual menus we served at dinner parties. Many of these menu pages also include the labels from the wine bottles you soaked off and taped to the page.

In 1983 you met Pat Donahue who was selling a product to Shell Oil, something that had to do with the production of gasoline. You and Pat became immediate and best of friends. We went out to dinner with Pat and to various cultural events. You had gone skiing with him at Vail on what you called a "boondoggle." We decided to reciprocate and gave a dinner party for Pat and some of his business associates. We told him we would do the cooking if he would supply the wine. What a feast! The date was March 27, 1984.

~~~

Passed Hors D'oeuvres
Veal Meatballs with Caper Sauce

Shell Crab Mold (since you worked at Shell)

Brut Champagne—Veuve Clicquot Ponsardin

Appetizer at Table
Artichoke Tarts

Chardonnay—1981 St. Francis—Sonoma Valley

Entree
Chicken Breast in Phyllo

Accompanied by
Wild Rice and Apples in Brandy Sauce

Asparagus with Pecans

Puff Pastry Cheese Straws

Don's Caesar Salad

Chardonnay— 1981 Heitz Cellar—Napa Valley

Dessert
Strawberry Pavlova

Dessert Wine—1969 Sauternes—Château Suduirant

After Dinner
Espresso and Liquors

~~~

From that day forward your version of Caesar Salad would be part of our repertoire for our dinner parties. One Christmas I surprised you with the largest hand-turned wooden bowl, seven inches deep and thirteen inches across. I heard about a man who worked at Shell Oil. His hobby was making wooden bowls and other turned wooden items. I met with him on the sly in his woodworking shop and ordered the bowl. It's in a place of honor on one of the kitchen bookshelves. It was used only for your Caesar Salad and *never* washed with soap. However, from the first Caesar Salad you made, you were never satisfied with the consistency of the dressing and were always looking for the proper tool with which to smash the anchovies. You had tried using the back of a large wooden spoon and the bottom of a glass, but those techniques just didn't do the job.

In October of 1979, we took a vacation to Bermuda and had a stop-over in New York City. I had shared with you the story of how I had met Fred Bridge of the famous Bridge Kitchenware Store. Fred was notorious for his brusque manners. The rumor was that on more than one occasion a society woman had left his store in tears. His store was then located on Third Avenue between Thirty-third and Thirty-second Street. I met him when I moved into my own apartment on the corner of Park and Thirty-Fourth Street and had gone to his store to buy a set of pots and pans. "You don't buy a set of pots OR pans," he roared to me. "You buy a pot or a pan for a particular use." And, so I did! I continued to buy every kitchen item I needed from him. Even after I married and moved to Houston, I would call him up to order a particular something I needed, especially during the years from 1985 to 1987, when I freelanced as a food stylist in Houston. He would answer the phone and say, "Houston, how are you? What do you need today?" He never used my first name; he always referred to me as "Houston."

I knew I could never get you to go with me to Saks or Bergdorf's because you hated shopping, so I suggested we go to Fred Bridge Kitchenware. You could ask Fred for his suggestion as to what tool would smash the anchovies. I pleaded with you, "Look, Honey, try not to be the engineer and question him. Just buy what he suggests. If you don't like it, you don't have to use it. He doesn't like to be challenged." We arrived at his store and after I made the introductions, you started to describe how when you made a Caesar Salad you couldn't get the anchovies thoroughly smashed. Before you finished he interrupted you and yelled to his son who was located in a small office upstairs. "Ritchie, get the mushroom." The mushroom was just that—a large wooden mushroom-looking tool. Perfect! The large flat bottom was the perfect tool for you to use to smash the anchovies to smithereens. It also sits in the bottom of the salad bowl along with the yellowed, scotch-taped covered index card with your recipe.

~~~

DON'S CAESAR SALAD

(Serves 4)

Rub large wooden bowl with ¼ teaspoon salt
& 1 large garlic clove.

Add:

6 tablespoon best quality Virgin olive oil

2 tablespoon red wine vinegar

1 tablespoon fresh lemon juice

Blend well.

Add:

½ teaspoon Worcestershire sauce

3–5 dashes Tabasco

1 teaspoon dry mustard

1 teaspoon freshly ground pepper

4–6 anchovies (kind packed flat in oil in
    small can)

Mix well.

Add romaine & toss. (Wash the romaine early
    in day, spin dry and then lay in layers on
    paper towel. Roll in cylinder, refrigerate.)

Add:

1 whole egg yolk—coddled for 1 minute in
    boiling water.

Add:

3 tablespoon freshly grated top quality
    Parmesan cheese

1 to 2 cups homemade croutons, ½" in size.
    (Use baguettes—cut off crust, slice into ½"
    squares. Dry. Sauté in garlic butter.)

~~~

See even this, your favorite recipe calls for a dash of
Tabasco. You did master "pinch," "scant" and "dash." Not a
problem for the master sous chef!

My sister was always amazed when she would ask me during our phone calls, "Well, what did you two do last night?" Occasionally, I would tell her we had one of our dress-up dinners. To celebrate a special occasion we had spent hours cooking together; we would dress up—you sometimes in your tux or just your tuxedo jacket and a pair of jeans and me in a dressy outfit. We would set the dining room table, complete with the fine china, silver and candles. We would toast each other—chef and sous chef!

New Year's Eve 1987 – Dinner for Two

Chapter 75

January–White

$\sim$

White is everywhere. All I see is white. It is white outside my office windows where I spend hours writing this story. It is white down my front path. It is white down the driveway where the snow plow has piled the snow on both sides so high it looks like I am driving through a tunnel, and it is white up and down Greenleaf Way. The temperature has stayed so cold at nights, barely above the high teens, that it is still white on the trees.

This has been the worst January I can remember since we moved here in 1989. In fact, the weather channels report we have had four times the amount of snow this January 2008 than in many years past. Wave after wave of cold fronts coming in from the Pacific Northwest have pummeled our mountains with heavy snow. Ten consecutive days of snowfall has dumped more than eight feet of snow on Lake Tahoe with January totals topping fifteen feet. The Sierra snowpack was recently measured and it was well above average for this time of the year, actually 123 percent of normal. Truckee town folk could have spared the snow survey crew their trek into the high country. We all knew it was well above average after the second major snow dump. Don, since you are not here to do some of the snow management, I hired the handymen to help me. Last week they shoveled the roof outside the office so I could finally see out these windows. It was almost like being in an igloo, complete with the snow and icicles—the only things I could see when I looked out the windows.

Yesterday, I went to the bank. I was gone perhaps two hours. When I returned home, I hit the garage opener as I drove up our driveway through the tunnel of snow. I expected to see the garage door going up but it was coming down. I soon discovered why. When I left the house, I neglected to check if the door had come completely down, one thing you and I always tried to remember to do. It had not, and in the two hours I was gone, the snow was coming down at such a fast rate, there was close to a foot of snow inside the garage. Groan!

I'm remembering the game we used to play. You and I would write down on two pieces of paper the date we thought there would be no more snow on our property and place these in an envelope. In spring, we would take walks around the property looking for any remaining snow, and on the day when the snow was completely gone, we would retrieve the envelope to see which one of us had guessed correctly when the last of the snow had disappeared. We didn't bet anything. It was just another tradition we had.

My mind is a kaleidoscope of all our memories, colored ones and white ones. White is getting to be a bit much.

I am looking forward to green.

Chapter 76

February–February 10th

This day in Truckee was much like it was thirty-three years ago in New York City when I received the blind date telephone call from you on that Monday, February 10, 1975. Today was a brisk 44 degree. The sun was shining and the sky was the most beautiful shade of Tahoe Blue.

Earlier in the day, I sat in a patch of sunbeam coming in through the front sliding door writing and thinking and longing.

The snow is mostly gone from our forest of pines and firs. All the trees are now uplifting their branches with what seems to be an enchanted splendor. It was a beautiful picture, this forest of trees.

For the past seven months, I have been struggling and living in my own forest, of grief, not a forest of pines and firs. I am still wrestling to get through the trees to find my way out. I know this will come in time. Just when I think I have conquered this grief, an explosion of sadness comes over me. My heart feels as if a dam has given way. If it does explode, will it then release all of my grief and anger? I don't know. All I know is that the sadness from my missing you still lingers.

We would have made some celebration of this day. On a beautiful winter day such as today, we might have gone down to the Lake for a late brunch. It would have been too cold for you to meet your tennis buddies for your usual Sunday tennis match and definitely too cold for a ride on your Harley. I used to tease you when you took the bike out on a cold day for a quick ride and say, "Don, you better dress warmly today, you'll freeze your balls off." Yes, we had fun at bantering.

My new friends, Penny and Bob Fink, reached out to me. I drove to their home and we used the bone from the six-month-old ham and made split pea soup. It was one of your favorite soups. Several other friends had been invited, some you and I have known for years. We also made pizzas. Six balls of pizza dough, consisting of different kinds of grains were resting on a tray. Their kitchen even has a built-in wood burning bread/pizza oven, so as one pizza was baking, the rest of us were busy rolling out the next one and adding our special toppings. What an assembly line! Later, it was fun sitting around their warm kitchen enjoying the food we had just prepared and sampling the several wines that were offered.

I drove home and was greeted by our dogs. Today was February 10—how many moons ago was that phone call? *I am a strong woman,*" I say to myself as I am given an abundance of warm and sloppy kisses. I'm strong, but still lonely, not as lonely as other widows might be since I have these friends to help me cope with the special days. They help me to get through them and pass yet another milestone on my way to wherever. Perhaps the forest, which surrounded my heart after you died, is slowly starting to recede.

Chapter 77

February–Westminster

Cell phones were not as common in 1996 as they are today. Bev and I stood waiting for our turn at one of the pay phones in the hallway just outside the main show arena at Madison Square Garden.

I could barely punch the number buttons. I was still so nervous with excitement. The phone rang and rang and I was beginning to give up hope of reaching you. I thought, "Oh Don, please, please answer. Where are you? In one of the most important moments of my life, how could you not be home?"

Then you answered.

I don't think I even said "Hello" or asked how you were. I was on such an adrenaline high. "Oh, my God, Don, we won. We won. Spirit and I won the longhaired variety at Westminster just minutes ago." "Yeah, right, Diane," you replied with mockery in your voice.

I tried again to get you to believe me. "Don, really. It's true. You have to believe me. Spirit and I won." After the third attempt of trying to convince you, Bev grabbed the phone away from me and said with an authoritative voice, "Don, this is Beverly. Now sit down and listen. They DID win and *you* get

to see Spirit and Diane in the group ring tonight on television."
She handed the phone back to me.

When you heard my voice, you became overwrought and
almost started to cry into the phone. I could hear how emotional your voice was and I know you thought that this win
was almost beyond belief. After I gave a blow-by-blow description of what happened from the early morning hours when
Bev and I were grooming Spirit to posing with him for his winning photograph, I started to rattle off the names of friends I
wanted you to call for me and asked you to be sure to tape it.
"And, Honey, make sure there's a blank tape in the VCR. Past
track record and all of that, you know."

Spirit BOV   Westminster – February 1996 • *(Photo by Ashbey Photography)*

Bev and I had made the trip to New York City that February of 1996 with Spirit. He was four and a half years old and in his prime, but had "blown his coat," a term doggie people say when the dog isn't in his usual full and lush coat. Earlier that morning, we had washed Spirit and dried him with a hand held hair dryer trying to make his hair puff out. We even used a special mousse for dogs on his pantaloons and chest hairs in an attempt to make the hairs look fuller. "Bev, I'm going to pull him," I said to my sister. "He looks so naked." "No you're not," she shot back at me. "We haven't come all this way and spent all this money for you to not show him. I'm sure lots of dogs aren't in their best coat." I acquiesced to her, mainly because I didn't believe a longhaired dachshund had to be dripping in coat. The Breed Standard said longhaired dachshunds that have a profuse coat aren't desirable as it masks their type. The coat should give the dog an elegant appearance and Spirit was elegant. Every purebred dog breed has a Breed Standard that is written by the specific breed's national club. It gives a word picture of what the breed type for that particular breed should be in appearance, movement and temperament. It is a set of guidelines, and conformation judges judge the dogs in their ring against this Breed Standard. Details and definitions within breed standards for a specific dog breed vary for each purebred dog. Judges interpret these qualities and usually have their own personal tastes which play in the final selection.

When we finished grooming Spirit, Bev and I gathered up our supplies, put him in his kennel and wheeled him over to Madison Square Garden. Once there, we headed for the ring. What a madhouse trying to get through the hundreds of dog lovers who were already sitting and standing around the dachshund ring. I got my arm band from the ring steward and waited until we were called into the ring, trying to stay calm so my nervousness wouldn't run down the lead and upset Spirit. Spirit and I were toward the front of the lineup. The dogs went around the ring together, and then one by one they were examined on the table by the judge. Down and back and then around all the dogs went. The judge had Spirit move against practically every other dog in the ring. The more times Spirit went around the ring, the better he got. His adrenaline had kicked in. He was a show dog and he loved it! The more the crowd applauded, the more animated he became. All of the handlers and their dogs, twenty of the top longhaired dachshunds in the country, kneeled on the floor with our dogs stacked in front of us, as the judge walked up and down the line observing each one. The judge wanted to view the dogs in a perfect stacked position, and Spirit was such a chowhound, always looking for the bait. The judge went to the end of the line first and then started to walk back to where Spirit was. I was concentrating on Spirit, hoping he would keep his pose. Then I looked up and saw the judge's very long legs were directly in front of us. As he stood there, his finger pointed down towards Spirit and me, and he said, "And, you—YOU—are my Best of Variety." When I told you in our phone call that morning this was the most incredible moment of my life, you asked, "And, darling, what about August 23, 1975?" "Of course," I answered, "that was the most incredible *day*, but this *moment* is what a breeder, owner and handler of a dog lives for." You knew!

An amusing incident happened soon after I walked out of the ring. Bev was standing by my side and I was holding Spirit when a Japanese man approached me. He bowed and then began to tell us he had been commissioned by his client, who lived in Japan, to purchase the winning longhaired dachshund. He offered me $50,000. I laughed and said, "I am honored, but my dog is not for sale. He's not only my show dog, he's also my pet." The man bowed again and repeated his offer. Bev looked at me and shrugged as if to say, "Now what?" I gave a perfunctory bow to the man and said, "Not only is he my show dog and my pet, but he sleeps with me and my husband." Again, the gentleman bowed and repeated his offer, this time with much more emphasis on the amount of money he was prepared to offer. So, now what do I say to him? I bowed again and said in a more determined voice, "No, he is not for sale, not for any amount of money. Not only is he my show dog and my pet, and he sleeps with my husband and me, but—when he kisses me on the face, I don't wipe his kiss off." The man just stood there in bewilderment and then bowed one final time and turned and walked away in a defeated manner. When I got home and told you the story, you said, "Diane, what, you turned down his offer? I can't believe you?" For a quick moment I thought you were serious, but then I saw the slow grin start to form on your face and your dimples were a dead give-away. Of course, we both agreed no amount of money could buy our beloved Spirit.

You had saved all the messages of congratulations that were on the answering machine. You were proud of us and of our win.

That night when we toasted to each other and to Spirit with our glasses of Korbel champagne, you pulled me towards you, gave me a warm and tender hug and whispered in my ear, "Honey, when I saw you and Spirit on TV, I had tears in my eyes watching you both go around the ring. You looked fabulous and Spirit was so full of himself. I really am so proud of both of you and *that* was the most incredible moment of my life also."

Chapter 78

February–Hearts

You and I believed that holidays should not be celebrated just because they were promoted by card companies and florists. Valentine's Day was the exception; we always celebrated Valentine's Day, but in our own special way. We always gave each other a Valentine's Day card and would either go to a lovely restaurant for a special dinner or prepare one at home. On this Valentine's Day, some eight months after your death, I was recalling past Valentine's Days that were more memorable than others.

I remembered one special Valentine's Day; it involved our dachshund, Mystic. In March of 1986 I had flown to Florida to pick up our puppy from her breeder. For the next several months I showed Mystic at puppy matches and when I thought she had matured enough, I entered her in some AKC dog shows. I completed the Championship on "Rinac's Mystic Wonderous Star" on October 9, 1988. We knew we wanted to breed her and I had spent hours and hours researching pedigrees for a possible stud dog to use.

Four months earlier we started construction of our house in California. We soon found that the building of the house long distance proved to be more of a challenge than we had anticipated. Each change necessitated daily phone calls between the architect, builder and us. Each of these changes resulted in revisions to the blue prints which then had to be faxed to us. We tried to go to Truckee every few months to oversee the project; sometimes you would go alone, and sometimes we would go together.

The Dachshund Club of America's National was being held in Sacramento at the end of October 1988, two weeks after Mystic became a Champion, so we decided I would attend. While there, I would check out possible stud dogs for Mystic. After the show I would take the bus to Truckee to check on the progress of the house and then fly home from Reno.

While at the National, I spotted this magnificent flash of red go by. I asked a friend if she knew anything about the dog. She told me that it was Barbara Power's new "special"—CH Bermarg's Shoney of Boondox L. Shoney has just finished his Championship weeks before. He was only fifteen months old, and I had never seen such a gorgeous, flashy and correct long-haired dachshund. I approached Barbara and we agreed to the breeding of Shoney to Mystic. There was no contract, just a handshake. When I asked Barbara how much the stud fee would be, she told me, "He's a young dog and has not been used for stud. We decided on an amount. I'll send you a contract after the first breeding."

The next two years were filled with numerous setbacks. Contracts for the sale of our Houston house fell through and we didn't want to expose a litter of puppies to people coming in and out of the house. The house finally sold and we arrived at our Truckee house on Greenleaf Way to discover that the builder had not been truthful with us. The house was far from ready for us to move in. The hardwood flooring hadn't even been installed. The movers arrived the next day and put the furniture in the garage. We rented a small house across the street for a couple of months. We finally moved into our home and bred Mystic to Shoney on her next heat cycle, but no babies. By then Barbara Powers and her partner, Eva, had become good friends of ours, and we tried a second breeding. It had been two long years filled with heartbreaks. On a cold and snowy day, I drove to my vet to have an ultrasound. It was in February, a few days before Valentine's Day. The ultrasound showed there were no babies. I was devastated! All I could think was, "My God, two years of trying and trips down and back to Pasadena where Barbara lived, now what?" I drove home from the vet's office in tears the entire way. As I came into the house the look on my face and the dried up tears on my cheeks told you the unhappy news. You gathered me in your arms, then we both cried. After all, Mystic was a part of our family, and we both were looking forward to having a litter of longhaired dachshunds with the possibility of keeping one. You pulled away from our embrace and went to the hall closet. I wondered what you were up to. As you gave me this enormous box, you said, "Honey, this was supposed to be your Valentine's Day gift, but I think you need it now." It was the most luxurious long brown leather coat. We had tickets to attend the Kenny Roger's concert in Reno that night, and I wore my new coat. We agreed we would repeat the breeding if Barbara would agree. We were determined to have Mystic and Shoney babies. The third breeding was "the charm." The puppies were born on July 26, 1991. We kept the one and only boy—Spirit.

Another Valentine's Day I remember was more humorous, at least you thought so. We were still living in Houston and were very good friends with another couple; the husband also worked at Shell Oil Company with you. His wife and I had become friends and we decided it would be fun for the wives to plan a "blind date" for our husbands. My girlfriend and I made all the arrangements. All we told you was it would be a dressy occasion. Our friends picked us up and our first stop was at one of the fanciest restaurants in Houston. It was located on a main street going into downtown Houston and had only been open for several weeks. The reviews in the newspapers had been fabulous. Neither of us had been there and we were looking forward to this occasion. The restaurant's menu was from the Tuscany region in Italy. As we entered the main part of the restaurant, we were charmed with the décor. The walls were painted a very muted and pale yellow with frescoes as the focal point in the center of each wall. The floor was a white marble, cracked every so often to make it look old. There were festoons of greens and vines wrapped around old looking columns and in the center of the room was a gurgling fountain. The lighting was subdued with many flickering candles set at each table. My girlfriend and I smiled at each other because the entire room looked magical and we were happy we had chosen this restaurant for our Valentine's dinner. After we were settled into our chairs, the waiter came to our table for the drink order. Everything was moving along as planned. You and her husband had these big grins on your faces. But then the waiter returned and started to tell us what the specials of the evening were. The first entrée he described was some kind of dish that included rabbit. "I don't do bunny," I said as I explained that I used to have a pet rabbit and couldn't possibly think of eating "bunny." The waiter didn't skip a beat and proceeded to talk about the second special. It was a venison dish. My girlfriend quickly said, "I don't do Bambi." You looked up at the waiter and said, "No bunny—no bambi. What else?" Well, the laughter that followed after the waiter left our table carried us through to the end of dinner.

After dinner, the plan was to attend Mozart's "The Magic Flute." But, since I had purchased the tickets only days before, all the good seats were sold out. The opera was held at Jones Hall. As we climbed higher and higher to our seats, which happened to be the very last row, I heard you say to my friend's husband, not in a quiet voice, "I think I'm getting a nose bleed from the altitude." I was mortified. "Don, shhh," I said, "Keep your voice down. Someone will hear you." We passed two other couples who heard your comment and the men broke out laughing. Probably their wives dragged them to the opera, too. It was certainly a Valentine's Day we remembered.

I smiled to myself as I thought about those events on this, my first Valentine's Day without you. Somehow remembering you and your caring about Mystic as we tried to breed her, your wonderful sense of humor when I dragged you to the opera—these are the special memories have helped get me through this Valentine's Day.

Chapter 79

March–Spring

It's the beginning of spring. It's March 20th, the vernal equinox. At least the calendar, the spiral-bound Lake Tahoe calendar we bought at the beginning of each year, says it is spring, but the sky is gray and cloudy with a nip in the air. I still can't see any ground because there is about four feet of snow after a late February snow storm. I know I am on the downhill side of winter and feel jubilant with that prospect.

My summer of anguish and my winter of fears have now rolled into a spring of expectation. I had almost settled into an existence of some kind of strange acceptance or denial or both. But, spring is the season of re-birth. Spring was your favorite season. It meant tennis, rides on your Harley, and perhaps some fly fishing were within sight.

Now, it means I have made it through what the weather reporters say has been our worst winter in over twenty-five years; it means I have survived it alone. I told my friends if I survived *this* winter, I know I'll be okay in future years.

The blue jays have returned, a sure sign of spring; actually they are the Western Scrub-Jay. I saw some old yarn that had dropped onto the side deck. It was the wool yarn I had put out for them last spring. Then I saw one of the jays in flight with a small twig in his mouth.

Last year you constructed a square of wire mesh, about six inches by six inches, as a form of support so the jay's nest would not break apart and tumble to the ground below. You mounted it up high on the side deck, in the same area where the previous nest had been built by the jays, under the roof overhang so it would be protected. We watched the jays constructing their nest of twigs and roots and the wool yarn on top of the piece of wire mesh.

We would both eagerly watch for any signs of life and then one miraculous day we would witness it. The papa blue jay would come zooming in with a grub or other small insect for the mama blue jay, who in turn would feed it to one of the skinny heads that was bobbing up.

"Don's blue jays;" that's how you and I referred to them whenever one of us would talk about them to our friends. We actually took pride of ownership over "our blue jays."

For many days, we watched these baby jays develop and grow with the same regularity and dedication as if we were watching one of our favorite TV shows. We didn't miss a day. At times it was a frightening experience. We would be watching them and one of the babies would perch himself high up in the nest and start to flap his wings. "Diane, quick, come look," you would call to me, "I think they are ready to fly the coop."

In early June, some seventeen or eighteen days after mama had laid her eggs, we saw the first baby jay fly away. He didn't go far, only to a pine about ten feet away. There he was, holding onto the branch of the tree with his tiny legs trying out his wings—ready for the world.

In years past, we could tell which jays were "our" babies. We talked to them when they were still in the nest. As I would come into the kitchen, I would hear you cooing through the screen door, "Now, don't go falling out of the nest. You'll be Coyote Breakfast, if you do." As the baby jays left and went out into the world on their own, we could tell which ones had been born that year. Over the next weeks, we could see their feathers getting longer and longer and their little bodies starting to fill out.

The blue jays even tolerated the dogs and didn't seem to mind their barking at the squirrels that scampered up and down the trees and over the pine needles on the side lot. They took it in stride.

Now on this early spring day, a year later, they have returned and are in the process of looking for twigs, yarn and other items for their new home.

Maybe, so am I.

Chapter 80

March—The Home in Old Southwest Reno

It was the end of March, and I was in the shadows of my winter grief when I drove to Reno, Nevada, only 35 minutes east of Truckee, for my annual mammogram. A new machine, digital, was used. It detected a shadow. Another mammogram was scheduled. And after that, I had scheduled an appointment with the x-ray technician and then my regular gynecologist. She suggested I could have either a needle biopsy performed or surgery. As we sat in my gynecologist's office and discussed the options, she kept saying the surgery would be performed by the best surgeon in town. Then she said, "She is the best." Shortly after, my gynecologist said her first name. My mind started to do cartwheels. How many woman surgeons could there be in Reno who have an unusual first name? My doctor must have read the expression on my face and asked if there was a problem. I told her this woman was the surgeon on call who had admitted you the morning you were airlifted to the hospital in Reno. "I can recommend another surgeon," she said. "No, I want her," I answered.

A couple of days later, I sat in the surgeon's office, me on a sofa and her on a chair just a few feet away from me. I could tell she was trying to place my face and finally she said, "I know you from somewhere but can't remember where." I told her the story of the night and morning of June 23. She placed her hands on my knees and said, "Oh, my dear. I can arrange for another surgeon to do the procedure." "No," I told her, "You just showed me your compassion by placing your hands on my knees. I don't need another surgeon."

As I drove back home to Truckee, questions started to go around in my mind. My friends were scattered, some worked, who would be able to drive me to Reno for the procedure and wait for me to drive me home? *"Another obstacle of living in Truckee,"* I thought to myself. Plans were made for the surgery, and my Truckee friends came through for me, but the thread kept going through my mind that my life in Truckee was becoming more of a hardship.

After the procedure I met my girlfriend Lory for lunch. She suggested a wonderful, small and yummy Austrian restaurant where they made tasty goulash. I was driving west on a beautiful tree-lined street in the old section toward the address of the restaurant when I spotted the sign, "House for Sale by Owner." It was a house I had known for years in an area of Reno I loved to drive. You and I made weekly trips to Reno for one reason or another; and I would say to you, "Honey, drive through Old Southwest, I just love that area of Reno." Now, here was this house for sale.

I arranged to see the house. The first time I went through the house, I knew it was meant for me. The house was filled with charm. Our home in Montrose was built in 1905, and this house was built in 1917. I love old homes. I walked through the foyer into the living room to the back patio that was more like a "Secret Garden." I was filled with a sense of peace and serenity. When I turned to take one more look at the back patio—I saw it. The antique sun face was hanging amongst the 80 year old wisteria. An omen!

Later that evening I called my daughter-in-law, Joan, and I started to tell her about this house. I have great love for Joan, as you did, and I felt her connecting with me. When I finished telling her about this house, she quietly said to me, "Diane, a house will talk to you when you walk into it." And I told her, "Yes, I could feel that also and perhaps this is what I am supposed to do."

I have stopped asking why. I am in the process of healing myself, and I think I have reached a plateau from which I can start to feel certain equilibrium. Whatever happens now will be in my hands, or in the hands of faith. I cannot be kept down. Life goes on and it continues to be renewed. I kept hoping for calm in my life. Maybe now, I have found it in this wonderful old house in this old neighborhood.

I am a survivor. I am alive.

Chapter 81

April–The Ring

Last year Good Friday was April 6. I ran down the stairs looking for you. You were at the kitchen sink, cleaning up the dishes from breakfast. You turned around and looked up at me when I entered the kitchen.

"Do you believe in miracles?" I had tears in my eyes as I asked you this. You dropped the sponge, rushed over to me and put your arms around me. "You found my ring," you said. "You found it. Didn't you." "Yes," I said and handed you the ring.

You lost the ring the previous September as you raked up the pine needles that had accumulated on our property. This was part of your preparations for winter. Once you had the pine needles raked into piles, you would bag them in heavy black plastic, forty gallon leaf bags. You had filled more than twenty bags when you came inside for lunch. You went over to the sink to wash your hands and it was then that you realized your wedding ring was not on your ring finger. "Oh my God, Diane," you cried out to me. "The ring—your grandfather's ring. It's not on my finger. Oh my God, where did I lose it?"

We hoped you might have lost the ring inside the pair of work gloves you had been wearing. You walked over to where you had left the rake and your pair of gloves—no ring.

Both of us went over to where the bags of pine needles were stacked. We took handfuls of pine needles from a filled bag and put them into a clean plastic bag as we looked for anything that looked shiny and gold. Bag after bag, we repeated this as we searched and searched. It took us over two hours—no ring.

A few days later I drove to Reno and borrowed a metal detector machine from a friend's husband who was a contractor. It was a heavy-duty machine and very hard and cumbersome to handle. You carried the machine down to the side deck of our house, where you had taken down the hanging flower planter boxes. Back and forth you went, over an area that was eight feet wide and more than thirty feet in length. All you picked up were more than a hundred carpenter nails that had been used to attach the redwood siding to our house when it was built—no ring.

The next spring, as the snow began to melt from the edges of our driveway, I poked among the plants that were starting to appear—no ring.

Our housekeeper was at our house the day before Good Friday. She could never clean the entire house in the four hours she was there. I asked her to leave the central vacuum in the office and I would clean that room the next day. As I approached the computer corner desk with the vacuum hose, I had to move out a wire file crate from underneath. It was on four tiny wheels where dog hair had accumulated. In the mass of hair, I saw an object that looked like a round, thin wire. I thought, "I better not suck this up with the hose. If it gets stuck, Don will be mad at me." So, I bent down and reached through the pile of dog hair for the object.

It was your ring. It was the wedding band I placed on your ring finger on August 23, 1975.

I cleaned the dog hair from the band and with tears in my eyes ran down the stairs into the kitchen.

On Good Friday, eleven weeks before you died, a miracle happened.

Chapter 82

April–My Stages of Grief

Perhaps Spirit's death on April 18, 2005, helped prepare me for the grief over losing you. During a routine blood test, there was an increase in some of the values which signified kidney disease; a disease he battled courageously for two years. After he died, I wrote a story about him, "Spirit—A Tribute to a Legend." It was published in one of the hardbound dog books. The picture of him on the cover was painted by Maggie Graham.

Spirit was the "Dog of a Lifetime" to me. He was born on July 26, 1991. My friend Lory helped whelp the litter. She handed him to me so I could cut his cord and I rubbed him dry with a washcloth. It was love at first sight!

Spirit's first show was in March of 1992, when he was only six months old. I hung up his show lead in 1997. He was one the top five longhair dachshunds in the country for 1995, 1996 and 1997   and always handled by me. We were a team and he loved to show.

Spirit's image is all over our house. A photograph of him taken at the field trials in Vacaville, California, is the "wallpaper" on our computer and various shots of him are used as a screensaver slide show.

After Spirit's death I grieved for months, perhaps until the day you died. Then my focus was grieving for you. Photos of you are now added to the screensaver slide show and the fabulous shot of you taken at the dedication of the Truckee bypass in 2003 is tacked on the wall behind the computer.

Writing Spirit's story was a form of therapy for me. Now, writing about you and reliving all of these memories, I know in my heart of hearts it has been a help. It has been my catharsis. Even though many of my hand-written pages are splashed with tears, I was brought closer to you as I typed these notes into the computer.

Grief is a gradual process. I keep saying I am taking two steps forward and one step back. The process of grief, of bereavement, needs to be worked through. It's a series of small steps and it's not always predictable because the tears can appear at any moment. Any small thing can trigger them.

Others much more learned than I, have written about the stages of grief. Actually they list them and they are much the same in several books that I have read about widows and grieving.

Shock
Numbness
Bargaining
Pain
Depression
Anger
Resentment
Self-pity
Denial
Acceptance

I believe I have been through all of these stages, except for the last stage, acceptance. It is still so hard for me to accept that you are gone. I remember reading, "Grief is like a circular staircase." However, I see grief as a revolving door. I ask myself, *"Can I accept the reality of your death while I am living my life?"* I guess that's the real question. I know I have to if I am to have a life.

Tears still fill my eyes from time to time as a thought of you comes crashing into my everyday life. These moments have become less and less or perhaps it is because I am better able to control them. I really want to fast forward through this stage, acceptance, but I know I have to go through it in its own time.

It is a stage of my grief for you.

Chapter 83

April–The First Time Ever

What memories this day stirred. They came to the surface of my conscious mind from the minute this day began. I saw the rays of the morning sun making reflections on the pendant which hung around my neck—the solid gold pendant that I have worn these past ten months.

Ten months ago I said to you, "Don, can you believe it was thirty-two years ago we met face-to-face?" You answered, "Sometimes it seems like it was only yesterday and other times it seems a lifetime ago we met."

How do I remember these past ten months—like a *yesterday ago* or a *lifetime ago*?

This was not the original pendant I gave to you. That pendant was made of sterling silver. I wanted to give you a "happy" to celebrate our one-year anniversary of our meeting face-to-face for the very first time. I had a local jeweler in Houston make a free form pendant. On one side was engraved, *"THE FIRST TIME EVER,"* and on the reverse side was, *"APRIL 23."* You wore this around your neck, tucked inside your shirt, every day until the weekend we visited friends who had a cabin on Lake Conroe. You dove off the pier into the water. When you swam to the surface of the water and climbed back onto the pier, you realized the pendant was gone. The water was much too murky, too deep and after many diving attempts to find it, you had to give up.

I went through my collection of old gold pieces I had saved and had another pendant made for you, same wording, and same free form. I used to tease you that you had intentionally lost the sterling silver pendant because your taste had changed to gold in the short time we had been married. This pendant remained around your neck until ten months ago. As I sat by your side in the hospital, the attending critical care nurse handed me a small square box. It was made out of yellow plastic and was about one inch in diameter and about three inches long. In it was the pendent on its broken chain. I don't know when the chain broke. Perhaps, as the medics were moving you from the floor onto the gurney or perhaps when you arrived at the hospital and they removed your t-shirt to place you in a hospital gown. At least the pendant wasn't lost.

I took it to a local jeweler, the same one who resized your wedding ring smaller just weeks before. He knew how anxious I was for it and had the chain soldered back together by the following day. "No charge," he said to me as he handed it back to me with tears in his eyes.

Now the pendant hangs around my neck.

Chapter 84

April–Sometimes

Sometimes in the middle of the night when all I hear is the breathing of my two dogs lying next to me, I can remember your breathing, the soft noise you made after I would gently nudge you to turn over on your side if you had been snoring.

Sometimes in the middle of the night, when all is silent and still around me, I can almost feel your gentle touch on my shoulder, your way of reminding me of your love for me.

Sometimes in the middle of the night, in this same stillness and quiet, I wake myself up with a soft sob.

At these times of quiet desperation to remember you, sometimes I reach for the pillow that was yours; the pillow that still has a faint scent of you. I pull it to my face and bury my face into it, as I used to bury my face into your neck falling asleep.

How does one really heal a heart that has been broken? Two hearts broken, yours and mine. A piece of jewelry is designed as two broken hearts. One person wears one part of the heart; the other person wears the other part. If both pieces were put together, they would interlock to become one heart.

The experts all say it will get better; it is, day by day. Not great, not perfect, but better day by day, sometimes.

Life is made up of moments or a string of connected dots that can change your life forever. This is not "sometimes;" this is for sure.

Now, as I write down these words about us, all of these memories are conjured up by my remembering even the mundane events of our life from these past months without you.

I remember you, my darling. I bring your face to my memory. I remember the intimacy we had. "Spoons," I would whisper in your ear as I curled my knees in the well made by your bent legs as we fell asleep.

As I bring your face to my memory, I search for these words which I scribbled on a piece of paper months ago. I can't remember if I copied them from something I had read or if they were my original words.

~~~

Will you come to me in the night as I'm lying all alone?

Will you gently touch my shoulder as I turn on my side and

stare into your moonlit eyes?

Will you come to me in the night as you did on those

eleven thousand and six hundred and twenty nights?

What I would give for just one of those nights.

Sometimes

~~~

Not alone, I can go on, but with your image engrained in my memory for some time.

Chapter 85

April–Tennis

As I was driving down Northwoods Boulevard to run some errands in Truckee, I noticed the tennis courts at Tahoe/Donner were finally open after a long winter. A few weeks ago, I gave your tennis rackets to your old tennis partner, Andrea Otto. She was so pleased.

You had high hopes I would be able to be your tennis partner, but it wasn't meant to be. I played some tennis while attending college and when I lived in New York City. You played at the River Oaks Tennis Club when we lived in Houston before it was closed. You had various partners, but I think your favorite partner was your friend Tom Rushing.

After you and I were married, I decided to take some lessons because we both thought it would be a fun activity to do together. I went out and purchased one of those cute tennis outfits, a pair of those lace-trimmed pants and a pair of white tennis shoes with good arch supports—not the sneakers I wore in New York City. How in the world could any sane person play tennis outside in hot-as-Hades Houston at any hour of the day. I was on the court for only ten minutes, dripping wet and ready to call it quits. Serving wasn't my expertise. The end of my tennis playing days in Houston came quickly!

When we moved to Truckee, you encouraged me to pick up my racket and give it one more try. "Oh, come on, Honey, it's not as hot and humid as Houston and I'll be easy on you. I promise I won't smash any balls into you. And, you won't have to serve. Just hit the ball underhand to get it in play." "Okay, I'll give it a try," I said. Besides the courts at Tahoe/ Donner were beautiful with wonderful ambiance and the majestic mountains in the background. Why not?

The tennis outfit still fit, as well as the frilly pants, and I found my old tennis shoes. You made reservations for a court and promised we would just hit the ball over the net back and forth, nothing too strenuous. The only court available for the time we wanted was Court One, the court everyone walked past and the court most in view of spectators sitting up on the deck.

It was a beautiful day as I recall, another Tahoe Blue day and the temperature was in the low 70's—perfect. You were very gentle, returning the balls to me almost directly in front of me so I wouldn't have to run much.

After about twenty minutes of play, I looked down and noticed these tiny specks of white. They were all over the court in front of where I had been standing as I hit the ball back to you. I called you over to take a look, and you just started to howl. My old tennis shoes had literally disintegrated—all over the court. "Oh my God, Don," I said. "Quick, get a broom or something."

I was so embarrassed and you handled the entire situation with such aplomb as you swept up the bits and pieces, trying so hard not to laugh. "Nah, this isn't my game," I said to you. "I think I'll stick to dogs."

Chapter 86

May–The Stent

One year ago today you had the cardiac stent placed in. How could that be? How could that have only been one year ago? I keep asking myself *that* question as I go through this day.

Where is my life at this moment, this day, this May 3 without you? I ask the question, but receive no answer.

I am still going through closets. I am selling things on Craig's List and trying to downsize in case, in case I get this house, this house I so desperately want. Yes, this house I *need* to have.

"Don, Don, Don"—I keep asking you, "Be there for me, honey. Be there and look down on me and help me move on because it is so lonely without you. Tell me if I am doing the right thing. It's going to be a drastic move. I am terrified just thinking of all the complications that I might be facing. So please come to me in some thought and tell me I am doing the right thing."

Life is so fragile, as I have learned. I've thought that so many times these past months without you, especially today, May 3. A year ago today, who would have dreamt my life would be so different on May 3rd of the following year? It's May 3, 2008, I wonder where my next May 3 will find me?

One of the national television channels recently had a special feature on what is the best way to proceed if you have been diagnosed with heart disease. Is it better to have a stent placed or is it better to have open-heart surgery? I remember the surgeon's comment to me when I asked him how many of these procedures had he performed. "Yeah, I'm the best," he said to me.

I sometimes wonder why, this surgeon who studied "indifference" in medical school, pushed for the stent instead of open-heart surgery. Who knows?

I wish I had suggested to you, "Honey, let's load up the dogs in the car and drive down to Phoenix. We can stay in Polly's guest house and have the Mayo Clinic give you a thorough exam."

If we had gone, they might have discovered what was really wrong with your heart. *If*—but as you sometimes would say to me, "Diane, *if* a cow had wings, it would fly. Or, was it a pig—*If* a pig had wings, it would fly." Who knows? *IF*?

The stent—yes, it all started with the stent.

Chapter 87

May–Did You Know?

Did you know you were dying? Did you know your days on this earth were numbered?

It was soon after the stent was put in I started to feel anger coming from you and directed towards me. I couldn't do anything right. You seemed to criticize me for everything and anything. I took it in stride because I knew you had just come through a life-altering experience. You must have been scared, frightened of what was ahead of you; but, it did start to wear me down.

I remember one night when I couldn't take it any longer, and I thought, "I'll give you some space. I'll just pack up what I need and take the motor home and leave for a while." I was so tired of the senseless and needless bickering between us that I just wanted to escape for a few days, for a week, for a month. In time, I thought, the anger would be behind us. We would get back to our life; the life we knew before the stent, before the scare of what was going to happen to you next, to us.

I would ask myself in the quiet of the moment, "Don, don't you know you are my world, how can you berate me like this?" I knew it wasn't the real you.

I was reminded of the times when I was living my single life in New York and would go to visit my folks in Florida. On the very last day of my visit I would pick some senseless argument with my parents. A psychologist friend of mine explained to me this behavior was my inner defense because I really didn't want to leave them. My parents were my strength, my safety net, my cocoon, and I would be returning to the insecurity of my single life in New York. So, was this your inner defense? Did you know you were going to die? Could that have been the reason you were angry at me after the stent was put in?

Should I have picked up on this? Should I have suspected you felt something was not quite right?

The week after the stent procedure I took my Jeep into Reno for servicing. While I waited, I looked at some of the new cars. Earlier that day while we were having breakfast, I said, "Honey, I really need a new car. My Jeep had over eighty thousand miles on it." You replied, "No, Diane, you don't need a new car, you want a new car." When the repairs were finished, the salesman gave me a print-out showing the service I would have to do to my Jeep in the next few months. The list included a new set of tires, replacing the differential and other minor repairs. The bottom line showed it would cost close to eight thousand dollars. The blue-book price as a trade-in on my Jeep was around the same dollar amount. When I returned home, I showed you the print-out of needed repairs and the trade-in price of my Jeep. You looked at me and said, "Guess you need a new car." You started reviewing the write-ups of new cars in Consumer Reports and suggested I should test-drive a particular brand the next time I was going to Reno. This brand of car was a couple thousand dollars more than a new Jeep. When I asked you why you were insisting on it, you said to me, "Diane, I want you to have a car with the best warranty and best service record. You never know." During the family memorial, when I told Joan, my daughter-in-law, how you insisted on this particular car, she said to me, "Diane, I bet Don knew he was going to die."

The week before you died, you even took down the Christmas lights that were around the house. I had been out doing errands and when I came home, I found you high up on the ladder. I asked you why you didn't wait so I could hold the ladder for you. We had always put up the lights together and taken them down together because it was a tedious task of stringing out the lights. You simply replied, "They have to come down."

Then that last week of your life it seemed that all the planets were aligned; everything was going so right for us. We were back on track, no more bickering and no more arguments. We had fun together. You laughed. You smiled. You told me jokes you had heard at one of the meetings you attended that week. We laughed together as we experimented cooking our low-fat dinners. We played games before dinner. In the evening, you sat and hugged the dogs while we watched some of our favorite television shows. You hugged me. We sat outside and watched stars. You teased me about some trivial thing, and your lascivious smile returned to your face. We shared tender moments together. You even wanted to have our friends over for dinner on Friday night since the weather had turned spectacular and we loved sitting out on our front deck.

Yeah, I love my home....I love my life...WHAM!

Chapter 88

May–Truckee Here We Come

There is a small blue and white sign on the side of the interstate about three miles driving west on I-80, after leaving Reno, that says, "Welcome to California."

I remember the day in May 1989 when we first saw the sign, May 6 to be exact. We were moving from our Victorian home in Houston where we had lived and loved for fourteen years to a brand new mountain-style home in Truckee.

We were so excited as we crossed into California heading for Truckee. The historically rich mountain town of Truckee, named after a Paiute chief, was our destination. In our car were some of our most fragile, prized possessions we didn't entrust to the moving company. Mystic, our other prized possession, was sleeping in her kennel and oblivious to everything.

Many of my friends asked me, "Why Truckee?" I told them about your decision to take early retirement from Shell Oil Company. It started when we visited our good friends, the Dygerts, who had moved from Houston to Truckee in 1985. We visited them many times, either to ski or backpack, and we fell in love with Truckee. We loved the small-town atmosphere, the mountains, the gorgeous scenery and you loved the year-round sports. Besides, I told them, you were ten years older than I. If retiring to an area that would keep you healthier longer, well, I was all for that. Some of my friends couldn't quite understand how I could take the jump from the sophistication, glamour and excitement of New York City to Houston, a laid-back city with an almost cow-town atmosphere, and then move to small quaint Truckee, which they only knew for its annual snowfall amounts, not measured in inches but in feet and lots of them.

Before our visits to the Dygerts, we spent our winter vacations at our timeshare in Heavenly Valley, California, a ski resort located on the California-Nevada border in South Lake Tahoe. You had skied there before with your first family and loved it. My skiing did improve somewhat, but I never considered it to be "my" sport. I was always glad and relieved when I made it to the base, with you following behind me. You would call over to me, "Hey, Diane, that was awesome! Come on, Honey, let's do that run again. You were great." Hmmm? I was thankful I made it down the mountain in one piece and was ready to sit out a couple of runs by the warm and cozy fireplace sipping a Hot Toddy.

After thirty-eight years of working for the Shell Oil Company, one day you came home from work and said, "Honey, I need out. It's stopped being challenging. I want to spend more time with you before I'm too old to enjoy life and you." You were only 54 and didn't want to wait until 62 to retire. When we started to think of taking early retirement, we made a list of places where we might like to retire. We both knew we did not want to remain in Houston for many reasons; mainly it was too hot and humid. One summer we went on a car trip to visit some of the other places on our list besides Truckee. These included Durango and Santa Fé. We both decided on Truckee.

On one of our visits to Truckee, we met with architects and builders. In August of 1985, we purchased the lot on Greenleaf Way, two lots away from our friends. It was in an area of Truckee called Tahoe Donner: a destination resort which offered tennis courts, an 18-hole golf course, a small downhill ski area, cross-country trails, a riding stable and a club house with pools and a restaurant. The next year we purchased the lot in-between our two lots and converted the lot to acreage

Diane and Don on "Cocktail Rock" – Winter of 1988

which gave us a lot and a half on which to build our dream house. On June 3, 1988, we started construction of our house.

There was a rather steep hill behind our house which we named, "Cocktail Rock." We had to push our way through mesquite and crumbling rocks and shale to reach the top, and over the next eighteen years, many bottles of champagne were uncorked on top of this rock formation, either shared with friends or by ourselves.

In May of 1989, you turned in your resignation to Shell Oil Company where you had been employed for forty-two years. You were fifty-eight years old, a young fifty-eight. On the same day, I closed my small business which involved public relations and advertising. That same afternoon, we met with the realtor and closed on the house on Mount Vernon. We spent that evening with our friends at the party Penny hosted for us and left the following day for our new life in Truckee.

For the eighteen years we lived in Truckee both of us were involved in our true passions in life, which we discovered after moving here—you in local politics and me in the world of dogs and judging. Truckee made all of that possible. In a letter I found which you had written to family members in February of 1989, a couple of months before we actually moved to Truckee, you wrote.

~~~

"The next years will likely be the best of all those remaining. Retirement is one of the greatest changes one makes in life... There are lots of things we want to do, both at home and other places, and we enjoy doing them together. The old saw about "for better or for worse, but not for lunch' doesn't fit us. We have no plans for further work effort, although we wouldn't rule out a community effort of some kind. We have put a lot of thought into retirement, because we recognize the significant emotional aspects and adjustments. As I said, we are ready and anxious"

~~~

Yes, Don, you prophesized the life we would live in our mountain home in Truckee. It has almost been an entire year since you died. You are gone and I am here without you to "celebrate" my living in the Sierra for nineteen years, the longest I have lived anywhere in my life. I know I cannot endure another winter...in solitude...in our big house...alone... with my dogs and isolated from people.

It's May 6, the very same date we drove into Truckee to start our new life.

Today it's a momentous day for me in another way. I am trying to move on with my life.

This house, our home on Greenleaf Way, our dream retirement home, now has a "For Sale" sign in front.

Our Dream House – 12373 Greenleaf Way - Truckee, CA

Chapter 89

May–White Russians

This story would not be complete without mentioning "White Russians." You made and served me my first "White Russian" shortly after we were married and they certainly became a part of our life.

It is the second week in May and on this particular night the dogs and I curled up on the long sofa watching a movie on the Hallmark channel. We didn't move for two hours.

After watching the movie I was still encapsulated with my thoughts and decided to go down to the hot tub. The night was still early, a little past eight and the sky was that wonderful shade of pale indigo. The pines and firs towered into the sky; they have grown so much in the nineteen years I have lived here. As I slowly lowered into the hot tub, images of us taking a White Russian out to our pool in Houston or into our hot tub here came to my mind. My mind skipped to thoughts of Gypsy. Gypsy, who was the sweetest, most gentile dachshund of all, would have literally killed for a White Russian. Somewhere in our archives of photographs is the one you took of her with her snout half hidden in one of our tumblers slurping away.

I haven't had a White Russian since you died and thought

maybe one night I would just have to resurrect your "tried and true" recipe. Of course, it will have to be a special occasion although when we indulged, it was just any old night.

Throughout our married life, the White Russian was to be one of your specialties. I can remember those hot, humid but balmy nights in Houston when we would end the evening by taking a dip in the pool. You would disappear and come back in minutes with a tray of White Russians.

When we moved to Truckee and continued the tradition of taking a White Russian down to the hot tub, we swore to each other we would be careful and so we used the crystal glasses. The gods were with us—never a broken glass.

We had White Russians at other times. When we were in San Francisco we would go into a bar and order one to finish off the night. They never tasted like the ones you made for us. I asked you many times, "Don, why are your White Russians so special?" You would just laugh and tease me and say something stupid but endearing like, "Ah, Diane, it's the special mixing of the vodka, Kahlua and cream." One night, a few years ago, as I came back into the kitchen to retrieve something to take down to the hot tub, you were not aware I had come in the room and there you were—with the nutmeg grinder in one hand and a whole nutmeg in the other. THAT was the secret ingredient!

A sprinkle of fresh ground nutmeg.

Chapter 90

May–Garage Sale

The garage sale had been planned since early May. I made up a tentative list of items to include and checked out other garage sales to see how I could make mine better. I am the "organizer," so I knew that aspect of putting on a garage sale would be no challenge.

I cleaned off some of the shelves on your side of the garage to house the books for sale, in case of inclement weather. A week before I started going through my extensive collection of cookbooks and carried out the books I would have no use for in my future life. I tackled the bookcase in the living room with all those hardback copies of the latest novels written by the "in" authors, books you bought the week they hit the market, until we discovered our local library purchased the same books.

The pantry was next to clean out. I took out the items I knew would be useless in my next life: the coucouserie, the ice cream maker, the pasta machine, the bamboo trays for steaming Chinese dim sum delicacies, and the asparagus steamer.

I smiled in remembering the asparagus steamer. It was a wedding gift from the woman who introduced us, the woman who had given you my name and phone number. For whatever reason, once we had decided to marry, she turned against us, especially you. We never knew why. How surprised we were when a box arrived after we were married. In it was the asparagus steamer with a note, "I hope your decision will be a happy one." It was such a ludicrous message that I have remembered it all these years. In fact, the many times we used the steamer, we would toast to each other and say, *"Here's to our happy decision."* Now, it is amongst the rest of the dispensable, the discards;,the items that will NOT go with me into my next life, my life without you.

Many of the items are things that were in the motor home. Along with all the teal bedding items, were four silverplated cocktail tumblers. I can't remember when we got them, but for some reason they made their way to the motor home. On the few occasions you went with me to dog shows, you would use them for your White Russians. Now, that I am trying to simplify my life, I decided they would "go."

All of these items I placed along the edge of the driveway, covered with tarps, awaiting their new owners.

But, on May 18 when I received the call from my sister that her husband had died from a lingering illness, I wanted desperately to soak in the hot tub with some brandy, Kahlúa or something. At eleven o'clock, with only the rays of the moon shining on me, I tiptoed out to the driveway and found the silverplated tumblers. I carried them into the kitchen, washed one out, filled it with some ice from the bar and some Kahlúa and went down the spiral steps to the hot tub. The tumblers will go with me. They were a small part of our life, but now, they have become very much a part of my new life.

My girlfriend Lory came from Reno to help. It should have been beautiful weather. The day started out cold, blustery, rain fell intermittently and then it turned to snow. At one point Lory and I fished out two pairs of your Sherpa lined slippers to put on. We brought some space heaters from the house into the garage and wrapped the teal quilt over our laps. Hours later, the sun came out. The crowds were fairly good. Some of the items for sale were big ticket items such as two outdoor propane heaters, the generator and the telescope.

Lory and I decided we would not have the sale hold over until Sunday. The good items had sold. The stuff that did not sell I would donate to the thrift store.

At the end of the day after Lory left, I went outside and brought back into the garage all the items that didn't sell. They were covered with debris from the trees and were rain blotched. I wiped off each item as I put the items on one of the shelves. It was a lot of work, and I made a fair amount of money on the items that did sell. I vowed I would never again have another garage sale.

Chapter 91

May—The Friends & Family Walls

In the Truckee house, the friend and family walls were in the extension of the craft room above the two small day beds that were placed to form an "L" shape. It was often the highlight of the tour when we would take new friends, who had never seen our house before through our house. They always wanted to linger up there and hear the story behind each and every photo—many photos—many stories—many memories.

This was your favorite spot in the house, Don. You would curl up on the day bed, directly under the large round window with a view of the pines and firs and where the afternoon sun would come through. You would start reading a book you had just checked out from the Truckee library. With the sun warming you, you would drift off to sleep.

How many photos? I counted them as I started to pack them away but then lost count. This process of packing up these photos is part of the "get rid of clutter and personal effects" campaign realtors advise when a house is being shown. They will travel to my new home and I'll hang them in another location. After all, they were part of my life, our life, for almost thirty-two years.

One of the early photos is of baby Mystic. She was three months old in this photo. We were living in Houston and had taken a drive with Judy and Fred Brunk to the hill country to see the famous Texas bluebonnets. Bluebonnets, or lupines, are the state flower of Texas where they grow wild on the hillsides. The tag on the back of this photo says it was Easter Sunday, March 29, 1986. The bluebonnets were in their full splendor then. They bloom anywhere from the last week in March until the first few weeks in April and are more beautiful if there has been a bad winter. In this photo we are surrounded by acres and acres of rolling hill sides covered with thousands of wild bluebonnets making it look like a river of purple. I remember after we took the shot, we walked back to the car. We were holding Mystic on our laps when she started to cry out in pain and tried to lick her belly. Oh my God, we had been sitting in a mound of fire ants and her belly had been bitten by them.

Diane & Don with Mystic – March 29, 1986 • *(Photo by J. Gray Photographs)*

Here's another shot of one of our dachshunds from the time when we lived in Houston. This one is of Gypsy sitting in a field of butter cups but only her face is peaking through the flowers. I can see her muzzle has started to turn gray. Her eyes are shut as if she is concentrating on remembering what must have been a former glorious day for her. Here she is sniffing the air and having a splendid afternoon.

Of course, the photos from our many backpacking trips are here on the wall, some of the most beautiful scenery that one can only see when they are high up in the wilderness: no cars, no roads, just one breathtaking view after another.

Here's a photo of the "Hiking Group." Several of our friends gathered at the new home of Barbara and Buddy Hunt in Nevada City, California, to celebrate the 50th wedding anniversary of Sal and Frank Bulkley. We were the group who went hiking together, as you used to say, "We are the hiking, dining and drinking group." Most of our hikes were day hikes

Hiking Group – October 10, 2002

in and around the Sierra Nevada Mountains where we would hike on tranquil trails during the day and then gather at one of our homes later in the evening for a potluck dinner. One weekend in the fall of 2002, we rented cozy cabins at Sorensen's Resort on the eastern edge of Hope Valley. You and Kath did some catch and release fly fishing in the West Fork of the Carson River.

Don & Kath Eagan – October 20, 2002

Here's another of my favorite shots. It's a black and white image of you and your mother, Rainy. There's a scattering of sail boats behind you. It was taken at one of Rainy's favorite spots, Jimmy Walker's, a seafood restaurant in Kemah, Texas, where we took her many times for Sunday dinner. The drive from our Houston home to Kemah on Galveston Bay was less than an hour. We would always arrange for a table facing the water. The windows were always left partly open, so we could hear the waves crashing on the rocks, smell the salt air and hear the fog horns to warn the boats they might be coming in too close to the pier. When Rainy died, we spread some of her ashes there. It was a foggy night and we could hear the low bongs, two notes from the fog horns. We placed some of her ashes in two tissues and walked out to the end of the pier. We looked around to make sure that no one was close by and gently opened the tissues to drop her ashes into the water. You squeezed my hand as we watched the ashes spread on the waters.

One of your favorite photos was taken of the two of us at the restaurant, the Robert E. Lee on a barge along the banks of the Mississippi River in St. Louis. I never did like this photo of me, my eyes are half shut, but you are looking at me with such intent and the biggest smile full of love. We are both smiling and so happy. There is a sign behind us that reads, "Captain's Dining Room—Plate Lunches."

Don and Diane in St. Louis – June of 1984

Another one of you and Rainy rolling out pasta through the pasta machine. After rolling the dough at least four times, the final step was to put the dough through the machine, but this time with the blade that produced tiny thin ribbons of pasta. We would take these ribbons and drape them on the backs of our ladder-back kitchen chairs so that they could dry for a minute or two. One day as you went to the chair to retrieve the pasta, it was gone. Sitting on the floor at the bottom of the chairs was our ever faithful dachshund. A few days after this episode you walked into our home carrying a package from the local kitchen store. It was a pasta drying rack about twelve inches high with six or more racks. This new gadget allowed us to take the pasta ribbons from the machine, drape them over the dowels, then place them on the rack high up on the counter above the reach of a dachshund's nose.

Don and Rainy Rolling Out Pasta – Houston – July 1981

All of our relatives are in at least one of these mounted photographs: my parents spending Christmas with us; your sister Ann and her husband Tommy high up on the precipice overlooking Donner Lake.

Here is the photo of Pat Donahue sitting with us on our front deck. Our typical dinner with Pat was always steaks and your Caesar salad tossed in that big wooden bowl of yours with the infamous "mushroom." Pat was your best friend. He spent many weekends with us before he married Stacy in November of 2003. When we visited with them at their condo in San Francisco, many times as we were driving back home, you would moan to me, "Oh, Diane, I drank too much." "A true debauchery," I would say to you. "But, oh didn't we have a great time!"

Pat Donahue's Visit to Truckee – July 1997

The wall would not have been complete without photographs of one of our favorite couples, Sarah and Neil Hill, from Houston. They were part of our New Year's celebrations beginning in 1999 and would arrive a few days after Christmas to stay with us for over a week. It was great to have a couple staying with us that played bridge. We would wake up and you would ask, "How about a BBBG?" − *Before Breakfast Bridge*

Game. We would gather in the kitchen and while we waited for our meals to cook, we would squeeze in several hands of bridge. One vacation we took to Houston in September 2005, you talked about for the next two years. We spent a few days with Sarah and Neil at their new house in Spring, Texas, doing our usual: playing bridge, eating and drinking. Then we drove down to their bay house near Palacios. Neil couldn't wait to show you the forty-eight foot lighthouse he had constructed by the side of their house. We had such fun.

Our Visit to Hill's Bay House – 2005

Our wall would not be complete if it didn't include a photo-graph of my sister, Bev, and her husband, Art; they were a very big part of our life. This photograph was taken at Boat Works, a shopping center located on the shore of Lake Tahoe when they flew out to help us celebrate your 75th birthday.

Bev & Art Morgan – October 1, 2005

Here's the last of the photos to be packed and it's the one of us you loved the most. It was taken in Houston when we attended an art opening of Audrey Dygert in their home. The watercolor in the background is called "Mountain Tapestry." She painted it on the backpacking trip we took to the Wind River Range in Wyoming in 1978.

Diane & Don – Dygert's Party – Houston 1979

These mounted photos tell a lifetime of the happiest of times, from our fourteen years living in Houston to the eighteen we shared in Truckee, living and loving with our family and friends.

So many happy times; so many remembrances of a lifetime of love.

We were blessed, Don. We were blessed!

Chapter 92

June–Quilt of Many Shirts

Your sons went through your clothes during the week everyone was at our house for the family memorial. I told them, "Help yourselves to anything, but please don't take any of your father's 100 percent cotton shirts. I want to make them into a quilt."

Most of your clothes fit Bruce; the only alteration needed would be the shortening of your slacks. "Boy, Dad sure had some neat looking rags," Bruce said.

When he tried on your steel gray cashmere sport jacket and beamed because it fit him so well, I related this story: "*Your father used to say, with pride, he bought this cashmere jacket with his very first Social Security check. Then he would pause and add— the whole check.*" Before Bruce flew back to Cody, I came across the original sales receipt from Nordstrom and the business card of the very dapper salesman who had waited on us. Bruce tucked the receipt and the card into one of the pockets. The cashmere jacket was one of your most prized possessions.

I packed all of your shirts in three white cardboard moving boxes. I didn't think I would have time to quilt before I moved. But, this morning I needed the calming influence that I knew would come to me through quilting. As I took the first shirt out of the box before I had cut into it, I held it up to my nose and I could still smell you, your scent, you, even through the countless cleanings. I arranged the shirts on my cutting table into piles from dark to light—your shirts: the stripes; the checks; the ones with the Harley motif; and the ones that I loved the most, the paisleys; short sleeved; long sleeved—all of these shirts of so many colors. Not only the Ralph Lauren's, the Bill Blass' and the Calvin Klein's, but the Patagonia's and the Eddie Bauer's. Your shirts ran the gamut just like your take on life. You loved all people and could relate to all. It didn't matter what one's position was in life, be it the president of a major corporation, the local waitress, or our housekeeper, you could connect with anyone.

As I started to cut the shirts into strips and sewed them into squares and then into blocks, I remembered the words I said to you before we were married, "I don't iron shirts," to which you immediately replied, "I don't cut grass." The grass that had been our front lawn at our Houston home was soon replaced with landscaping that required little maintenance. Our Truckee home had a forest floor surrounding it.

Before I knew it, I had been in my sewing room for hours, cutting and piecing, and I realized the cutting up of your shirts into these strips was not painful, but comforting to me. These shirts are part of my memories of our life. One day these squares and blocks will become a quilt for my bed. The metamorphosis continues.

And... when the quilt is finally completed, I will remember the words a friend said to me soon after you died, "Don was interwoven into your life."

Quilt of Many Shirts – Completed 2010

Chapter 93

June–Father's Day Weekend

I had an appointment to see a book dealer in Grass Valley. While driving there, I listened to an audio book, "A Good Year," by Peter Mayle; a story about a man from London who inherits his uncle's estate in Provence. My thoughts turned to the house I saw in Reno, designed by a French architect; it reminds me of a Provence home with its country French charm. It's always on my mind, lately.

When the audio book ended, I hit the button for the local radio station. They were playing music and not just any music, but bluegrass. I heard the twang of the banjos.

I had forgotten until I heard the bluegrass music that it was almost a year ago, Father's Day, when we drove to the Nevada County Fairgrounds with friends to attend the Blue Grass Festival. Those were idyllic hours, walking around the fairgrounds, holding hands, sitting on the grass listening to the various groups perform, and eating salmon burgers in keeping with our new diet of limited red meat. How quickly these hours have evaporated.

Now, all I have left of that wonderful afternoon, the last Sunday spent with you, are the memories.

Chapter 94

June–Je Táime

A simple act like packing up all the needlepoint pillows I've made can trigger a feeling or recollection. I have a specific spot for them in my new home—if all goes well with the real estate transactions. They will be displayed on the antique bench which will be placed in back of the love seat in the living room. Sometimes these recollections are predictable as they come flooding into my memory. They come when I hear someone talk about things you and I used to do. The simple acts with no one else around to precipitate these emotions, these are the ones that are the hardest. They strike without any warning.

I made this needlepoint pillow for you in the fall of 1975. It's rectangular, about 14" by 20" and the colors are in shades of pale greens and creams with the lettering in blue. The colors were chosen to go with the upholstery fabric on the antique fainting couch. The pillow has no design on it—only these words.

~~~

JE T'AIME

PLUS

QU'HIER

MOINS

QUE DEMAIN

At the bottom I had needle pointed

2-10   4-23   8-23

~~~

Those were the three dates we always observed. The first, 2-10, was the day you called me all those years ago when I lived in New York City. The second, 4-23, was the day we actually met face-to-face for the first time. And, of course, the third, 8-23, was the day of our wedding.

My darling, Don, I did love you more each day than the day before and less than the day to follow.

All these memories haunt me, now.

Chapter 95

June–Regrets

D o I have regrets of things we should have done, of things I should have done, of things I should have said or not said? Or course I do.

I regret the time I spent away from you. Facing these lonely nights without you now, I can imagine what you experienced those weekends when I was away at some dog show showing the dogs or at a dog show judging dogs. I knew you were missing me. Even though you knew I would soon return, I'm sure those were still lonely weekends for you.

I regret all the time I spent on the computer working to defeat the anti-legislative bills. You told me that my being the Canine Legislative Liaison for several of the dog clubs had become practically a full-time job. I had become driven, almost compulsive and spent hours sending out emails, faxes, and letters. I even had you licking stamps. But, it was time not spent with you, even though you were just a room away, curled up in your favorite spot, reading a book.

I regret the pissy fights we had over the use of the computer. "Diane, when will you be through? I have things I need to work on that are just as important as those dog bills," you would holler up to me. Why didn't we buy a lap top for one of us to use while the other one was on the office computer? You could have even played your favorite solitary game of Sudoku on it. And, why didn't we each have our own email addresses like many of our friends do? Hindsight.

I regret not demanding and taking you to the Mayo Clinic or some other place highly regarded for their treatment of heart patients for a second opinion. We spent hours taking our dogs to UC Davis for a second opinion and follow-up treatments. Why didn't I insist we do the same with you? It was your heart, not a simple surgery for a hand or a knee replacement or hip—but YOUR HEART! That's what I regret the most! I remember when I suggested to you we should get a second opinion. You said, "No, I don't think that's necessary." Then again, you probably died from an aneurysm and it probably would have happened anyway.

I regret our not kicking up our heels more often and going out on more "dates." We did have dates, but not that often. Every time you and I went out by ourselves one of us always said, "We need to do this more often, just the two of us, alone. We always have so much fun when we go out. Why don't we have more dates?"

I regret not taking more vacations with you, even though you said you would rather stay in Truckee. The vacations we did take together were filled with so many memories and we always enjoyed ourselves tremendously once we arrived at our destination.

More than anything, I regret not giving you the moon, the sun, the universe—because you were all of those to me.

Chapter 96

June–Opening Doors

I am sitting in the rays of sun, coming through to the back patio from the canopy of the Dutch elms at my home. In Old Southwest Reno. I am waiting for my broker to go over some last minute details before I officially open escrow in a few days. This will soon be my new home.

When I mentioned to your friend, Ted Owens, that I was thinking of moving because I had a "need" to move, he said to me, "Don't worry, Diane, Don will find you, and it might not be at your Truckee home." How prophetic he was.

I know you will find me—here on the back patio is one of the places where I feel you now. I continue to think of you. How can one erase from their mind, from their innermost depth of their soul, memories of someone who was their life, their focus, their raison d'être for thirty-two years? Everything I do now still reminds me of you. Every time I turn around, there is a reference of you: something we did, something you said, some look, some gesture. I am hoping that by moving to this new house and this new town, I will make new friends and will have new experiences with them. This move will help me not be reminded of you every minute of the day—and night—because you never lived here. I won't see you walking through the door into the living room or sitting in one of our chairs on the back patio or crawling into bed at night.

I am thinking of a passage from Kahlil Gibran's "The Prophet"—

~~~

And ever has it been that love knows not its own depth...
until the hour of separation.

~~~

Last night as I sat looking at the piles of notes I've been collecting over the past months, the thought came to my mind that I am opening doors. That will be the title for the chapter I knew I would write sometime during my healing process. Can I turn back time? No, of course not! I must go on. I must open doors.

Now, what I used to think of as being the past has dissolved into the present. My past is what I lived with you, but the present is what I am experiencing now—without the physical you. My future—who knows? It will continue to evolve... endings that bring new beginnings.

"Time"—sometimes the sound of time passing by me these past months was so loud and I alone heard it. The old saying that time passes by too quickly is trite, but true. In the beginning after you died, I would say, "It's been one month." Then I would say, "two months, then three months, and then six." When does my counting the months since you have gone become more a part of my past and not part of my future? Does counting the months mean I'm frozen in time? I hope not.

As I sit on this back patio, I hear the sounds of the song birds that are darting in and out of the trees and I feel the high desert wind on my face as it blows across. I smell the scent of peonies, roses and honeysuckle that did not grow in Truckee, but are everywhere around this house. I take a deep breath and say to myself, *"My life here is not my life there, but it is life."*

A dear friend of mine, Beverly Brahe, told me shortly after your death, "Diane, if you were made of iron before Don died, then you will most certainly be made of steel when this is all behind you. You will be able to move on, you know, and you will only get stronger and stronger."

There are many things that are different for me, now. *Because, I am on my own, again.*

Before you died, I would talk to you about a major decision I needed to make and ask, "Honey, what do you think I should do?" You were my sounding board. The same confidence and self-reassurance I had in New York City is slowly returning. *Because, I am on my own again.*

Now I make the simple decisions. What I should make for dinner, if anything? What time I will get up in the morning? Do I want to sew until midnight? Do I want to visit friends and take my dogs with me? All of these everyday decisions are mine, alone. *Because, I am on my own, again.*

Now, the last and final decision is mine, alone. I am now in control of my own destiny. *Because, I am on my own, again.*

I guess I never realized how much you and I relied on each other for these day-to-day decisions. I have the sole responsibility of running my house. I will hire handymen to do the "honey-do list," and a lawn service to mow the tiny patch of grass in the front of this house, and an electrician to hang my chandelier that you and I had since we lived in our house on Mount Vernon Avenue. *Because, I am on my own, again.*

To go on with our lives after there has been a death or separation, we each need to find our passion for something. I am fortunate; I have two passions. The first is dogs and the second is being creative through sewing, quilting, gardening, cooking—anything that is creative.

You said to me once, "Diane, you are so driven. I don't think you can settle for a second or third "best" in life. You want it all or none at all and you want it *now*." "Yes, you are so, so right," I answered you. "My passion drives me. But,

Don," I emphasized to you, "That's why our marriage has also worked all these years. We have passion. We believe in our marriage and we will defend it to others to the very end. We are committed to each other. We are alive in our marriage because of our passion."

Why do each of us need to have a passion in life? Ask yourself, "What would I do if I woke up tomorrow and was alone?"

You need to find a passion for something, because...nothing is forever; nothing is permanent.

Chapter 97

June–June 23rd, 2008

In one year, I feel as if I've spent a lifetime's worth of emotions: sorrow, grief, anger, happiness, fright and oh so many more. Many times during this past year, I've had a sense of another life, moving alongside this one—a parallel life. Has everything in this past year been leading up to this—the ending of one narrative and the beginning of another?

This morning I stayed in bed watching the sun come up through the forest of pines and firs; these trees that will not be part of my mornings when I move in a few weeks to Reno.

Last night I stayed out on the front deck for hours, watching more than a thousand stars. When I thought of you, my world seemed to stop. I felt a rush of longing for you so intense, so real. I had to actually shake myself to remember the reality of this past year.

As I was sitting on the deck, a shooting star shot across the sky; it was such a spiritual moment. It reminded me of June a year ago, in the wee small hours of the morning, as I was driving into Reno with our friends, Lisa and Debbie. I silently screamed to God, "Please, dear God, let him live." Through my despair I was pleading with Him. And, then when I knew it was hopeless, I asked Him, "Please stay with him through his journey. Don't let him go alone."

I have waited for the bell to toll. Today I will spread some of your ashes up on Cocktail Rock. As I actually type these words, I feel as if someone is stepping on my heart.

I called some of our dearest friends—Kath, Jim and Lisa—to come over today to help me spread your ashes and to toast your memory with a glass of Korbel Brut. It was a last-minute thought.

Before our friends arrive, I opened your box of ashes and took out one of the four packets. I picked the smallest of the four. I put them in my jean's pocket and then went about doing chores.

Then I remembered I wanted to include some of Spirit's ashes in with yours. I took his tiny cedar box and carried it to the kitchen table. I took the bag with your ashes out of my pocket and added some of his.

Kath arrived first and I took her around the house to show her what has been done to the house. It's down to its bare bones. I casually mentioned to her, "I have Don in my pocket." She immediately responded, without a bit of hesitation, "Diane, haven't you always had him in your pocket?" Yes, perhaps I did.

Jim arrived a few minutes later and then Lisa. I told them I had made some notes for the epilogue of this book and thought maybe it would be fitting to read it up on Cocktail Rock, as we sprinkle your ashes.

I can't remember the last time you and I were up on Cocktail Rock. I know it wasn't when Spirit died because I couldn't part with any of his ashes until now. We four climbed up the rocky path through the thorny manzanita, and I remarked, "I better not fall and break my neck," and Kath answered, "You better not, I have a full week ahead of me." A bit of laughter.

We saw the sign that our neighbor made for "Tasha's Path." I was taken down the "memory path" of all the animals and birds and loved ones whose ashes were sprinkled on what we called hallowed grounds—Alphie, Harry, Taffy, Coach, Rusty,

Gypsy, Rainy, Mystic, Sky, Tasha, Goose and Giggle. Some of Spirit's and some of your ashes will now be added to this sacred spot.

A butterfly kept flying around us, a swallowtail butterfly. It wouldn't leave us alone. It went from one of us to another.

A sign, maybe?

I read my notes from the epilogue, and then we took turns sprinkling some of the ashes. We talked about your wonderful character and shared and relived stories about you. Just as the bag was handed to Lisa, and as she was about to sprinkle some of the ashes, a gust of wind came up from nowhere and blew some of the ashes back in her face. I quickly said, "Lisa, watch out." She replied, "It wouldn't be the first time that McCormack got in my face."

The swallowtail butterfly kept flying around us.

Was it you? Was it your spirit?

We toasted to you with the Korbel Brut champagne and I sprinkled the last of the ashes from the bag. We climbed back down from Cocktail Rock and all went our separate ways. You would have said to me, "Well done, Honey, simple, small, but meaningful."

Later, as I was getting ready for bed, I stood at the back glass door and looked up to Cocktail Rock. I knew I couldn't push any of it back...

No time...

No day...

No night...

No grandfather's clock banging at the one o'clock hour.

I wondered where the swallowtail butterfly had gone.

Chapter 98

June–Epilogue

This is the last chapter. It's time to close. You have been in my thoughts every day for the past year as I wrote down our story. I have made either a written or mental note of each day, each week, each month. Now, the year has ended. In a way I have made witness of the changing of my life, as you slowly left it. The reality of my life has changed; every aspect of it has been altered. My life stopped being the same life it was the minute you died.

I have tried to tell our story and many times the words just came tumbling out as I spent hours typing away on my computer. Many times I just got hung up with tears. I started this tale when I was thirty-four years old and you were forty-four. Our thirty-two years of life together went by so quickly—too quickly. I want to relive them again with you holding my hand, but I know I cannot. For the past year I have filled some of my loneliest hours touching you, remembering you, by writing this book. There are so many thoughts, so many questions, that I have now as I write this epilogue. My future days and years are yet a mystery. How I choose to fill the days does matter to me. After all, I survived. I do have a life. I will go on. Life is for the living.

My friends tell me I need to make space for my unknown future. It is unknown and probably will be full of surprises. They tell me my heart has to be open. They tell me your death didn't end my life—it only changed the last several chapters of it. Who knows?

As to my future life without you, what will my choices be? How will *my* life unfurl, and what will be *my* legacy? Who can say or who really knows or who can predict what I will leave behind when my life is over?

These words I have written about you, about us, about our marriage, and about "D & D" for the past year tell about *our* legacy, if only in some small way. When your life was over, my life as "me" began. Writing these words was my catharsis, but it was also my tribute to you.

You were such an incredible man, Don—an incredible human being. You were an observer of human nature, a leader in town politics, a teacher to some, a mentor to many, and a friend to all. Though you are gone in the physical sense, you left a legacy that is eternal. You touched so many, many lives, that I could not let you go without telling about you.

You were *my* husband, my friend and lover for all those years. Our thirty-two year marriage is a long story, a story not only about a marriage, but about a love affair. I can't bring you back, but I need to keep your vision alive through this book. You may have left us in body, but your spirit will always be with many of us and will always be in my heart.

Thank you, my darling, for having been a part of my life for thirty-two years. Thank you for sharing your life, your dreams and your goals with me. Thank you for making that call on February 10, 1975, for writing that first letter and for telling me all so many years ago, "I'm a toucher."

Yes, you were a toucher, in the physical sense, but you were also a toucher in other ways. You touched so many lives: mine, your children, our families, our friends, the Town of

Truckee. We are all better for your having lived.

There are some things one can never say goodbye to, I know I am writing the last words. I have to lift the veil. My girlfriend, Ellen North, told me Jewish law demands a year of mourning and then the veil is lifted from the tombstone. The year is up. The mourning is over. One year, twelve months, three hundred and sixty-five days have passed. I am lifting the veil. Life is for me to live now.

I was hoping I would know how to close these pages. Perhaps, it's with the words that you and I wrote on each and every card we gave each other after we were married, and just under the words "I Love You, Darling."

Forever and Always...

Chapter 99

June–Widow Advice

Some personal and non-professional advice I would like to pass on.

* Make a notebook of all pertinent information to include:
    * Wills and/or Trusts including information and copies of your and your spouse's Durable Power of Attorney. If you have Long Term Health Insurance, include this information.
    * Insurance policies.
    * Pension information.
    * Tax information—most CPA's suggests saving at least the last five (5) years of tax returns.
    * Bank account numbers and any passwords.
    * Yours and your spouse's Social Security numbers.
    * Brokerage account numbers and name and phone number of your stock broker, if any.
    * Money market fund information, if any.
    * Property deeds or House Mortgage information.

- Credit cards—Photocopy fronts and back of each one.
- Car title and registration information and location of extra key.
- Safety deposit box—location of it and the keys. Include birth certificates, divorce papers, if any, passports, copies of your Will and Testament and/or Trust, name and phone number of law firm and lawyer who helped prepare the will.
- Information on each of your parents. Include date of birth and death and where they were born and died. This is needed for the Death Certificate.

Your trustee should have access to the above information and a house key.

* Make a list of computer ID and passwords.
* Make a binder on all the instruction manuals for your home appliances.
* Know where the electrical switch or junction box is located and mark what each switch is for.
* Let your heirs know of your wishes before your death. This is especially true if there are children from different marriages involved. It will alleviate any hurt feelings and unhappy surprises after you die.
* Write your own obituary. It could save your spouse a lot of added grief and at least most of the information will be accurate.
* If you have a pre-paid funeral plan, make sure your heir(s) or trustee(s) knows this. Your heir(s) or trustee(s) should know your wishes upon your death: cremation or burial; memorial service or not; specific church, if any and type of service; any special uniform you wish the funeral director to have, should you wish a burial and viewing.

* Learn how to do the simple maintenance on things around the house that the spouse did such as checking the spa/pool for chemicals, programming the sprinkler system, setting the timers, etc.

* Make a list of handymen you can count on. Make a list of service and terms already contracted.

* Sit with your spouse when they are organizing information necessary to prepare your income taxes, even if prepared by a professional accountant. Know who that person is. You might even want to contact the same accountant your spouse used, if one was used, after the death and find out the items that should be saved.

* There will be significant changes in your finances. Talk to your spouse about this; is there an insurance policy and for how much. If there isn't an insurance policy, should there be one?

* Remember, if you both are receiving Social Security monthly checks, you will be receiving only one after the death of your spouse.

I also have some personal advice I want to pass on.

- If and when the day comes, take notes on everything that is said, instructions that might be given to you, all the details—because you will be totally overwhelmed.

- Set your own pace. Don't let anyone tell you that you should stop grieving or to "get on with it." Cry or laugh when YOU need to.

- Keep moving forward, even if two steps forward and one step backward.

- Keep in touch with your girlfriends. They can be your lifelines.

- Happiness is derived from other people. Sort out people you don't need in your life and move on with your life because it's your life.

- Some of your friends may want you to pretend everything has been unchanged. They might expect your life will simply roll on—right over death. You will be in pain and if they can't understand that, perhaps they were never your friends in the first place. Your true friends will be there for you.

- You will be entering a voyage of self-discovery when you become a widow. Pursue your own happiness.

- Find your passion in life before you become a widow.

- Remember, grief is a process. None of us is ever prepared for grief, especially when it's instant. Grief hits hard. WHAM! You need to be kind to yourself as you take those first steps towards recovering from what you might be feeling now, which probably is the sense of having lost everything.

- Get a dog or a cat. Cry in their fur. Laugh at their antics. My dogs are the mirrors of my soul.

Chapter 100

$\mathcal{A}$uthor's $\mathcal{N}$ote

While walking away from the town of Truckee memorial on July 22 of 2007, Linda Brown and Ruth Hall approached Kathleen Eagan, who was one of the two speakers at the town of Truckee memorial. They said to her, "That was really a powerful tribute you gave to Don. We think his principles are valuable and should be preserved as a legacy to his memory." Kathleen explained to them that her words had actually come from the tribute I gave during the family memorial, and my words came from notes I found in Don's files on "Leadership in Local Government." He had given a talk on "Leadership," perhaps at a town council meeting, and this talk included many of Don's principles of life. When I called Kathleen to ask her to speak at the town's memorial, she asked if she could use his notes. I sent her a copy.

The wheels were in motion.

These three women continued to meet and work on the format for several months. Much of the funding came from the Tahoe Truckee Community Foundation, of which Linda Brown was a founding board member and Past President.

Tahoe Truckee Community Foundation is a philanthropy organization in North Tahoe. At the time, Ruth Hall was with Sierra Nevada Children Services, an organization that helps low income children, as well as being Chairperson of Friends of the Truckee Library. Ruth first met Don when the Truckee library was in financial trouble. Ruth told me, "Don helped the library when it was in danger of closing. Kathleen Eagan, the first Mayor of Truckee, had her own history of working with Don. I can honestly say that not only did Don respect her but he loved her. The three women met at the school district office, polishing the sentences. Then they approached Rich Valentine of the TIP Printing & Graphics who also donated to the project.

A framed copy of Don's, "Ten Principles of Successful Leadership" was presented at an airport board meeting. Unframed copies were handed out at community coalitions and collaboratives, where individuals participating in group decision-making would benefit from Don's Leadership Principles. Small wallet-size reproductions of Principles were also printed and passed out.

Don McCormack lived by these words.

As I said at the family memorial, *"If we can learn something from his death, let's try to remember his philosophy of life. We will be better people for it, we will have better relationships with our friends and with our families...and we will always be true to ourselves."*

~~~

TEN PRINCIPLES OF SUCCESSFUL LEADERSHIP
1. **Have Vision**
2. **Take Initiative**
3. **Build Consensus**
4. **Develop Good Working Relationships**
5. **Use Interpersonal Skills**
6. **Get the Facts**
7. **Seek Compromise**
8. **Forget Your Ego**
9. **Make Right Decisions for the Right Reasons**
10. **Be Persistent**

~~~

TEN PRINCIPLES
of Successful Leadership

1. HAVE VISION
Think outside the lines

Look for impact into the future

2. TAKE INITIATIVE
Drive to make things happen

Have confidence in yourself

3. BUILD CONSENSUS
Recognize there are other valid views

Change your position, if necessary

4. DEVELOP GOOD WORKING RELATIONSHIPS
Respect others and their basic beliefs

Speak well of others and harbor no grudges

5. USE INTERPERSONAL SKILLS
Communicate clearly

Listen carefully and openly

6. GET THE FACTS
Be inquisitive Evaluate, compare and consider all factors.

Avoid preconceived decisions

7. SEEK COMPROMISE
Adjust your own priorities

Remember nobody is right all the time

8. FORGET YOUR EGO
Be unconcerned for your own welfare

It's not about your basic belief

9. MAKE RIGHT DECISIONS FOR THE RIGHT REASONS
Consider what's best for the whole

10. BE PERSISTENT

Don McCormack's
Philosophy of Life and Leadership

Don McCormack, as public servant, sat on the Truckee Town Council from 1994 through 2002 and served as Mayor in 1996 and 2001. Known for his rapid fire questions and boundless curiosity, he led by example. Don McCormack, the person, was much more: from Harley rider to husband and father, from voracious reader to skillful bridge partner, from hiker, skier, and casual tennis player to attentive friend---Don will be remembered for a life fully lived and for his eternal optimism. ~ Truckee will miss him.

Thanks and Gratitude

I didn't set out to write a book; it started as scribbles on pads of paper placed around the house where I wrote down thoughts, emotions, and memories after my husband's death, as a way to hold on to him. One year later, after I moved to Reno the note pads filled two moving boxes. Over the next four years, I continued to jot down remembrances and tossed the pages into one of the boxes. Some of my friends suggested that I needed to tell our story.

I don't "acknowledge" but give "thanks and gratitude" to those who read this manuscript in its numerous versions, made helpful suggestions, pointed out passages that needed to be tightened and mostly gave me neverending encouragement. Six years later the manuscript and I have made it to the finish line.

I am forever grateful and appreciative to...

Beverly—my sister whom I love with all my heart. We agree we "march to different drummers." Bev and I have shared secrets, intimacies, and memories for many years, including the years we bred and showed our standard longhaired dachshunds, the "sister trips" we took visiting family and friends, our trip to Alaska, and our sojourn to Eastern Europe, as a tribute to our Aunt Irene. We spent a week touring Hungary.

This trip culminated the day we visited our maternal grand-father's birth town, Ipolytarnoć. I know we will continue to trace our past and make new memories as we travel to new adventures in future "sister trips."

Sarah Hill—my dearest friend since 1985, when we met at a dog show. Sarah was on the first flight out of Houston after she received the call from me the morning Don died. She stayed with me for the next three weeks, helping me get through the raw grief. Sarah is my "other" sister and my "extra" sister. She will forever be known to me and many of my friends as "Saint Sarah."

Penny Douglas—another of my lifeline sisters from our days in Houston, whose phone calls and visits after Don died filled me with not only her love, but with her wit and humor. As I sent her various chapters for comment, she offered her wisdom and experience. She held me in her heart while I navigated my life after Don. Penny is a constant in my life, especially since we own dachshunds that descend from my beloved Spirit.

Lory—my treasured friend I met those many years ago after Don and I had moved to Truckee when I was looking for someone to instruct me in dog obedience. Lory read parts of this story as it was becoming alive, and through her remarkable expertise and laser-sharp vision for rightness of tone, gave me different perspectives. Lory and I are old souls and Scorpio sisters. Our friendship bonds deepened, as we shared each other's personal griefs through our dark days and nights.

Ellen North—one of my friends I've known the longest. Our friendship dates to my days when I lived in New York City and has continued over five decades. Ellen is one of my friends who also read parts of my book in the early manuscript form and always made me view things in a different light and kept challenging me to do better.

Cindy Chandler—another friend of mine from my life in New York City. She was the first person I met the day I walked into the lobby of The Wool Bureau for an interview. We have remained friends all these years.

Polly Savage—whom I also met through our dachshunds and who became my immediate friend. Polly helped me get through many *"firsts"* the year after Don died, when "the *first* of everything is so hard to do."

Barbara Cox—who lost her husband two years before Don and became an important friend of mine after Don's death. We knew we could call each other in those dark hours when only another who has experienced the same depth of grief would understand.

Julie, Carlie and Clair—mother and daughters, who were there for me, not only after Don died, but who drove all the way from Vancouver, WA to help me make the move to my new home in Reno. Not only do we share the same blood lines in our dachshunds, but we share deep respect and love for each other.

Ann Powers—my sister-in-law, a supreme source of the family history and who shared with me many of the innuendo's, regarding Don's side of the family history. Ann listened to me as I read to her the chapters that dealt with the Powers family history and was insightful and enormously helpful.

Joan—my daughter-in-love whom I love as dearly as if she were my daughter and who cried and laughed with me when I would recite certain chapters and passages to her.

Bruce, Dan and Mary Beth—for helping me keep the circle of family complete. I give thanks to Don's children for remaining in my life.

Jinny, Maggie, Katie, Betsy, Beverley, Susan, Darlinda, Carla, Donahue, Ivy, Barb, Paula—and all of my other friends who have remained close to me over the years.

Kath, Jim, Stef, Lisa, Debbie, Kathleen, Ken, Buddy and Barbara, Sal and Frank and other friends—including my friends from the "Truckee Ladies' Bridge" group—Ina, Marilyn, Pris, Iris, Sharilyn and Lorrie—from our days in Truckee—who have remained in my life by continuing to reach out to me.

Katie Salo—whom I met one Sunday while attending the Methodist Church in downtown Reno. Katie and I discovered we lost our "others" the same summer—that summer of 2007. As she said to me one time when I was reading one of the chapters to her, *"That summer is forever etched in my memory."* Katie was also one of my proof readers and gave me astute advice.

Friends from the First United Methodist Church in Reno, Nevada—too many to name, whose support and kindness formed a circle of love around me from that first Sunday in August of 2008 when I walked from my new home to the church. Their friendship continues to uplift and overwhelm me.

Peggy Jeanes—my friend from my days in New York City. Peggy was the Managing Editor, back in the 70's, of the trade division at Harper & Row Publishers and helped me immensely with the first edit of my manuscript.

Donna Quante, Janet Andrews and Ena Estes—whose editing and proof-reading on the many rewrites saw things that others had missed and encouraged me to rewrite chapters and paragraphs.

Renate Neumann—for her many suggestions on the cover design. I met Renate and her husband shortly after I moved to Reno and I thank them for their continued support and friendship.

Vision and Mirage, my two longhaired dachshunds—my constant comfort from the moment I heard the clashing of the clock's chimes in the wee small hours in the morning of June 23, 2007. One minute they were kissing the wet tears from my face as I relived painful memories and minutes later made me roll over in laughter with their playful antics.

Jack Bacon—another lover of longhaired dachshunds and my publisher, who guided me through the final steps of making my manuscript into a book.

So, I lift a glass of vino or Scotch.

To old friends and new friends.

To those who questioned why I was determined to write this book.

To those who gave me the encouragement to finish writing this book.

I love all of you from the bottom of my heart.

COLOPHON

Text is set in Carmina Medium and Bold.

Carmina was designed for Bitstream by
Gudrun Zapf von Hesse in 1987, all of whose
typefaces exhibit the spirit of calligraphy.

~~~

Chapter Heads are set in Poetica Chancery.

Poetica was designed in 1992 by Robert Slimbach.
It is modeled on the elegant Italian Renaissance
scripts which are credited with forming the basis for
italic type and calligraphy in the modern era.

~~~

Book design by Jim Richards.
Cover design by Diane Young McCormack